SAS WARLORD

"SHOOT TO KILL"

SAS "SHOOT TO KILL"
WARLORD

TOM SIEGRISTE

FRONTLINE
NOIR
PUBLISHING

Dedicated to our darling Swiss mother
LINA LILLIAN SIEGRISTE
from all of her children

Published 2010 by Frontline Noir Publishing,
An imprint of Books Noir, Scotland.
Reprinted 2011 (three times)

ISBN 978-1-904684-95-4

Printed and bound in the UK

CONTENTS

Author's Note 7

Chapter 1 Shoot and Scoot 11
Chapter 2 The New Kings of Falls Road 35
Chapter 3 A New Quarry 49
Chapter 4 Spoils of War 65
Chapter 5 Balls up 85
Chapter 6 Thompson Twins 100
Chapter 7 Pulp Fiction 111
Chapter 8 Crime and Punishment 124
Chapter 9 Busted Flush 137
Chapter 10 Super Sniper 154
Chapter 11 Remember, Remember… 178
Chapter 12 On the Road to Bruin 203
Chapter 13 Hanging by a Fred 224
Chapter 14 One Final Foray 244
Chapter 15 The Mything Force 267

Epilogue 279
Glossary 295

Author's Note

This is not a textbook. This is not a military history. It is the story of some very brave men.

Sometimes when truth emerges, it is painful. Sometimes it is dangerous, as sometimes the authorities will not allow things to remain in the past. Other times they make sure they do, as is the case with this story, which successive British Government's have tried to bury in the mists of time.

The British soldiers that were involved and are still alive are now old men, but believe this is a story that must be told – so that it can never happen again.

The year 1972 was a very long time ago. However, 500 died in Northern Ireland that year, 5,000 more were injured. The bereaved and those whose lives were shattered have long memories.

With that in mind, certain facts in the story – some names and places – have been distorted to protect those involved. The operational techniques of the unit have not. The changes are to protect those who have lost loved ones, as we have no wish to look back either in anger or with false sorrow.

Remember what happened in 1972 happened in a different age. Today's sensibilities do not apply to this story.
The Special Forces involved were not from a peacetime Army.

They were the soldiers who had never stopped fighting Britain's secret wars. Any blame for their actions or tactics must be with the politicians and senior officers who let loose these dogs of war.

Orders were orders in that Army – they simply could not be questioned. Army doctors put the one man who did try to raise the alarm, and today would be hailed a "whistleblower", in a mental hospital.

The real lunatics, however, were those who deployed the MRF death squad in a United Kingdom sectarian civilian population. Their actions were like pouring petrol on a flickering candle – but perhaps for their own misguided reasons they wanted to inflame the Irish situation beyond any reasonable comprehension. Perhaps they wanted to solve it "once and for all".

There are no official military records available to researchers or to the public about the MRF, and what has been written about the unit up to now has for the most part been fantasy or at best fanciful.

If you are British and decide to buy this book, be prepared to be shocked and upset by the actions that were taken in your name by Her Majesty's Government in 1972 and 1973.

Tom Siegriste.

THE MRF

1972

By Tom Siegriste

Belfast: a sectarian nightmare, but a dream, target-rich environment for the SAS-trained operatives of the MRF – the Military Reaction Force. Working undercover, between early 1972 and late 1973, they were too successful for their own good and were disbanded before nervous politicians started to ask too many questions.

Did they have a licence to kill?
Were they the British Army's Death Squad?
It certainly looked that way…

This, told for the first time, is their story…

Chapter 1
Shoot and Scoot

Listen.

Carrying a gun does not make you a man; it does not make you a soldier. It makes you a target. In Northern Ireland, just a glimpse of gunmetal on the streets meant the clock was ticking on your destiny – especially once the men of the Military Reaction Force were on your case. And with their SAS training, any weapon makes you a killing machine – even when that weapon is your bare hands.

Monday 20th March 1972: today's weapon of choice is the Thompson sub-machine gun. It sits on the armoury shelf incongruously among the weapons of the modern age. It may be almost an antique but it sure packs a punch. The fifty .45 calibre bullets from its round magazine promise the potential of a St Valentine's Day Massacre every time it leaves the armoury for an outing.

Its life started in the 1920's in New York as a gangster's "enforcer". It crossed the oceans in the thirties with one of the five crime families to Cosa Nostra, Sicily. In the forties it had somehow arrived in mainland Italy and was "liberated" from surrendering German troops at Monte Cassino by a British SAS Major whose son now wears the red beret of the Parachute Regiment on the streets of Belfast.

• • •

Location: The MRF Briefing Room in Palace Barracks, Holywood, Belfast.

Time: 1900 hours.

A group of casually dressed male figures between 20 and 35 years of age wearing bomber-jackets, blue jeans, jumpers, desert boots or Doc Martens gather in front of a "rogues' gallery" of the 50 "most-wanted" IRA terrorists in the Belfast area.

Intelligence Sgt. Roy Mackay speaks.

"OK! Pay attention – the mission tonight. These six IRA bastards are out there walking the streets today. They were identified by Army Land Rover Patrols who 'could not stop' to arrest them. I want them taken out of circulation as soon as possible so keep your eyes open. Here are some individual photographs for each car. Memorise them now – it will be dark. Do not make any mistakes that you, or God, cannot correct later. That's an order.

"Call sign Nine-Zero. Sergeant Major, sir. The Commanding Officer of 5 Field Regiment Royal Artillery would like you to pay him a courtesy call this evening. The unit's location is McGuigan's old industrial site in Andersonstown. There has been lots of activity in his area recently, especially around Anderstown Park Road and Anderstown Park South Road, so proceed with caution."

• • •

The MRF Armoury: a steel-reinforced door in a brick built structure at the end of a recently erected prefabricated hut. A bang on the door with the side of a fist, and a small metal slit slides open revealing dark brown eyes belonging to Jeff, the armoury Corporal. He quickly recognises his casually-dressed visitors and opens the top half of the door that gives entry to his private kingdom. The MRF team know that what lies beyond Jeff is "verboten". Each MRF man ID's his personal weapon.

Corporal Alan Marshal, 2nd Battalion Lancashire Fusiliers, steps up to the opening looking much younger than his 27 years – eight of which have been spent in the Army. He is good looking, fit, agile, with short blonde hair and some serious attitude, dressed in a black T-shirt worn under a black plastic bomber jacket. With his faded blue Levi jeans, he favours black Doc Marten boots with high lace ups. No-one has ever seen him smile but he is "always happy to help".

"SMG [sub-machine gun] Number 20 please."

"Ok SMG with two mags [magazines]. Sign here," Jeff replies.

"Right next one."

Sergeant Peter Adams, hippy-length dark, curly hair, moves forward. He looks every one of his 29 years and, with the odd grey hair showing, appears to have borrowed a few more from somebody else. He's a strapping lad from Yorkshire – broad shoulders, a round face, dark blue eyes set back in his face – an experienced Royal Marine Commando. He does not joke – he is tough and shows it. A very good man to have around in a sticky situation.

"SMG Number 21 please."

"Done – next."

Bombardier Bert Cousins, Royal Artillery, is up next. A fit 25 years of age, short curly black hair, dark features, brown eyes, and the broken nose that says "ex-boxer". From Preston in Lancashire, he is light on his feet, quick-witted and talkative with a cold heart of gold.

"9mm Browning [pistol], armoury ID seven please."

"Two empty mags."

"Done!"

"Next."

Sergeant John Benson, Royal Military Police, aged 30, 6 foot 2 inches, moves forward. He has piercing blue eyes, thin eyebrows, a "fashionable" Tony Curtis-style blonde haircut and moustache. He is self-assured and speaks with a Belfast accent because he is from the Shankhill. Always well turned out, he thinks of himself as the "player" of the team. God's gift to women and the younger the better. With his looks and impressive voice, he says he could have been a pop singer and maybe a TV star like David Cassidy if he had not been a soldier.

"Same again. With knobs on mate!"

"No bloody cheek, you'll get what you're given – Browning 9mm Number 8, two empty mags. Next!"

Corporal Joe Lock, Royal Engineers, aged 23, small, barely 5 foot 4 inches, it was joked that "he stood on someone's shoulders to get into the Army". A Scouser (native of Liverpool), with long fair hair, a narrow nose, a square face with round shoulders and a deathly white complexion as if he'd never seen daylight. The boys call him "dead already" but he more than stands up for himself. He is the joker in the MRF pack and he always has the last word if not the last laugh.

"Me too. Number 9 9mm."

"Done."

"Next!"

Welsh Guardsman Taff (Steve) Morgan moves forward.

"SMG Number 13 please."

"Unlucky for some..." Jeff, who is now beginning to lighten up in light of the infectious banter from the boys, apes a

Welsh bingo caller he had heard on holiday at Butlin's Barry Island, the spot he and the missus had travelled from Birmingham for a week's break last year.

"That's not funny Jeff, you know I'm really superstitious..." Taff said and muttered something in Welsh under his breath.

"*Mae dy fam yn llyfu cociau mul.*"

Well that's what it sounded like, if you listened carefully and could speak the "language of heaven".

Steve is your typical Welshman. Acne, fair skin, Celtic hair – not red, not brown. He is just 20 years old, with a Nationalist chip on his shoulder the size of the Isle of Anglesey – or Ynys Môn, as he likes to call it – a chip so big you wondered why he was fighting for the English Army and not against it.

If the Free Wales Army actually existed – beyond the M15 and Special Branch "agent provocateurs" who whipped up the adolescent fervour of students and a few misguided hotheads in Aberystwyth and Bangor – he would have volunteered. However, as a misfit whose Welsh Guards Sgt. Major was glad to see the back of him, the MRF was now the only show in town.

Perhaps he should not have had a live round up the spout when he was on guard duty at Buckingham Palace. Unsurprisingly, that night does not appear in the regimental history or the records at the Ministry of Defence.

"Corgis are Welsh dogs, see – for the Welsh not for the English..." was his only explanation for his quite random canicide.

"Next!"

Sgt. Major Jack Gillespie Royal Artillery (ex-SAS) is, at 35, the old man of the outfit. He has a fresh complexion, short brown hair and brown eyes, with a Roman nose, tough-looking lean face and strong jaw line. He is Glaswegian – and although you may need a translator present to understand him after he's had a few drinks, you will definitely know when he is serious.

He's a leader of men. Jack's smile wins hearts and minds – but he can be at his most dangerous when he's grinning. Sensible people stay out of his way.

Today he wears a well-worn sleeveless suede photographer's jacket. It is jerkin-like and covered in pockets – some zipped, some buttoned, some filled with empty 35mm Kodak film containers. Somewhere in one of them, there is a spiral notebook, and protruding from the pocket over the left side of his chest is a 1972 National Union of Journalists Press Card in a clear plastic sleeve. Just the word "PRESS" is visible.

By day, he is a press photographer covering the Northern Ireland conflict for the *Glasgow Times*. For tonight's mission, he will later change into a dark blue denim bomber jacket, dark brown corduroy trousers and desert boots.

"Thanks for your help Jeff, I'll take an SMG... Hold head, what's that wee weapon over there?"

"That's the boss's Thompson he brought over from Scotland – why, do you want it?"

"I'll think I'll have a look at it – pass it over, Jeff."

The gun changes hands.

"You beauty! I haven't seen you for a wee while. Solid, heavy. Holding you in my hands like this makes me feel top of the world. Pass the magazine over, Jeff, I think she is in need of an Irish outing."

"A drum or a normal magazine Jack?"

"A round gangster mag thanks – you never know might need the extra firepower."

"Why? Where you going?"

Jack touches the end of his nose.

"Need to know, need to know," he taps.

Jeff nods and closes the green armoury door. First, a Chubb padlock is clipped closed, and then another key turns in a deadlock. The armourer then selects another key from his copious bunch and walks towards the ammunition store a few yards down the concrete slab path.

The MRF team wait patiently for him at the door, shuffling their feet in the cold evening air. The smokers were a few yards further away in the kind of huddle that 20-a-day-plus men adopt to give their habit an almost Masonic reverence.

"Choking smokers, don't you think the joker laughs at you," Jack recites under his breath.

Keys engage and the two heavy steel doors swing wide open. Jeff quickly gets the usual 9mm ammunition boxes out and places them on the hard standing. The MRF men open them hastily and the contents are disgorged.

Each SMG magazine's capacity was 28 rounds – although you could push 30 in with a strong thumb. If you did however, you'd risk a "stoppage" (jam) when you attempted to fire the first couple of rounds. This could have potentially fatal consequences in a contact situation. You might as well just stand there with your dick in your hand. So 28 it was – no more, no less.

Those MRF soldiers whose personal weapon is the SMG know this well and they empty the 9mm rounds from the small cardboard inner boxes, count 56 out and put the excess back into the ammunition containers. None of them can imagine a situation in Belfast where you would need more than two mags.

For the MRF, contacts invariably never lasted more than a few seconds. Several short sharp bursts of three rounds on automatic usually proved decisive or the IRA targets would be lost – melting back into the native population as quickly as they appeared.

A 30-second "contact" was an SAS tactic – "shoot and scoot" they called it. It meant the MRF would always leave the scene of the firing and then the Royal Ulster Constabulary would usually appear some minutes after the event, sometimes taking 10 or 15 minutes to arrive.

In that sort of time, republican sympathisers would have removed all evidence of illegal IRA weapons, spent cartridge cases or any incriminating materials like roadblocks. Just the bloodied bodies would remain in their innocence – stripped of their guilty secrets.

There was never an occasion when the MRF stayed on the scene waiting for the security forces to arrive.

The dead or wounded terrorists would lie, attended by local women screeching loudly of the "*murdering UVF* [Ulster Volunteer Force] *bastards*" who had just assassinated their unarmed men-folk right in front of their eyes.

Never for one minute did it cross their minds that these "murderers" were in fact regular British soldiers, ordered by those at the highest level to take on the terrorists at their own game, on their own turf.

Little wonder the UVF had such a deadly reputation and instilled fear into the toughest IRA terrorists when captured.

But now, Jeff has a problem. The .45 calibre rounds for the Thompson Sub-Machine Gun are not standing up and saluting him.

"Where are you? You bastards..." he mutters as he rummages around the armoury.

The specially requisitioned box of US Army ammunition had arrived late the previous day. Jeff had hurriedly pushed it onto a top shelf, out of sight, out of reach, and out of mind, to a place where he thought it would remain undisturbed for the duration of "The Troubles". The Troubles was the quaint English understatement for the "civil war" breaking out in the United Kingdom just a couple of hundred miles from London.

Now here was Sgt. Major Jack Gillespie asking for those very rounds. A coincidence or what?

The heavy 2ft. by 1ft. brown steel box bearing yellow-stencilled US contents markings strains the armourer's out of condition biceps as he pulls it down from what he had imagined would be its final resting place.

"Never thought I'd have to get it back down again," gasps Jeff.

"You didn't think of giving me a hand then Jack?"

"Sorry. Didn't think I was allowed in your ammo store."

"Even by special invitation?"

"Rules are rules," says Jack.

Jeff carefully peels back the airtight heavy foil covering of the ammo box, revealing tightly packed small cardboard boxes of .45 calibre rounds.

"Two boxes Jack?"

"Foreign weapons familiarisation range firing Jeff – two boxes and a 50- round drum magazine".

The team quickly charge their magazines.

Corporal Alan Marshall is all fingers and thumbs, dropping a few rounds onto the concrete. He picks them up wipes them clean with the edge of his jacket before slotting them home. The MRF drivers leave to check their "squad" cars.

The British Racing Green 1966 Morris Oxford Estate looks heavy on its leaf-spring suspension. No wonder – its front doors and the full width of the rear passenger seat is reinforced with composite armour plates, including ceramic inserts capable of stopping both high and low velocity rounds.

Corporal Joe Lock, the driver of call sign Nine-Zero – Jack's driver - approaches the Farina-styled Series 6 Traveller model. Its chrome grill and bumper catches the compound's lighting, scattering the beams over the 12-foot high, corrugated steel-clad walls that surround it.

Beneath the bumper is its Antrim registration plate, BIA5949, that replaced the UK mainland number it bore when it was "borrowed" from a Liverpool backstreet a few months earlier and delivered to the Royal Electrical Mechanical Engineers (REME) for "hardening". It is about to make its first appearance on the streets of Belfast.

Joe kicks the cross-ply tyres with all the skill of a professional tyre kicker. He steps back and taps each in turn with the side of his instep. Then he gives a nod towards the approaching members of the MRF team that, in his "expert" opinion, this wagon was ready to roll.

"Rock and roll baby – all the way from the Delta to the DMZ," he apes the US troops he'd once met at RAF Upper Heyford on a NATO exercise. He flays his hips Elvis-like and attempts a Yankee drawl but it ends up sounding like an ultra-nasal John Lennon.

He should have stopped while the going was good, but Joe can't resist going for a high five with one of the approaching smokers. Completely mystified by the ritual of a foreign culture, the potential recipient just stares at him.

"Scouse twat."

This just about sums him up.

Bombardier Bert Cousins, driver of call sign Nine-One, has already started up the "back-up" car, a dark-coloured Mark I Ford Cortina GT BIA2278. Also "liberated" from the mainland, it has the go-faster stripe of the more powerful Lotus Cortina model. But its four doors are what matter to the MRF – it is impossible to fire weapons easily and effectively from the rear seats of a two-door car with no wind down rear windows.

The two teams turn left on to Sydenham Highway heading for Belfast. They join the Newtownards Road, then cross over the Queens Bridge, left into Victoria Street and right into Grosvenor Road. They enter Falls Road and head on south to Andersonstown Road, "recce-ing" the area to see if the highways are clear.

In fact, three cars are out tonight: call signs Nine-Zero, Nine-One and Nine-Two. The first two call signs are supposed to travel together, and Nine-Two is to move independently, do a general recce of Lower Falls Road and afterwards head in the general direction of Glen Road where they will all meet later.

Wanting to attract as little attention as possible, Jack decides Nine-Zero and Nine-One will head for the safe haven of the Victoria Hospital car park. Call Sign Nine-One will hold position there and Nine-Zero will then go on alone to see the CO of the unit in Andersonstown.

Having radioed the MRF Ops Room to ask them to warn the Army unit of his imminent approach, Jack's team drive, with the headlights switched off, across a grass field to covertly enter the rear entrance of the fortified McGuigan's Yard, away from the prying eyes watching the front gates.

The Duty Sergeant is waiting for Jack when the Morris Oxford arrives.

• • •

McGuigan's is a typical builders' yard. In its heyday it prospered in supplying materials for the construction of the local Catholic area. Now its occupants are the focal point of the community's destructive wrath.

The British Army has done some interesting building work of their own, on the premises since moving in at the beginning of the Seventies. Mr Sandbags and military fortifications now replace Mr McGuigan's supplies of sand and cement for sale. Corrugated steel tops the brick walls to stop distant snipers seeing any movement within the perimeter and coils of barbed wire deter any entry by direct assault or stealth.

A watchtower dominates proceedings, looking down Kennedy Way and into Andersonstown. The silent barrel of a general-purpose machine gun routinely follows any suspect movement in the vicinity. Someone once had come near enough to scrawl "IRA rules British fools" on a wall nearby and the crude rhyme is good enough to leave for the Irish rain to wash away.

But tonight is a clear one. At 2100 hours, stars are blinking but a chill breeze deters study of them for too long in the open air. Only those with evil intent would be out tonight, that's for sure.

The Ops Officer introduces Jack to the CO, Lieutenant-Colonel Michael Tomkinson. He is tall, standing at 6 feet 3 inches, thin, and slightly gaunt with a narrow nose and brown eyes. His brown hair, parted on the left and combed back, shines with a hint of Brylcreem that makes it look darker, almost black.

Michael is a "Rupert" – the enlisted men's derogatory nickname for the British Officer – and a typical product of the Sandhurst conveyor belt.

With a few notable exceptions Sandhurst – the British West Point – could take a good bloke from a middle class Grammar School background and, in a couple of fraught years, turn him into a slightly-confused upper class twit whose first words to the troops were usually: "Right then chaps, what's going on?"

In the British Army, if you were lucky, you'd have a good Sergeant Major who kept the Ruperts in line and you alive. A good Sergeant Major like Jack Gillespie.

The MRF has no Ruperts on the streets of Belfast. In fact, at that time, the only MRF soldier with pips on his shoulder never left his office.

Captain Arthur Watches, Parachute Regiment, and ex-SAS, rose through the ranks and has never seen the portals of an elite officer academy. It was blood, sweat and tears that won his commission and the men respect that. Nevertheless he now "drove a desk" as the liaison point between the MRF and the conventional forces of 39 Brigade, the Headquarters of the Army in Belfast and the surrounding area as far as the border with the Irish Republic. The HQ at Lisburn also has some "cuckoos in the Army nest" stationed there: MI6 – the British Secret Intelligence Service.

Tonight, Jack has to stand and listen to the wisdom of a Grade A Rupert.

"Now look here. The situation is this: we know from intelligence reports that there are gunmen on the junction of Anderstown Park Road and Anderstown Park South who are illegally stopping all traffic. If we send an army vehicle, those IRA Johnnies will hear us coming and simply skedaddle into one of the houses on the junction."

"It's just like playing cat and mouse."

"I would like you to confirm that these activities are in fact happening and report back to me forthwith."

Tomkinson's face breaks into a wide smile. He has delivered his orders with authority and panache – "by the book" – without a trace of the upper-class stutter that he tries so hard to hide from his men. His efforts are in vain, however, as his unit's favourite pastime is to impersonate their glorious leader's speech defect behind is back.

What Tomkinson doesn't realise is that the man who stands in front of him in civilian dress and who talks to him on equal terms – and has the potential to bring a quick solution to all his problems – is in fact a member of a Gunners regiment.

Tomkinson had requested the MRF's help to get out of the strategic stalemate his regiment is now in at McGuigan's Yard. Their ineffectiveness was proving a personal embarrassment that threatened his prospects of a rapid rise in the regimental hierarchy.

The next time the pair meet, Tomkinson will bear the Royal Crown and three pips of a Brigadier of the British Army as testimony to Jack's handiwork. A Brigadier is the British rank, which stands between a full Colonel and a Major General – the highest field rank or the junior General appointment. He will return the favour and save Jack's skin many years down the line but, for now, he is just a prize Rupert.

"I'll do my best sir."

Jack returns to the Morris Oxford, which waits silently in shadows of the yard. The Nine-Zero pair dispose of their Benson and Hedges butts. Joe Lock has chain smoked since their arrival and Cpl. Alan Marshal, who is, to all intents and purposes, a non-smoker, has joined him for a few puffs of a fag just to be sociable.

Jack does not like the smell of tobacco on his clothes. Only guns smoke when he is around. He picks up the microphone handset of the military radio. The coiled lead stretches out of the car door and his breath is visible in the cold night air.

Usually, he would sit inside on the front passenger seat, activate the transmit button with his left foot and speak through a small button microphone concealed to the side of the Morris

Oxford's beige sun visor. Incoming transmissions would be heard via speakers hidden under the seats.

This set up enables the MRF Call Signs to communicate covertly with base, or each other without detection, even in the most crowded urban street or traffic jam. Just a glimpse of a hand-held mike in the Lower Falls Road would have deadly consequences and any squad car thus compromised would have to be scrapped. However, in the safety of McGuigan's Yard the auxiliary microphone ensures clarity of the message he speaks to Nine-One.

"Nine-One this is Nine-Zero… Over."

"Nine-Zero, this is Nine-One …send. Over."

"Nine-One, this is Nine-Zero. Go to RV-Zebra. See you in 10 minutes. Over."

"Nine-One. Roger. Out."

MRF messages were open transmissions that anyone could hear, but only those at the previous briefing would understand their meaning and be able to act upon them.

RV-Zebra was the pre-arranged mission rendezvous point – a lay-by on Kennedy Way just before its junction with Glen Road; a quiet spot in Catholic West Belfast.

• • •

Nine-Zero moves out of McGuigan's yard the same way they entered. Vehicle lights off until they rejoined Kennedy Way, travelling north. As they approach RV-Zebra, the Ford Cortina GT of Nine-One appears through the darkness. It is parked in the lay-by with its lights off. Two men are sitting in the car; a third is concealed in a hedge with his SMG to protect the location from an IRA drive-by assault.

The Morris Oxford pulls in behind the Cortina and its 1660cc engine falls silent. Even though it is barely 2130 hours, there is no other traffic or activity.

Normally the MRF squads would drive into a small parking area shielded by trees, just off the highway, to ensure complete concealment, but Jack's instincts tell him that no-one is about tonight. On Ulster Television that night a TV special of the hard-hitting current affairs programme *World in Action* called *Waiting for the Package* – Tory (British Conservative Party) Prime Minister, Edward Heath's peace proposals for the Province – was screened, and proved compelling viewing for the population. They are unaware that Northern Ireland was just days away from the announcement of direct rule from London.

World in Action was a British investigative current affairs programme made by Granada Television from 1963. It frequently took risks and gained a reputation for its unorthodox approach and campaigning journalism.

Jack motions for the men to gather around. He smiles.

"Okay boys this is the plan. We're to go to the junction of these two roads, Anderstown Park and Anderstown Park South where we believe IRA gunmen are stopping the public from entering. We'll go and confirm this is going on and report our findings to the local Army ground commander. Any questions?"

Joe Lock, a relative new boy, gives his boss an uneasy glance.

"So what happens if we're fired upon?"

Jack smiles again.

"You know the Rules of Engagement, Scouser: if fired upon, you return fire, and withdraw."

A snigger breaks the silence. Jack spots the culprit.

"Yes, Benson, that means get the hell out of there or suffer the consequences. Remember the drill – only fire in self defence, or if you think that you, or someone you are responsible for, is in danger of being killed or seriously wounded."

Jack takes a breath just in time.

"You open fire to avoid this danger. Any more stupid questions?"

He is met with silence, so he continues: "I will be in the front car and you, John, as commander of Nine-One, will stay at least 100 yards behind me."

Corporal Lock nervously fingeres the safety catch of his 9mm Browning before putting it in his shoulder holster. Jack "recruited" him on the basis of his exceptional ability as a driver and car thief, who learnt his craft not in the Army training centre in Bordon but on the mean streets of his native Liverpool.

The rest of the team are an experienced and well-organised patrol – their training having kept them alive on the streets of Belfast in some pretty hairy situations up to now.

True, they're not SAS, but Jack's expertise as an SAS Instructor has produced a fair facsimile.

The team are tense, but it is a clear night and with lady luck on their side, this task would soon be over and they would be preparing for the next one – looking for trouble elsewhere. Maybe at the pub.

Jack tells his men to cock their weapons. This means putting a round into the chamber of the weapon, making it ready to fire, or in the case of the SMG with its fixed firing pin, drawing back the working parts and applying the safety catch.

Jack now sits in the front of the Morris Oxford fondly cradling the Thompson sub machine gun. The black gunmetal feels cold even through his corduroy trousers – the wooden butt tucked under his right arm, the drum magazine filled with its 50 .45 rounds ready for action. Corporal Alan Marshal is in the back with his 9mm SMG.

Windows down, the Morris Oxford silently leaves the lay-by, followed, once it has moved 100 yards down the road, by the Cortina GT.

They head south-east down Kennedy Way. When they reach Andersonstown Road, they turn left into it. The target is about half-a-mile further on. Approaching Anderstown Park on their left, Jack can see two or three men talking in the street. There is a red and white wooden barrier across the road on trestles.

The MRF squad knows what they have to do – if necessary.

"Get ready," says Jack.

"We may be in for a bit of bother."

Jack gestures for Corporal Lock to drive towards the barrier and follow the proven tactic of turning across the roadway as if intending to make a three point turn. The car stopped side-on to the barrier – 20 feet away.

On spotting the roadblock, Jack uses the radio transmit foot switch and tells Nine-One to close in on Nine-Zero immediately if they hear shots, as they may need extra fire power. Nine-One "roger"s that.

One of the IRA men starts to raise a rifle in Jack's direction. Another motions as if to fire a pistol, the third man turns and runs towards a house. Two shots hit the MRF car.

Jack jumps out, does an SAS forward roll and comes up shooting with the Thompson sub-machine gun on automatic. Three low-velocity .45 calibre bullets leave the Cutts Compensator attached to the end of the Thompson's barrel.

This was not a silencer, as many people thought, but a device that has a bullet-exit hole slightly larger than the bullet. Inside is a marginally enlarged chamber with ports, or "saw slots", above and crossing the axis of the bore. The escape of a portion of the propellant gases through these slots pushes the muzzle downward, thus counteracting the natural tendency of the muzzle to "climb," particularly on full automatic fire.

The first burst of fire the Thompson had spat in anger for some years sends staccato rounds towards the enemy. The sound of the .45 calibre is different from the usual British Army low-velocity ordnance. The 1927 Thompson sub-machine gun with its Cutts Compensator has a sound all of its own – one for the connoisseurs of automatic weapons – a *swoosh-thud*. The same trained ear could tell it was a burst of just three rounds fired by an expert marksman that found its target.

One man drops.

The rifle he had held and fired just a fraction of a second earlier clatters on the paving stones. Jack's years of training and experience now initiate an instinctive reaction.

The first IRA man to move: threat now eliminated.

Jack sees the other man starting to run for cover, and although his cone of focus is on the targets, the peripheral awareness honed by SAS training to ensure battlefield survival means he knows that the other members of the MRF team are now in play.

The metallic stutter of Cpl. Alan Marshal's Sterling 9mm sub-machine gun fired from the back of the armoured Morris Oxford breaks the silence.

It is a multiple round burst: a fault due to excitement that Jack will have to correct in continued contact drill training on the firing ranges in the days to come – but today it fits the bill precisely.

The IRA man never completes his turn; he simply falls forward, in a lifeless heap.

"Good shot Alan – change magazines," orders Jack.

Jack quickly gets back into his car to exit the scene. Suddenly, to the left, the Cortina GT of call sign Nine-One skids to a halt.

The IRA man who had bolted to the nearest house seconds earlier now appears in an upstairs window holding an Armalite AR-15 automatic rifle.

Obviously an experienced gunman, he only exposes enough of his upper body to fire a quick and lethal burst. Approximately 20 of the rifle's .223 calibre high-velocity rounds speed at 3,200 feet per second to greet the Nine-One newcomers.

Seemingly sharing the exact same moment to open fire as his IRA adversary, Alan lets rip another over-long burst from his SMG.

The target falls back out of sight, and Jack shouts: "AWAY!"

"CASUALTY!" screams Sgt. John Benson from the front passenger seat of the Cortina GT.

As the car's wheels swing away from the scene of the fight, Sgt. Benson presses his transmit button:

"Nine-Zero. This is Nine-One. Casualty. Repeat. Casualty. Over."

"Nine-One. Nine-Zero. Roger your last. Proceed RVH immediately. Out."

MRF HQ "Zero" enters the transmissions to confirm they had heard the emergency call:

"Zero. Nine-Zero, Nine-One. Roger. Out."

The two cars turn off Grosvenor Road at the cobbled forecourt of the Royal Victoria Hospital. Designed in 1899, it was completed and opened in 1906. Before becoming known as the main casualty unit for The Troubles, its claim to fame was to be the first building in the world to be air-conditioned.

The IRA usually took their casualties to the Mater Infirmorum Hospital off Belfast's Crumlin Road. The Royal Victoria was favoured by the fighting men of the Ulster Volunteer Force and the other East Belfast para-militaries, although it was used by both the Catholic and Protestant communities.

Through "official channels" the Royal Victoria Hospital has been put on standby for the "civilian" casualty about to be in their care.

• • •

Arriving at the hospital, Jack runs towards Nine-One's Cortina and sees Taff Morgan slumped in the back. Sgt. Benson and Bombardier Cousins are trying to get the Welshman's body out. He is bleeding from a gunshot wound to the upper body and sucking in air to his lungs through a hole in his chest.

Pulling his man onto the ground, Jack rips Taff's Western-style shirt apart and pushes a shell dressing into the wound in an attempt to seal it. He applies mouth to mouth, though the blood flooding out of the Welshman's lips makes Jack's task near impossible. Nurses eventually have to pull him away. Orderlies take Taff on a stretcher. Swing doors open and butt closed.

Jack moves to follow but, covered in blood, he goes into a washroom. As he looks into the mirror, he sees the steely darkness that now blackens his brown eyes. He glances at the blood already coagulating on the stubble around his mouth and quickly flushes cold water across his face.

The crimson-streaked liquid swirles around the porcelain of the sink and into the drain that gurgles as it greets this grisly effluent. He reaches out for the paper towel dispenser and wipes his face. He rolls the towels into a paper ball and, banging his fists together, propels them toward the waste bin, the missile just catching the side of the rim before dropping inside.

This is an action he has repeated it many times before and will repeat many times again. It is his absolution – his justification. He could train soldiers in the skills of slaughter and survival, but Jack is no superman, merely a mortal who made his own luck through his skills and training. Like Taff's, one day Jack's would run out. But no, not today. Today was routine. It would take some great alignment of misfortunes to get Sgt. Major Jack Gillespie.

• • •

Guardsman Steven (Taff) Morgan from the small village of Meidrim near Carmarthen was the MRF's first fatality. The RAF flew his body home. There was no announcement. No honours accompanied his coffin, no military funeral. How could there be – he died fighting for a unit that did not exist in a war that was never declared.

Yes, thought Jack, this was war, but *never should its name be spoken*.

It was a politician's war.

Jack should know. He had fought them for Her Majesty's Government since the fifties. British soldiers lost their lives. British politicians simply lost their seats.

Now ever closer to home, as the British Empire waned, this was a war on the mother of democracy's doorstep. Jack Gillespie was that mother's prodigal son, home on "civilian leave".

His rules of war? Well, there were no rules.

The MRF were a force on unfamiliar ground; the enemy was on home territory and knew every cobblestone, every back alleyway. Jack's men were "jungle-trained" and now fighting the natives of an urban jungle. Jack was the "SAS Warlord" who had turned Stone Age head-hunters into a modern guerrilla force that struck terror into the regulars of the Indonesian army.

Now they had asked him to do it again.

This time it was in their own backyard.

In their own house of cards – a pack of jokers and discards that had been folded by the Army and picked up by Jack, which would now deal out summary justice on the streets of West Belfast, day and night, in a no-rules game of Killer. On behalf of the Queen, they would be the new Kings of the Falls Road.

If no one interfered, Jack knew this was a war for the winning. Moreover, for the MRF it was not a case of the gloves being off – they had never been on.

• • •

Before the night could be put to bed – consigned to the Black Book Jack kept just in case the Army decided to sacrifice him as the scapegoat for the Government's so-called illegal "shoot-to-kill" policy – there was the formality of going down to deliver a statement to the Protestant-dominated Royal Ulster Constabulary.

Something had rattled the cage of the normally supine RUC. They hinted officiously that Jack had used unnecessary force in Andersonstown, even taking into consideration the MRF casualty.

"Was it the Tommy Gun?" Jack asked them. "I just had it in the car when we were fired upon. I signed it out for foreign weapons-familiarisation range firing – we have intelligence that the IRA has one or more of these weapons and we need to know what we are up against."

The big black lie returned the smile to Jack's brown eyes.

As Jack turned to leave, an Army Intelligence Officer, a nondescript MI6 spook from 39 Brigade HQ Northern Ireland, arrived.

"There are questions being asked in the 'House', especially

because of the fact that we lost a man," he told Jack. "I just want to run through the events with you, in your own words."

In precise detail and without a hint of emotion, Jack recounted what had happened. The Intelligence Officer listened in silence then imparted the message he had been despatched to deliver from *on high.*

"We have to now.... start a period where we are going to have to be more – how can I put it – *defensive.* In particular," he lowered his voice "*not going out looking for trouble.* Your MRF have done a superb job and we appreciate the fact that the IRA are fearful of our covert cars. Reports coming in indicate that their gunmen are going to be seen less on the streets at night, especially in the 'no go' areas."

With that, the member of what the SAS call "the slime", left as anonymously as he arrived and another chapter in the short history of the MRF began: *armed non-agression.*

Chapter 2

The New Kings of Falls Road

It was Top of the Pops – it was Number One in the Hit Parade. The whining strains of the Harry Nilsson ballad *Without You* echoed around the MRF accommodation in Palace Barracks at Holywood, Belfast. However, this version did not sound anywhere near as tuneful as the US singer's original.

Jack was back. The men didn't know where he'd been, and certainly hadn't missed him for a minute. But now that he was back he was in for some real stick.

It was the post orderly's fault. A package had arrived for Jack and mysteriously "opened itself", its contents falling into the wrong, very wrong, hands.

The shiny black vinyl of a 45-rpm single record had been exposed and taken into protective custody by the men of the MRF who had by then perfected their own, very own, version of the chart topper which they used to serenaded their boss.

"*Can't die if dying is without you, Can't die can't die anymore...*" shattered the silence. The words "cats" and "chorus" came to mind but the immortals of the MRF had found their theme tune.

• • •

The song itself has death links for another reason apart from the discordant and desecrated version adopted by the men of the MRF. Both the composers, Peter Ham and Tom Evans, committed suicide. But in 1972 Belfast it was a belting ballad and had won the hearts and minds of the MRF.

It was pure coincidence that only hours before Jack had been passing through the composers' hometown of Swansea in South Wales. "Passing through" was the best thing to do to the town of Swansea. It was Dylan Thomas's hometown. He called it a pretty, ugly town or something along those lines. Others knew it "as the place where ambition went to die". But with the filthy Carbon Black plant belching out a pure soot welcome to travellers arriving from the east and the incessant acid rain, Jack just thought of it as the arsehole of Britain.

Aside from the Adelphi public house at the bottom of Wind Street, that is, where you were always sure of a grand welcome, as long as you left all your money in the till. Landlord George Hopkins and his son ex-Para Les (the Bear) Hopkins would see to that. Les's grizzly presence made sure there was never any trouble at the Adelphi. It was a pub for real men and real ale.

The tiny village of Meidrim just outside Carmarthen, some 20 or so miles from Swansea, was a different matter. It was a rural idyll. Jack had stood silently watching the parents of Cpl. Steven (Taff) Morgan as they left their cottage in mourning clothes for their son's funeral. Jack would not be there at the graveside, nor would any representative of the Welsh Guards, the regiment his parents were sure he had served so proudly.

Jack had seen their grief and it was real. Viscerally real, unlike the war brave men like Taff fought just a few minutes flying time from where they stood, across the Irish Sea.

Somewhere in the distance, the beautiful lilt of a Welsh male voice choir had broken the still of the afternoon. They sang the lament *Llys Ifor Hael* in Welsh. It was a fitting tribute to Taff, a true son of Cymru, who always stood his turn at the bar and led the singing. The discordant remainder of the MRF choir would sorely miss his voice.

Jack didn't lose many men in action, but when he did, he saw them off in his own way. It was personal. Every time. He had failed, not them. A few minutes of quiet reflection standing at a distance, but in range of the emotions of others, and he was away – back to the frontline wherever in the world it may be.

If there was a war memorial in the community, Jack would carefully write in the name of the secret conflict that had claimed the life of his comrade, and, the name of the fallen, in Chinagraph pencil on the polished marble. He would also leave a sum of money with the local publican so that the unknown war's fallen could buy one last round for his friends.

He did this for Taff at the New Inn, Meidrim, where an hour later the newly raw throats of the tenors and baritones of the funeral chorus would be soothed and slaked with bitter ale.

• • •

Back with the living and breathing, why were the MRF's out of tune bastards now giving a live performance, singing their hearts out at Jack's expense?

The only clue lay in the wrapping paper that now littered the polished red lino of the barrack room floor. The shards and tattered chads of an emotional greeting card were visible in the detritus.

Pieced carefully together they revealed the words, written in love-red biro: "Lots of kisses for my huggle-bunny love Pam XXX P.S. Please listen to the words of the song".

On the front of the shredded card, given enough time, a dedicated forensic science officer would have painstakingly pieced together a picture of further incriminating evidence. Two cute bunny rabbits, pictured explicitly, carnally entwined in an infinite embrace. Damning. The sender certainly did not buy a greeting card like that in John Menzies or W H Smith.

The reality of the relationship between Jack and Pam could not have been further from that suggested by the bunnies. After the main event was over, just a bare 10 minutes in the front row of the theatre of love was *way* too long for Jack to be in Pam's company. Her "huggle-bunny" or not, for Jack it was shoot and scoot.

After all, the fleshpots of the almost neutral Newtownards area of east Belfast and the coastal resort of Bangor were easy prey for a fit British soldier. Jack was even working undercover under the covers.

Perhaps the past was to blame. If Jack stayed too long in a comfortable bed, the tattooed face of the Murut head-hunter Radu Ulan, Jack's blood brother, from the covert four-year war that Britain fought against Indonesia in the jungles of Borneo and Kalimantan would appear in his dream-wracked sleep, beckoning him to keep marching on:

"Jack, my brother, stay one step ahead or face certain death. Jalan! Jalan! Move on! Move on!"

"Every step you take brings you closer to the enemy and nearer to immortality."

• • •

At the MRF compound, everyone was running for cover. There could be heavy casualties.

"How the fuck did you lot get your dirty little hands on my personal mail?" stormed Jack.

"It certainly looked like a suspicious package boss – couldn't take any chances," Corporal Joe Lock piped up.

"It needed just a small controlled detonation to be certain – some of the innards of a thunderflash you understand – and it were made safe."

"We didn't want you to get hurt boss. It's just that there was some pretty dangerous stuff inside as it turned out – well it was dangerous when we read it – but its OK now, Huggle-Bunny, all your secrets are safe with us. Nice tune that record though. Once you listen to it once you can't get it out of your head."

The mere mention of the melody set off another chorus from the men. The Huggle Bunny beat a retreat.

Joe did have a point about all the romantic stuff, thought Jack, and the banter showed good morale considering they had just lost a mate. He wasn't too sure about the singing though.

"Carry on men," he shouted down the corridor as he left for the mess.

After enjoying lunch – steak and kidney pie and chips – Jack was sitting in his office going through the top secret "Sitreps". These were the details of what had been happening operationally while he was away on his Welsh pilgrimage.

He read today's date: Thursday 30th March 1972. He turned on the transistor radio to catch the local BBC Radio News. The Direct Rule from London announced by the Tory Government on Friday March 24th had started. The Stormont Parliament of Northern Ireland prorogued.

The main reason for the suspension of Stormont was the refusal of the Unionist Government to accept the loss of law and order powers to Westminster. William Whitelaw was now the first Secretary of State for Northern Ireland.

Tuesday 28th March 1972, while Jack was away, saw the second day of a strike organised by the paramilitary Ulster

Vanguard Service Corp. A rally was organised at Stormont that was attended by an estimated 100,000 people. According to the Sitreps, MI6, MI5 and MRF men had mingled with the crowds tailing IRA suspects.

Dark days indeed.

Jack shook his head then looked up.

It was a beautiful morning, one that suggested spring was on its way. The sun was shining through the six panes of glass of Jack's office window, forming a stretched grid of shadow on his desk. Half a dozen black and white "most wanted" mug shots were illuminated as the westerly winds moved a wisp of cloud off the winter sun's disc.

"What am I doing inside on a day like this," he thought. "It's a beautiful morning."

He looked at Belfast.

"It's a beautiful place for me to start."

There was no time to waste.

As far as Jack was concerned, outside that window,the enemy had had 72 hours of freedom to do what they liked on the streets of West Belfast. Holiday over, tonight it was shoot and scoot time again for the MRF.

• • •

The footfalls of someone approaching in the corridor interrupted Jack's thoughts. There was a gentle tap on the door.

"Hello? Come in," Jack ventured.

Pud from the Op's Room craned his head around the side of the door and spoke.

"Good Afternoon Sir. The new boss would like to see you at your convenience."

New boss?!" exclaimed Jack. "What happened to the old Boss?"

"It was very spooky. He simply disappeared in a puff of smoke while you were away," said Pud, gesturing extravagantly. "The bottom line is that am told to forward all his correspondence to Century House in London."

Corporal Lewis "Pud" Price hailed from Brighton. He was a switched-on guy, and despite his lowly rank was the dynamo that drove the MRF's intelligence machine, which worked like clockwork except at the times when the Ruperts thought *they* knew best. The men knew Pud had all his ducks in a row – his nickname an affectionate reference to his wobbling waistline. And yes, he was a bit of a ducky himself – but the MRF boys, fiercely heterosexual to the last, didn't mind that, because professionally the 'gen he gave them was pure gold. You could bet your life on it. They often did. What he did behind closed doors was up to him. He was their Mrs Moneypenny.

"Thanks Pud, I'm on my way," waved Jack.

Jack tidied away the Sitreps he'd been reading, and put them in his safe. Then he carefully locked his office door and walked the short distance to the boss's office. Switching the six mugshots he carried into his left hand, he knocked on the pine door.

"Enter!"

The new boss, a fresh-faced 25-year-old Captain Hamish McGregor MC, greeted Jack with a large smile.

"Please sit down Sergeant Major," he gestured, "I have a request",

The over-generous smile was due to the fact Captain McGregor's father was Jack's old squadron commander in the SAS. Jack had not twigged that yet.

"How can I help you Boss?"

"It's really nice to meet you Sergeant Major. I have been waiting for you to return from your absence. The thing is this,

I'd like to go and take a look at the Falls Road area, and perhaps then do a quick recce of Andersonstown. What do you think?"

I've got a keen one here, Jack thought.

"Suits me boss. When would you like to go?"

"How about in half-an-hour – does that suit you? Can you sort out a good driver?"

Jack sensed nervousness, or perhaps it was just anticipation, but as a fellow Scot, let it pass. In true Parachute Regiment-style McGregor obviously, unlike his predecessor, who shared the same cap badge, wanted to lead from the front.

In his SAS career, Jack had some bad experiences with Parachute Regiment officer-types. His judgement had been prejudiced by one Para Major who had joined the SAS and, by his treachery in breeching the confidentially of the bar room confessional, had earned the nickname "The Rat". He would take the NCOs out on a bender around the bars of Hereford, get them well and truly plastered and, while they were in an alcoholic haze, ask them what they really thought of him as an officer and a gentleman. His sin was that the next morning he remembered what they had said and they did not. He made sure he never let them forget it. Just like that other little Emperor, Napoleon, the men made sure the SAS's King Rat was soon exiled to St Helena, or some island or other.

Nevertheless, that Rupert ruined some fine careers in the process, so Jack was wise not to take any chances with the new Pegasus-badged man in his life.

He left Captain McGregor's office wondering whom he should use to impress the new man "in command". All Jack's drivers were good or dead. In the MRF, there was no middle ground between the gun and the grave.

"Drivers – let me see now?" Jack looked at the MRF duty roster.

Royal Marine Commando Sgt. Peter Adams was the obvious choice. He had bags of experience; bags of guts. Jack would make sure he was behind the wheel.

Peter was reading newspapers in the rest room when Jack found him. He was quickly briefed on the task ahead, told to find a suitable car, report to the armoury, and be ready to move in 30 minutes.

Jack moved over to Pud in the Ops Room and reported the plans for the Boss, Sgt. Adams and himself. Pud wrote down the details.

"Have a bona trip," he called after Jack had left the office.

The next stop was the armoury, to see what weapons they had available. He noticed the Thompson sub machine gun resting on the weapons rack. He did think about taking it along, but because this was only a recce patrol decided not to. The Thompson was better for more offensive engagements, he reasoned. After all, the MRF were currently practicing "armed non-aggression" – whatever that was. Settling for an SMG, Jack then also selected three 9mm Browning pistols for the boss, Peter and himself.

Sgt. Adams drew up outside the armoury in the same Morris Oxford Estate the MRF team had used on their outing in Andersontown, which, despite coming under fire, had escaped unscathed. The Ford Cortina GT in which Cpl. Morgan had perished was now swimming with the fishes in the murky depths of Belfast Docks.

After loading their weapons, and putting one up the spout, the new Boss's tragical history tour of Catholic West Belfast was underway.

They drove from Holywood towards Belfast on the

Sydenham Highway, and were soon winding their way through the city towards the Lower Falls Road. Jack smiled as they passed through without incident but both car and occupants were on the receiving end of a few hard looks as they halted fleeting, shortly after passing the wrecked Broadway Cinema, which sadly was still awaiting demolition following its fire-bombing by Protestants Paramilitaries on January 31st.

Approaching the Upper Falls Road, passing Waterford Street, which led to the notorious Clonard district, on the right and just before the junction with Springfield Road – both IRA strongholds – Jack spotted some unusual activity.

Women were taking their children by the hand and rushing them towards the safety of their front doors. Men were shouting instructions.

The MRF were rumbled.

Was it the car? Was it too conspicuous for the streets of Belfast? Had Peter swapped the plates? Or was it the UVF signature of three men in a car to blame? Anyway, no time to bother with such thoughts now – we'll leave them for the post mortem.

Jack knew his choice of words, even as thoughts, had been ill – the *debrief* was what he meant – but they had to get there first, alive.

As it transpired, according to informers, IRA lookouts in the Lower Falls Road, had indeed clocked the MRF vehicle as a UVF foray deep into the Catholic heartland.

Call sign Nine-Zero was in big trouble and things were getting worse by the second.

Jack had to do some quick thinking. A man, his face obscured by a black balaclava, jumped in front of the car to try to stop it. He waved his arms frantically.

Jack's luck was still good; the IRA ambush was not ready to swing its deadly trap closed.

Jack remembered the three Scottish soldiers, two of them brothers, murdered while enjoying a night out in West Belfast. IRA sympathisers lured the drunken soldiers to a flat in the Clonard with the promise of female company. Although there were no girls present, the Scots did not suspect anything was wrong and were plied with Irish whiskey until they were unable to walk.

IRA men arrived and the trio were shoved into the back of a van, driven to Ligoniel, the hill to the north overlooking the city of Belfast, thrown into a ditch and murdered in cold blood.

Each body had two shots in the back of the head – the hallmarks of a professional executioner.

Jack did not want his new boss to leave the MRF quite so soon. It would be a bit embarrassing to lose a Rupert just like that. *Not good form, old boy.*

Jack's instincts clicked on.

"Do not stop!" Jack ordered. "Run him over!"

At the very last moment, the hooded man jumped out of the way. Ten yards further on, other men, with black hoods over their heads had begun rolling metal beer barrels off the pavement to block the car's escape route.

Sgt. Adams braked – the car slowed down.

To his right, Jack saw a man, his hair Brylcreemed back, reaching into his unbuttoned three-quarter coat. The terrorist drew a huge .45 Calibre pistol from a shoulder holster.

Two shots rang out.

The IRA man who'd fired twice at Peter from point blank range somehow missed with both bullets, but now all hell broke loose. People were shouting and guns were appearing in hands as if by magic.

Jack looked straight at the man with the .45. The man's face froze as he saw the barrel of Jack's SMG spit the first three-shot short burst. It tore into his abdomen, and as the successive rounds climbed higher, Jack saw half his face swept away in a bloody mess.

Jack glanced at the boss. Captain McGregor had his head between his knees in the front passenger seat. He wasn't hit. Meanwhile Peter *was* doing a good job driving. Beer barrels bounced off the car as the snarling Morris Oxford ploughed on. The rear view mirror revealed two men crouching, arms extended, holding handguns, firing into the back of the car. There was an almighty bang as Jack let rip a long burst through the back window, shattering the toughened glass. Through the gaping hole, he saw the two men fall backwards. Other men came from the sides to help them.

Even though Jack had 14 rounds left in his SMG's magazine, he ceased fire.

The job was done.

• • •

Jack directed Peter to the nearest security post, just off Broadway, and reported the successful contact to Pud at MRF HQ. He happily rogered that.

However, the local area commander, an Infantry Major was not amused.

"You people come into my patch, which had, until your unit's formation been quite a quiet area, and, time and again, set off a fucking hornet's nest. Just what do you think you are doing? Having a jaunt to see the natives? If I had wanted you I would have called you..."

Captain McGregor stood ashen-faced as his superior officer continued bawling without drawing breath.

"Didn't they teach you anything at Hythe, Sergeant?"

Captain McGregor accepted his unintentional demotion gratefully. The anonymity of his civilian dress saved his invisible blushes and the raucous dressing down was absorbed unnoticed in the post-traumatic stress, which now accompanied the vivid flashbacks overloading his brain.

Did it enter the Major's head that if the ambush had been successful he would now be out recovering three stripped and mutilated, murdered bodies of British soldiers from a patch of waste ground?

No, he was just busy calculating whether today's irritation would hurt his chances of leaving the bare, frustrating plateau that was the rank of Major in the British Army for the lush pastures occupied by the ranks of Colonel.

Finally, after what seemed an eternity, Captain McGregor regained his composure, revealed his true rank and used a phone in the Major's Ops Room to file a Sitrep.

Two cars were sent out from MRF HQ to pick up their men, two of who were by now having a quick cuppa and a joke with the Greens that manned the security post. The other sulked in a corner.

Jack and Peter returned to the armoury, cleaned their weapons, and handed them back in, knowing that interviews with the RUC were now on the cards.

After they had made their statements to the RUC in the MRF Rest Room, the police informed Jack that one man had been killed and two had sustained serious gunshot injuries in the Falls Road incident.

There was a buzz in the air when Jack and Peter returned to the Op's Room. The MRF, ambushed in broad daylight by a significant number of IRA terrorists, had come through unscathed.

The UVF had taken the blame, the armour plating fitted in

the boot of the Morris Oxford that protected the rear seat had done its job and the words of the Jack's men's serenade earlier that day had been proven more relevant than they anticipated.

"Can't die..." filled the air again.

Not a bad day for a Huggle Bunny, thought Jack.

The spray of a shaken bottle of best Irish Republican Guinness filled the air in the Sergeants' Mess. Some stray residue slowly dripped onto the mug shot of an IRA "most-wanted" target abandoned on the bar – now with a red Chinagraph "X" firmly driven across it.

CHAPTER 3
A NEW QUARRY

The noise of the SLR distracted the six men for a split second. They raised their Armalite rifles to their shoulders and each fired a single shot. The volley echoed around the lichen-covered gravestones of Milltown Cemetery in Andersonstown, West Belfast.

Had the SLR been a 7.62mm FN self-loading rifle they would all have been as dead as the comrade they were saluting while the funeral director's men lowered him six foot under.

However, on this occasion Sergeant Major Jack Gillespie was looking through the viewfinder of his 35mm Canon camera. Today, Jack was Gillespie of the *Glasgow Times*, covering the "military funeral" of the IRA murderer he had helped through the gates of Hell a few days earlier.

His MI6-forged National Union of Journalists Press Card hanging from a lanyard around his neck replaced the British Army dog tags he normally wore in battle as his shield. The media were the messengers, and you certainly do not shoot the messengers in a propaganda war.

This was spring 1972 – before the IRA took their war of terror to the streets of the British mainland – and when the UK's national, or even Scottish, media took an interest in The Troubles, the Republicans gave them every assistance. Hence today's "photo opportunity". It was a conflict that needed column inches to raise its profile as well as military and civilian casualties.

Of course, you had to go through a tough accreditation to become the part of the furniture that Jack was now.

For Jack, the process had been a little different.

He had met Jean at a party in the "neutral" area of Newtownards about three weeks before today's funeral.

Newtownards, seven or so miles from Belfast, was like Meidrim Jack visited in Wales – a rural village untouched by the excesses of the outside world. Here both sides in the conflict could get some of what the US forces call *R and R*.

To Jack and the boys of the MRF it was a place for a bloody good night out. A heady cocktail of booze, birds and bonking and no half measures. The Guinness flowed and other liquids followed.

Jean had been a lucky girl. She thought she had her met "Mr Right" but she could have not been more wrong. The choice of Jack Gillespie as her future beau virtually signed a death warrant for many of her Republican friends.

The Jack Gillespie from New Lanark near Glasgow that she met was not a trained killer. Quite the opposite, he was the perfect gentleman – the perfect *Scottish* gentleman and a Catholic, of course. Her deceased grandmother would have purred.

Jack's cover story ran deep and detailed. He was from the illegitimate line of Thomas Gillespie Stanton of New Lanark. This much was true. The Gillespie brethren had all left Scotland in the mid 18th century to seek their fortunes and escape religious persecution. Some sons went west. Some sons went east. Jack's great-grandfather just went bad.

Great granddaddy slept with Sarah the chambermaid in 1895 and begat Jack's grandfather, Tom, who also out of wedlock begat Jack on a whisky-filled night of debauchery in Dunfermline the home town of the great steel magnate, James Carnegie, who left the town to make his fortune in the USA.

The Western Gillespies had chosen the cold of Canada and the Eastern Gillespies the tropical heat of India. One Gillespie became the Chairman of a Canadian Bank another saved the Prince Regent from a marauding white tiger.

The tiger story was the one Jack liked to tell best.

It had been the day of the races and polo in Bangalore. The Prince and his cronies seated high on a dais watching the day's sport. Hundreds of the India population cheered from the sidelines. Suddenly a tiger broke cover from the jungle and started to devour a helpless spectator close to the Royal Enclosure.

Seizing his chance to leap up the ranks and social ladder, Jack's great, great grandfather, Robert Gillespie, wrestled a lance from a petrified Sepoy, jumped on a nearby polo pony and fearlessly speared the roaring man-eater through the heart.

He then gallantly dragged his lifeless trophy to the Royal Presence and offered his brave mount to the Prince Regent, modestly deferring the valour to the horse rather than himself.

It was a masterstroke and as the years passed, Robert Gillespie became a full colonel in the British Army and gave great service during the Sepoy Mutiny his guns and cavalry, killing 300 to 400 mutineers out of hand. He died a Major General eight years later in 1814 during a vain attempt to storm a mountain-top Ghurkha fortress.

Of course, Jack did not mention the entire British Army bit. As a Scottish Nationalist and journalist for the *Glasgow Times*, naturally he would have no shrift with them. The words "British Army" would never pass his lips. They were "murdering swine" – exactly the language of love that Jean Philomena McLaughlin needed to hear.

Now it was her turn to daydream in rapture.

My Jack, young, virile, handsome – with a distant look in his dark brown eyes which obviously hid the years of his longing which were now finally over. He has found me. He will not escape my clutches. I can already hear the wedding bells ringing out across Andersonstown from the belfry of St Patrick's Church and Father Monahan saying "Do you Jean Philomena McLaughlin... take the Devil into your heart? Into your mouth? Between your legs? You licentious hussy!"

She jolted back from fantasy to reality. She had had sex, yes s-e-x, with a man, a man she had not married. She would burn in the fires of hell for eternity. Her grandmother would die of shame.

Her anguish climaxed and subdued.

Sex with him had left her feeling complete. She was a woman who knew what her body wanted. It would be fine. Everything was fine.

But unfortunately, thanks to this carnal union, it wasn't fine for all those present at Milltown Cemetery on Friday April 7th 1972. Anything but.

Jack was as much a perfect a facsimile of a Scottish gentleman as his NUJ card was of the real thing. If anyone had bothered to open them up and look inside, they would have noticed something vital was missing. In the press card, it was the *Contributions Received* table. In Jack Gillespie, it was a heart.

Smiling both inwardly and outwardly, Jean now looked proudly towards her brother, his face hidden by the black balaclava of the IRA honour guard as the rifle volley salute rang out.

Jean had vouched for her lover, the journalist Jack. The publican of the in Springfield Vaults public house in Parkhead,

Glasgow, had vouched for his "regular" Jack when the IRA called him. The picture editor of the *Glasgow Times* had vouched for Jack. In fact, if the IRA had dug him up, Jack's imaginary father would have vouched for Jack too.

The carefully crafted cover story was watertight.

Now the motor drive of his Canon camera was red hot, whining and whirring as the shutter captured image after image of posturing IRA men and their supporters.

The camera kept clicking even after the ceremony was over and the balaclavas discarded. Jack's long lens captured the young faces of the quarry. More ugly mugshots to paste on the most wanted wall in the Ops Room in Palace Barracks. MRF targets for tonight, tomorrow and the day after tomorrow,

Jack saw Jean hesitate at the cemetery gate and look back towards him. Her Irish charms could wait until later – there was business to attend to.

He thrust his hand into an unzipped side pocket of his brown suede photographer's jerkin and pulled out a screw top Leica aluminium film container. He grinned as he carefully inserted the 35mm Kodak Tri-x black and white film cassette inside.

Gold dust, he thought.

"Got to get these on the wire to Glasgow poppet," he said to Jean without breaking step.

"See you later Dar..."

"Alligator," he cut her off.

Back at Palace Barracks, Military Intelligence senior NCO Roy Mackay took Jack's "gold dust" and refined it into the potential silver halide death masks of six more IRA men. The alchemy had created many of the 50 most-wanted mug shots on the MRF's Ops Room wall. One of the faces of the six hooded felons unmasked by Jack today matched one of those already displayed for dispatch to the hereafter by the MRF.

Confirmed at large in the area, his picture now took pride of place in the book of today's "death list six".

He looked young, sweet, and somewhat familiar to Jack.

Have I seen this murdering miscreant before? Or perhaps all these Irish bastards are beginning to look the same, he thought.

• • •

That night, as usual, the MRF team would be on the look out for trouble. If they didn't find it, they would make it.

Jack fingered the photographs and chuckled.

The door opened and Corporal Len Smith from Lincolnshire – a "ploughboy" – walked in, looking none too pleased. He had only been with the MRF a month and quite literally experienced a baptism of fire. An IRA bullet had shaved his scalp when a MRF covert car had come under fire near the Divis Flats (a notorious Republican stronghold) in the Lower Falls Road. It had shaken Len right to the core. He was probably suffering from post-traumatic stress disorder but his very unsympathetic mates just thought he was having an attack of the jitters.

He was a reject from the Royal Engineers – a bomb disposal expert. Handy to have aboard in the streets of West Belfast, but he was no good to anyone in this state, Jack noted.

This was nothing new – he had seen even the bravest of men contemplate the meaning of life after a close shave took millimetres from meeting their maker.

Kid gloves time, thought Jack.

"So what's troubling you then, Len?" he asked.

"Well, boss, it's like this. We're ordinary fucking folk and those out on the streets are ordinary fucking folk and we are turning this fucking place into a fucking shooting gallery. We shoot at any fucker that moves, they shoot any fucker that moves and everyone is fucking terrified of each other. Where is it all going to fucking end? That's what I want to know Sir. Where's it all going to end?"

Jack was fluent in Jungle Malay and this language: "Squaddie".

"Steady Len. It's like this. We are servants of the Crown. We serve her Majesty the Queen and answer to her alone. Her Majesty's Government is elected by a majority of the people of the United Kingdom of Great Britain and Northern Ireland.

"No-one has asked them outright yet, but it doesn't take a genius to work out that the majority of the people in Northern Ireland would democratically vote to stay part of the United Kingdom and moreover, they want these IRA bastards dead. The Queen, whose realm we protect from attack, has authorised her ministers to take appropriate action as they see fit to restore peace to this troubled land. Brigadier Kitson, her Commander in Chief, has decided that we, the MRF, are the solution to the whole Irish problem.

"We will take out the top 50 IRA men and see what happens. Then, we take out the next 50 and so on. Until it all stops and we can go home.

"The Greens can't operate in this jungle so it's down to us. So far it seems to be working fucking well for everyone. Except you my son."

"So I'm fucked then Sir?"

"Just stick to driving and leave the dirty work to us."

That sounded good, thought Jack. But Len was miles away with his own thoughts.

"The bottom line is we're ordinary folk who are being asked to do extraordinary things. And if you can't do it for the fucking Queen then do it for me and your fucking mates," Jack concluded.

"So what you are saying is that the politicians make the *right* decisions and it's up to us soldiers to make those decisions right, even if they are not right, and what we are doing is not right," said Len calmly.

"You've got it in one."

Innocently smiling like Tommy Steele fresh from the bull-ring, Corporal Joe Lock walked in rubbing his hands as if from an outside frost.

"Who do I have to fuck to get a cup of tea?"

"About turn and take your Sapper mate with you Lock," snapped Jack. He had had enough. Was it one F-word too many; is there a critical mass? He wondered what the atomic weight of element "F" was and where in the Periodic Table could it be found. Was it inert? He toyed with the thought decking them both – then decided against it.

"Hold it," Jack ordered. "I've decided we'll do something different today."

• • •

Jack wanted to try a new tactic that had recently become available to him, and had the potential to get some deadly results with just a little less drama than shoot and scoot.

Enter "the Freds".

The custodians of the Freds were MI6 – the British Secret Service.

Freds were IRA men persuaded or coerced to change sides and betray their comrades to the security forces for many different reasons. The main one being money.

MI6 surveillance had indicated that, like the Corporal, certain IRA men were having psychological or motivational problems, and with the right "incentive" would be only be too happy to blab like babies.

MI6 had recruited three Freds so far. They would be driven, their faces concealed, with MI6 men through West Belfast and point out members of the IRA and locations frequented by them. This tactic had worked for Brigadier Kitson in Kenya, Malaya and Aden, among others. Now it was Northern Ireland's turn.

MI6 would also take them to security bases in Republican areas and Freds would point out members of the local IRA from an observation point overlooking the streets. MI6 would then photograph them with telephoto lenses, and their pictures would gradually filter through to the death list gallery.

Jack planned to take things a little bit further. The idea was a simple one. Now, once the Fred had identified and named an IRA man the MRF would drive alongside the target, bundle him into the car, take him away and "interrogate" him.

It hadn't been tried in Northern Ireland before so it would be a big surprise on the streets, and doubtlessly have a destabilisation effect on the enemy.

• • •

The Fred set-up operated from an empty married quarter close to the MRF compound within the walls of Palace Barracks. Corporal Smith drove Jack and Sgt. John Benson the 300 yards to the building in a 1969 Volvo 164. Like its predecessors, it was another Merseyside crime statistic. Its powerful 3-litre engine and big doors made it the ideal kidnap vehicle.

Jack outlined his plan to the Spooks.

"My idea is to kidnap a known IRA man, fingered by a Fred, off the street, take him to an isolated spot on Cavehill and, posing as UVF men, interrogate him."

The MI6 boys jumped at the chance. Intelligence had

been drying up, and they were always keen to make life more interesting.

At 1900 hours, the MRF men met in the Ops Room to discuss their final preparations.

"I think we'll carry 9mm pistols," said Jack. "No need for the SMG, this will be a 'non aggressive' patrol, except for the time it takes for us to get the selected victim into the car.

"OK Len?"

After drawing their weapons from the armoury and loading their magazines, the MRF team were ready to go. The armoured Volvo drove them to pick up the Fred.

Even Jack was excited – it was his first kidnap. An old dog was learning new tricks certainly, and he was full of confidence for the coming confrontation.

The operation started with a trip to the familiar surroundings of McGuigan's Yard. The Fred was installed in the watchtower with an MI6 minder and John Benson, who would memorise the target and rejoin the MRF team in the car below.

A lone figure crossed the road just 10 yards from the front gates of the Yard and started to walk away towards a social club. Irish music leaked from the distant door:

"Oh, I am a merry ploughboy and I plough the fields all day
Till a sudden thought came to my head, that I should roam away
For I'm sick and tired of slavery since the day that I was born
And I'm off to join the IRA and I'm off tomorrow morn

And we're all off to Dublin in the green, in the green
Where the helmets glisten in the sun
Where the bayonets flash and the rifles crash
To the rattle of a Thompson gun..."

That's pretty ironic, Jack thought as he waited at the Volvo's front passenger door with his very own ploughboy sitting in the driver's seat, now shaking profusely. Jack's empty hands perspired; he missed the Tommy gun too.

The Fred was suddenly animated. The lone figure was a prominent member of the IRA in West Belfast. Beginner's luck.

Sgt Benson came down the wooden ladder like a bat out of hell. He shouted to the sentries to open the gates and was in the Volvo in a flash. The powerful Swedish straight six roared into life and its rear wheels spun as it swung left into the street

"The target is wearing blue jeans and a white top", he said.

"I can see him," said Jack his pistol drawn in the front seat. "Ready JB this is it."

Len brought the car to a halt just in front of the target. At the same time, Jack and JB leapt from the car.

The pair brought the IRA man down, but he was young and fit and fought furiously on the ground, kicking and flaying his arms wildly. One limb caught Jack full in the face. After a few more seconds of frenzied shouts and screams, he was subdued by martial arts blows from the two soldiers. More used to killing than capturing, it seemed a bit strange to Jack that for once his hands had not realised their potential.

They bundled their semi-conscious victim into the back of the car, laid him in the foot well and sat on him. Sgt. Benson put a bag over the prisoner's head and frisked him for weapons. Nothing. It was taking too much time.

"Make a sound," said Benson in his Belfast accent "and you're a dead man."

As the car finally sped away, a drunken figure staggered out of the social club and looked up the road directly at them. Jack wondered if the struggle to get the captive into the car had attracted attention. Yes, the music was loud in the club. but anyone at the entrance or leaving may have seen what was going on. Was there a roadblock now waiting for them up ahead?

The distant figure collapsed into the gutter. Maybe Guinness was good for the MRF. Still, Jack knew he would have to be more careful. Scoop and scoot was a little bit more difficult than it looked.

The man on the floor of the car was now pleading with them to let him breathe.

"Quiet you Catholic cunt," said Benson. "We're going to take you to a place we have where you'll answer a few questions."

Len drove the car along Glen Road, turned right along a small country road onto Upper Springfield Road towards a disused quarry a few miles before Hannahstown. Benson knew their destination well. He had spent his boyhood in this area.

The Volvo drove into the quarry workings and came to a halt behind a corrugated building. The ruts behind the car started to fill with water, erasing the tread marks. Len got out, did a quick recce of the area, came back and said, "All clear."

Jack dragged the man out of the back of the car laid him on his chest spread-eagle. His face was pressed into the gravel and water seeped through the hood and entered his nostrils.

Sgt. Benson gave him a couple of kicks in the groin. He cried out. Len pulled out a set of handcuff's and slipped them on the man's wrists. He was now pleading with them not to kill him.

"Mary Holy Mother of Jesus save me," he choked through the gravel.

• • •

Benson told him they were the UVF and wanted some information about the IRA in Andersonstown.

"We want the fucking names of the fucking district commanders,"

The names of the people who had been there when Taff was killed a few weeks before would be good as well, thought Jack, *but why would the UVF be interested in that?*

Either way it didn't matter – the IRA man didn't say a word.

Benson got a hunting knife out from under his shirt and pressed the cold blade on the man's bare skin. He asked the man his name. The reply came: Angus Maloney. The hood that pressed tightly over his mouth made Maloney sound like *Baloney* – which is exactly what it was.

Benson asked his address – he gave that too freely.

"Tell me," said Benson. "Who is the IRA Commander on the ground in Andersonstown?"

"I don't know."

Barely had the words got out of his mouth when Benson stuck the knife into the man's hand. He screamed.

Even muffled by the hood on his head, the piercing frequency bounced against the quarry walls and died in the light rain that had started to fall.

There was no one else to hear it except for the perpetrators.

"Listen you Republican bastard, we are the UVF and when we ask questions we want them fucking answered. Do you understand?"

He twisted the knife again.

"We know you have brothers, what are their names and which battalion are they with?"

"I have three brothers and they are IRA members but that's all I know".

He was terrified.

The captors stood him up and took off the hood. They put some masking tape over his eyes, and carried on with the interrogation. It was when Benson put a pistol to the prisoner's head and said "Goodbye Angus", that the smell was detected.

Len turned to Jack and whispered, "He's shit himself."

Headlights from another vehicle on a bend lit up the rain-filled sky somewhere close by. Too close. They could hear the engine. It was time to leave.

"Leave him there," said Jack.

"There's no way we want him in the car smelling like that."

"Why don't we just kill him?" said Benson.

It would have been a cold-blooded execution, and Jack wasn't up for that. He shook his head. In future, they would take all kidnap victims back to Palace Barracks and interrogate them there, he decided.

As for this guy, he would take a message back to his IRA cell that it wasn't safe for them to show their faces on the streets. Even in their own back yard.

The MRF men surrounded the prisoner and made him kneel down facing a wall, roughly warning him to stay where he was for at least an hour.

They left the quarry. There was only one entry, one exit, and if they had to fight then having a shit-covered IRA man in the car was the last thing they needed. And they only had 9mm pistols; not exactly ideal.

But the headlights of the other car had disappeared and the MRF simply sped away.

It was about 15 minutes later that Benson said, "I was just thinking..." He turned to Len. "Got the handcuffs, Corporal?"

"Oh fuck, they're still on that bastard's wrists," he replied.

"Schoolboy error!"

"We have to go back," said Jack. "And make it quick!"

It was now raining heavily. Acutely aware that there might be someone else there, they moved back toward the quarry carefully, with Sgt. Benson and Jack walking in behind the car, their guns drawn.

As they approached the area behind the corrugated shed they had left half an hour earlier, Jack saw the outline of the kidnap victim still on his knees, still shaking like a leaf.

The prisoner stiffened as Benson took off the handcuffs, and they left him there in the darkness, in the rain.

Jack took a final look around and joined Benson back in the Volvo. As they left the quarry Jack said: "Take two."

No one laughed.

All in all it was a bit of a balls up, thought Jack. *We should practice this next time in the Barracks before we hit the streets.*

But at least the IRA knew who they were dealing with – the UVF. Benson had rammed home that point at least. Unsurprisingly, the level of violence between the two communities went off the scale over the next couple of weeks. Jack and the MRF could just sit and watch as the two paramilitary factions hit six bells out of each other.

Back in the barracks, the patrol felt positive about the outcome. There were a few teething troubles but in general it was a successful mission which would be repeated in the future. No-one was hurt, and they recovered from Len leaving his Army issue handcuffs behind.

They would get it right next time, the next, and the next. However, in future leaving the victim alive might not be an option. The real UVF were not as humane as the MRF had been that night – and their imitation had to be dead on.

• • •

After debriefing with the Slime, Journalist Jack headed to Jean's home in Andersonstown. He fancied a late night rendezvous. The crucifix was in the window – their signal that she was alone.

He knocked softly – just loud enough to be heard inside but not disturb the neighbours. Mrs O'Reilly next door was a light sleeper and her dog was a yapper.

When Jean flung open the door, she was in floods of tears.

"Jack, it's my brother Sean he was kidnapped and badly beaten by the Prots... He's in the Sancta Maria and they won't let me see him. Jack help me... Please!"

Jack pulled her close to him and held her so tight she could hardly breathe.

"He's lucky to be alive darling. Those UVF bastards are merciless killers. How did he escape?" asked Jack.

"My brothers say he fought them off when they removed his handcuffs. He was so brave."

"They are with him now. Will you take me to the hospital and bring your camera? We will need to take pictures of his injuries."

More shots for the McLaughlin family album and the MRF Ops Room wall...

It had been a good night after all, thought Jack.

Chapter 4

Spoils of War

Lizzie lent into the car window as it stopped beside her on the Lower Falls Road. The three men inside seemed surprised at her brazen approach but were soon laughing and joking with her.

She looked much older than her 15 years of age. Most teenage girls did nowadays. "Jailbait" the MRF boys called them in the mess. Moreover, one or two of them admitted to having dabbled with these "devil's daughters".

This one was a proper little madam. She teased the bubblegum out of her mouth with a red-painted fingernail.

"Do you want to be my boyfriend?" she asked the car's occupants.

No one in particular had taken her fancy – but then, it was just *a bit of fun*. A wind up, as she tested her newly adorned femininity.

Her sister, Ali, was four years older and always making sure her sibling was "with it". She was responsible for the painted nails, and had made up Lizzie's face, especially the lying lashes, so that she now looked at least sweet sixteen.

Ali did not have her younger sister's good looks – not anymore. Her hair was shorn off and her previously flawless skin was now pocked and scarred. She would often remember the hot tar flowing down her face and neck and dripping on to her bare breasts that had been covered in goose bumps when the IRA commander had stripped her upper body to prepare her for punishment.

For a second she had felt a flush of excitement as her nipples hardened in the cold wind, but such a feeling was fleeting as the pain of the scorching liquid extinguished any false hope of passion.

A pillow full of feathers had been emptied over Ali's head and they paraded her in front of jeering and hooting men and women. She had screamed for mercy, Sweet Jesus, Mary – and her mother.

Ironically, she had suffered a punishment introduced by the British during the Irish Rebellion of 1798, and now used by descendants of those "Rebels" on their own people in May 1972.

Ali's crime was to be seen in the arms of a young British soldier in a field around the back of Casement Park. The fraternisation was commonplace. The girls from Catholic Andersonstown would walk along Moreland Park into Moreland Drive and meet soldiers near the perimeter of the sports ground commandeered by the British Army as a security forces camp.

Roger Casement, whose name the Gaelic Athletics Ground bore, would have been turning in his grave at their antics. He was an Irish patriot, poet, revolutionary and nationalist. He was also a British Consul by profession, famous for his reports and activities against human rights abuses in the Congo and Peru, but better known for his dealings with Germany before Ireland's Easter Rising. An Irish nationalist and Parnellite in his youth, he worked in Africa for commercial interests and latterly in the service of Britain. However, the Boer War and his investigation into atrocities in the Congo led Casement to anti-Imperialist and ultimately Irish Republican and separatist political opinions.

The British executed him for treason in August 1916.

Now, when the young girls lay down in the bushes just outside the perimeter fence of the park that carried his name, they were probably not thinking of Ireland or England. Tar and feathers were probably the furthest substances from their thoughts.

But for a few, that was the painful reward for their foolishness, for others perhaps more fortunate, the consequences came nine months later with the birth of a new "patriot".

Equally painful some might say. Ali, was unlucky on both counts. Her bump was getting bigger by the day.

Lizzie turned her attention to John Benson in the back of the car.

"You're a big boy," she started. "I like a man with a moustache..."

The others burst into hysterical laughter as her first efforts at seduction ended with a bubble of gum bursting in the large soldier's face.

A mixture of spittle and Bazooka Joe candy apple bubblegum now attached itself to the pride and joy that was Benson's tash. He thought the hours of careful preening made him look like Errol Flynn. The boys thought it made him look like a prat. They wouldn't say that to his face. But behind his back? Well that was OK.

Benson fancied courting young women; the younger the better. In fact, had the lads not been in the car with him, then Lizzie might well have been in moral danger.

Bubblegum and all.

Suddenly the radio crackled into life and it was "windows

up" before the transmission could be heard by the wrong ears.

Len Smith put the Ford Cortina into gear and they rolled away from the teenage temptress of the Lower Falls.

"Nine-Zero – this is Zero. Over."

It was HQ.

"Nine-Zero. Send."

"Nine-Zero proceed to Co-op Department Store in York Street. Bomb incident. Over."

"Nine-Zero. Roger Out."

Belfast-born Benson gave Len directions as they sped towards the large plume of black smoke – the tell-tale sign of an IRA attack.

This time the Provisionals had hit the jackpot. A small but effective device had ignited a fuel tank situated on the roof. The cascading oil combined with a series of additional incendiary devices placed throughout the store had a devastating effect as fire quickly took hold of the building.

The men from the Parachute Regiment patrolling nearby were the first on the scene, and the troops plunged fearlessly into the burning store. The staff had evacuated, but they needed be sure that there weren't any stragglers still inside.

The Paras had been searching for some minutes by the time that Jack and the boys arrived. Len, who was still jumpy, stayed with the car but the two other MRF men ran towards the scene.

The four-storey Victorian building was well ablaze. Smoke and heat filled the streets. The fire brigade were fighting a losing battle.

Jack and John noticed that some of the knee length smocks the Paras wore were bulging as they were ushered out of the blazing store by fire fighters. Either there were a lot of fat soldiers in the Regiment or they were concealing something underneath. Benson exchanged a glance with Jack and tripped one of the departing "heroes". The contents of his smock spilled onto the pavement.

"I'm so sorry," said Benson.

The men exchanged a few expletives. "Clumsy Irish bastard" or some such greeting mixed with the smoke in the air, making heads turn. The Red Devil picked up his pilfered possessions – some nice leatherwear and trinkets – and bolted to a waiting truck.

"That was the Parasite Regiment then," said Benson.

"They came, they saw, they did a little shoplifting..." said Jack.

He could imagine that when the Paras' tour of duty was over, there would be plenty of well-dressed soldiers in Maida Barracks, Aldershot, wearing the latest designer leather jackets, with Christmas presents for their wives' sorted well in advance.

"I suppose it's better than it all going up in smoke," Jack concluded, but he wasn't 100 per cent sure.

The millions of pounds worth of damage caused by the IRA bomb would make headlines around the world. Just the publicity they wanted. All that was left by the following morning for the 200,000 Co-op members, ordinary Protestants and Catholics, who owned the store, would be a tangled mass of twisted metal.

Scrap iron.

It became clear that the IRA perpetrators, if they had remained at the scene, had either melted away or were watching anonymously from the safety of the watching crowd. With no prospective fire fighting of a different kind, there was little Jack's patrol could do to help so they returned to Palace Barracks.

Jack only noticed the state he and Benson were in when they had already arrived in the Ops Room. However, it was too late to about turn and head for the showers.

"Sooty and Sweep," said Pud looking the pair up and down. "Mind you I've been up a few old dusty roads in my time – or perhaps you've been playing flaming arseholes in the mess again."

"We have just come from the Co-op," said Jack.

"Yes, so I can see. You're covered in it," replied Pud.

"I don't know about you but I've had it for today," Jack said to Benson ignoring Pud's last remark.

• • •

He had a shave and a long shower and headed for the Sergeants' mess.

The drinking game Blow Your Top was underway. From the state of the participants, it was clear that there were plenty of novices present. Jack knew the game well from his time in Hong Kong and knew you had more chance of converting the Reverend Ian Paisley to Catholicism than ending a game without tears. Or, to be more accurate, fisticuffs.

Corporal Len Smith was about to take a turn.

Just as in the SAS, Smith and all the MRF NCOs had acting Sergeant status, which ensured that the men who might die together could drink together without infringing petty rules, although some of the resident Royal Anglian Regiment Senior NCOs frowned on the arrangement.

The idea of the game was to blow a single playing card off the top of a complete pack, jokers and all, balanced precariously on the metal cap of an unopened beer bottle. If you did it – which was even difficult sober – then there was no penalty. If you failed, you had to drink a finger of booze for every additional card you dislodged. If you spilt the whole pack, you drank your whole drink. If you failed to dislodge any with the one breath allowed, you had to buy all those present a drink.

Smith approached the task with all of the delicacy of a Bomb Disposal School student. A student, that is, before the instructors discovered that even under normal circumstances, he had very shaky hands and frayed nerves and had waved him goodbye.

"He'll huff and he'll puff and he'll blow the pack down," chanted the MRF boys as they pulled faces and made obscene gestures to the man of the moment.

Smith did not disappoint them. He blew the whole damn lot across the table and onto the floor with the help of an encouraging back slap from Sgt. Benson.

"Down in one, down in one, down in one," the MRF men chorused.

Sure enough, a whole pint of Guinness disappeared down Smith's extended gullet.

Because the ex-Sapper had "blown his top" – decked the whole pack – he was up again straight away for another go. A pint of the black stuff put quickly on his mess bill and Smith prepared to face the ordeal again. He was getting the hang of it now.

Thwack!

The heavy hand of John Benson found its target again, but this time the encouragement measured nine on the Richter scale as Benson was himself propelled forward by a seismic shove from behind by Corporal Joe Lock. The pair hit the ground in a kaleidoscope of cards and beers.

Lock knew that he had bitten off more than he could chew as Benson launched himself at the Scouser. A six foot two missile of Belfast shipyard steel crashed into the white-faced Liverpudlian.

Amidst much cheering by the boys, Benson soon wiped the floor with Lock. A shake of hands and it was back to the bar. Jack decreed no more silly bar games.

"You stupid bunch of drunken bastards!" Jack chided his charges.

The Angle Irons present turned up their noses.

The MRF boys went back to their bar except, that is, for Len Smith who was fishing a lone playing card out of the half full glass of Guinness that he had somehow managed to clasp even when he was propelled forward. Jack turned just as Smith wiped away the white foam from the face of the card to reveal: the Ace of Spades.

"Lucky we're not superstitious hey son," said Jack putting his arm around the quivering Corporal.

"The next round is on me."

The bar fell silent.

No one had heard Jack say that before today.

• • •

When dawn finally broke the next morning it hurt.

A shaft of light had somehow found a pinprick hole in the blackout curtains in Jack's Mess bunk.

Alcoholic icon Dean Martin said that the best cure for a hangover was to keep drinking. The Rat Pack raconteur was not far wrong. This wasn't an option for Jack, however, as he was back on duty in 30 minutes and, in any case, the bars didn't open until noon. Jack had to dip into the SAS survival handbook for a regimental hangover cure: "A teaspoonful of the beef stock Bovril mixed in a small tumbler of Smirnoff Blue label vodka."

Jack fumbled around in his bedside locker and pulled out the ingredients. The tinkle of the teaspoon on the tumbler glass hurt. The effort of prising the metal cap off the Bovril hurt. Jack's right fist hurt and he did not remember how the hell that happened.

It was just another night in the MRF mess then.

Something stirred in Jack's army green boxer shorts. The shoots of recovery were emerging. The rest of the body just had to keep up. But as soon the "Bovka hangover cure" kicked in, Jack was up and running.

In the briefing room, the rest of the gang were in an equally bad state, some noticeably worse than others. Benson was the best of the bunch, so if West Belfast was buzzing he would be Jack's best bet.

Jack entered the Op's Room.

"Ooh! Look what the cat's dragged in," said Pud.

Pud's vocal chords were pitched an octave too high for Jack's delicate disposition.

"Don't say a word. I've heard all about it from the mess steward. Apparently you owe him for ten tin trays," said Pud. "I told him you knew the mess got them free from the brewery but he was having none of it. You are going to have to cough up big time."

Jack winced as a vestige of memory flashed fleetingly before his eyes.

"Sore head?" offered Pud.

"I'm not surprised. After you paraded your party trick of having the boys each hit you on the noggin with a tray, you bet them you could punch through a tray. You said you had seen Johnny Mason do it in the NAAFI in Nee Soon Camp in Singapore. Obviously, he was a better man that you because you just knocked the two men holding it into another dimension.

The tray lived to fight another day though. I had the great job of putting you all to bed."

Jack did a quick systems check – everything was as it should be. Pud just grinned like a Cheshire Cat who had had his cream as Jack tried to focus on the Sitreps.

A message had just come down from 39 Brigade in Lisburn that there was a crowd gathering on the Protestant Shankhill Road. The previous night, an IRA drive-by shooting had taken place and two locals were badly wounded.

"The Spooks say there is serious talk about a revenge attack on Catholic residents down on the Springfield Road," said Pud as Jack stared blankly at the paper.

"The boss said to make sure you knew about it. So you'd do something."

"Do 'something'? He's not a great one for detail then," said Jack.

Jack considered Sergeant Benson. He was from the Shankhill area. Jack would go and find the Irishman and then the pair would check the place out together.

Jack returned to the briefing room.

It was like the Mary Celeste without the mystery.

The men had deserted their posts.

Jack walked over to the Sergeants' mess accommodation. On entering, he quickly found the name Sgt. Benson marked on a bunk door. Knocking gently, he heard a muffled voice answer.

Jack opened the door to reveal a sleepy Benson, in the recovery position, fully clothed on the bed.

"I'll be back in a minute," said Jack.

He returned with a tumbler of the evil-looking Bovka and handled it to Benson.

"Down in one," said Jack.

"No way, José – that's how I got into this mess in the first place!" demurred Benson.

"That's an order," Jack rebuffed.

There were more than a few bears with sore heads in the briefing room that's for sure," said Benson. "Then the boss came in, all Pukka and proper, so we all made ourselves scarce."

General retreat.

Soon normal service from Benson, at least, was resumed thanks to the magic elixir. Jack and John decided that, as the UDA who controlled the Shankhill had not been any trouble to the MRF boys before, the pair would make their way to the Royal Bar on the Shankhill and see what was happening. It was an old watering hole for Sgt. Benson and he was a familiar face there.

They drew 9mm pistols from the armoury, selected a Cortina from the car park, tested their communications and drove off. The gates of Palace Barracks closed behind them as Benson greeted the lunchtime traffic.

As they approached the crossroads at Northumberland Street and Agnes Street in the Shankhill, they came upon a roadblock that was still under construction.

John stopped, almost out of politeness. They considered themselves still in a safe area. Immediately, some angry-sounding men told them to get out of the car.

Jack, who despite the Bovka still felt like death warmed up, was having none of this.

"This is the Queens Highway and you have no right to stop us!" he yelled.

"Drive on driver!" he commanded.

Oh, how that hurt his head.

The men took a step back and the MRF car sped away, followed with a squeal of tyre rubber, by two cars each with four men on board in hot pursuit.

Not wanting to get involved in a shoot out with the Protestants, and only armed with 9mm pistols and hangovers, Jack instructed John to drive to the nearest security forces' outpost – the Shankhill Road Police Station.

• • •

"Blow into this bag, please Sir."

Jack held up a Typhoo tea bag in front of Benson's nose in the police canteen.

The UDA or UVF men, or whoever they were, had given up their pursuit as soon as it was obvious that Jack and John were headed for the RUC post. Now the dehydrated MRF pair sampled the delights of the police canteen, making themselves a cuppa and crashing out until the coast was clear.

An hour later, they were in the Royal. During a talk with the locals, John discovered that no retaliation against the IRA was on the cards. The Protestants would leave it to the security forces to "investigate".

After leaving the pub, they drove to the upper Shankhill Road along Woodvale Road onto the Crumlin Road where they turned right and headed for the city centre past the Mater Infirmorum Hospital.

• • •

As they drove slowly past the Crumlin Road Gaol, Jack spotted two men close by behaving suspiciously in a stopped car. A man holding a clipboard and scribbling something on a white piece of paper sat in the passenger seat. Three IRA men had escaped from the prison in the past year, and MI6 believed the Republicans planned more escape attempts.

"You've got to be kidding!" said Jack and ordered John to turn around to investigate.

As they pulled up behind the red car, the driver looked in his rear view mirror, signalled he was pulling out and drove carefully down the road.

"They are on to us," said Jack.

Jack called the registration into the Ops Room for checking.

They followed the car waiting anxiously for a reply.

"Nine-Zero this is Zero. The number is registered in Belfast as a 175cc BSA Bantam motorcycle. Over."

"Nine-Zero Roger. Out!"

With that, the MRF car cut in front of the target forcing the driver to do an emergency stop.

Guns drawn, John and Jack dragged the two men out of the car.

One, much older than the other, dropped his clipboard and his glasses fell off as Jack slammed him against the side of the car.

"Legs apart, put your hands on the roof," said Jack.

The kid who had been driving was almost in tears as he stood at gunpoint while Jack roughly frisked his companion.

"What's this?" Jack demanded. He'd found a suspicious package around the man's waist.

"It's my colostomy bag," the man stuttered.

"You what?" said Jack.

"It's full of shit," the man replied.

"Just like you pair," said Jack. "Now tell me what the fuck were you doing outside the prison?"

"What prison?" said the younger man.

"Don't mess with us," growled Benson.

Now the boy really *was* in tears.

"I'm taking my driving test," he wailed.

"Its true," said the older man. "I'm a driving examiner."

Jack and John exchanged glances.

"Where're your L plates?" said Jack.

"They are on the car – front and back. Plain as anything."

John who had a clear view nodded agreement.

"Ok, so whose car is this?"

Jack had one weapon left in his armoury. He obviously was not looking at a motorcycle.

"It's the boy's father's," said the examiner.

"What's the number," Jack stepped away from the car and turned to the boy.

"1968NZ." He replied correctly without hesitation. "My father bought it when I was nine."

Benson shrugged and released his grip.

"Something doesn't add up here," he said.

An idea came into Jack's head – were they on an IRA delivery run?

"Is there anything hidden in the car? Are you carrying weapons or explosives?"

"You have got to be kidding. No," said the boy.

Jack went to open the boot.

"It's a Volkswagen, Jack. That's the engine at the back," said Benson, as he pulled open the bonnet storage compartment at the other end of the vehicle.

There was nothing there apart from a spare wheel.

Inside the car was bare too; there was just a well-thumbed copy of the Highway Code on the back seat.

"I cleaned it out especially for the test," ventured the youngster.

Jack spotted the RUC in the distance. HQ would have informed them of the "stop and search".

Jack and John had already attracted too much attention waving guns around on the street. They returned to their car and left. The pair vacating the scene before the police arrived would confuse onlookers as to their true identity, although their car was now compromised.

As they drove down the Shankhill Road and reached Peter's Hill, Jack pressed the transmit stud and rechecked the index number of the suspect vehicle.

"Nine-Zero that number is of a 1963 Volkswagen Beetle registered in Belfast. Over."

"Zero – this is Nine-Zero. Repeat. Over."

"Nine-Zero this is Zero. Perhaps your earlier transmission was at sixes and sevens after you had one over the eight. Over."

"He means we are still pissed from last night," said Benson.

"Cheeky bastard," said Jack.

"Better head back to base – it's nearly opening time."

• • •

The next morning a fresher and more fragrant Jack turned on the radio in the Mini Cooper.

"Happy First Wedding Anniversary Mick and Bianca Jagger. We love you Mick! Happy Anniversary from all of us here at wonderful Radio One."

Jack joined in with the chorus of the Rolling Stones' *Lets Spend the Night Together* as he sped towards Jean who he had arranged to meet in a café in Andersonstown.

"*Let's spend the night together*
Now I need you more than ever
Let's spend the night together now"

The words matched Jack's feelings exactly. It was all getting a bit macho around the mess. He needed some skirt now and he was sure Jean McLaughlin would be only too willing to oblige.

He parked right outside the café and could see her waiting through the window.

On the table in front of her was a package.

"It's your birthday present," she said as he sat down.

"It's not my birthday… Is it?" said Jack.

"Well if you don't know when it is, who does? Is it a state secret or something?" she flustered. "No, it's just you never told me what star sign you are so I took a guess you were a bull – Taurus. So you have either just had your big day or it is very soon."

"You are a remarkably intuitive woman. Yes, you're right. It's tomorrow night," Jack lied. "Are you doing anything…?"

"You can open your present now and wear it tomorrow," she continued ignoring his question.

He ripped away the wrapping and revealed a black bomber jacket of the finest leather.

Jean was puzzled as the first thing Jack did was look at the label. It said Skincraft.

"Aren't you going to try it on then?" What's your problem?"

"Yes I am. It's just, I was looking at one exactly like this in the Co-op last week," said Jack. "Just before it burnt down."

The jacket fitted a treat. So did she.

• • •

By nightfall, Jack was out on patrol with call sign Eight-Zero. They had a few new members who were having their first foray on the streets of West Belfast. A "familiarisation tour" was the correct military jargon.

Jack was on board call sign Eight–One sitting in the front with a new driver and new rear gunner in the back. Taff Watkins, a Royal Military Police Sergeant and the commander of call sign Eight-Zero was taking the lead on the night's operations.

It was his show. Jack was just hitching a ride. The Nine-Zero boys had a few days off. He would join up with them later on or maybe tomorrow, if his "birthday" celebrations fizzled out early. Perhaps, as often happened when her mother, Katherine, was feeling lonely, Jean McCinderella would have to be home by midnight.

It had been that way since Katherine had seen her husband, Jimmy, knocked down by a Number 22 bus driven by a Protestant. It was a genuine accident but there was no way that anyone in the McLaughlin clan was ever going to believe that in a month of Holy Sundays.

• • •

Call sign Eight-Zero, commander Taff, as the nickname suggested, was another MRF Welshman, originally from Cardiff. He was a tough Celt who took no prisoners – literally. A shoot first, ask questions later soldier. As long as *he* was alive at the end of a fight, nothing else mattered. He knew how to drink hard and he knew how to fight hard, so he was ideal material for the MRF.

If Jack had one criticism of Taff, it would be he was more than just a little trigger-happy.

"So long as I don't meet myself coming the other way, I'll be fine buddy boy," he used to say.

Jack had joined the patrol as they were preparing to leave Palace Barracks. He still had a 9mm pistol from earlier in the day. There had been no enemy activity since an IRA sniper had killed an 18-year-old Green on the Lower Falls on Thursday afternoon, and a man kidnapped from his home had been found a few miles away with three gunshot wounds in his leg – a standard IRA punishment.

Maybe Friday night was going to be quiet – but in Belfast,

anything could be waiting just around the corner. The MRF had to be the masters of their own destiny and the two cars bristled with arms just in case their SAS Warlord's luck had run out.

The Falls Road was quiet and Jack's car, a blue Austin Cambridge, driven by new man Corporal Denis Cosslett, drove straight over the Kennedy Way roundabout and into Andersonstown Road.

There was nothing happening.

Cosslett reminded Jack of Corporal Jones of *Dad's Army*. He almost expected him to run around shouting "Don't panic, don't panic!".

Corporal Cosslett used to think Jack was like Captain Mainwaring but for some reason or other never got round to mentioning it.

Wise boy.

The other new lad was just as green. He was quiet as a mouse; Jack could see he was just a petrified teenager. He was gripping an SMG so tight his knuckles were white. Where did they pick him up? He'd obviously been reading the morning newspapers as the army death toll reached 77. Perhaps he thought he was to be number 78.

A couple of miles hence, Jack gestured for Cpl. Cosslett to turn left into Finaghy Road North. Up ahead, opposite a row of shops near the junction of Riversdale Park Road, half a dozen men seemed to be preparing to stop traffic entering the estate. There were four on one side of the road and one on the other. They were all holding automatic weapons.

He radioed call sign Eight-Zero following some distance behind.

"Eight-Zero. Eight-One. Over."

"Eight-Zero. Send. Over."

"Eight-Zero. There is an IRA VCP on the junction of Finaghy Road North and Riversdale Park Road approach with caution – these men are armed with rifles. Over."

"Eight-Zero. Will investigate. Roger. Out."

Thirty seconds or so later, Jack heard automatic gunfire. First some sporadic fire and then the unmistakable sound of a Thomson sub-machine gun spitting death.

"Eight–Zero this is Eight-One. Automatic fire heard from your direction please report. Over."

An agonising two minutes later Eight-Zero replied: "Eight-One this is Eight-Zero contact. Future ints. RTB. Over."

"Eight-One. RTB. Roger. Out"

With that it was all over.

Back at Palace Barracks, there was the usual buzz that followed a successful shoot and scoot.

Five suspected IRA men were down. And the hospital had reported one man dead on arrival to the RUC. The RUC, who the boys had christened "Green Bottles", would interview Eight-Zero but for the call sign Eight-One new boys a bar and a beer beckoned.

Jack had his plans too. Perhaps a second helping was available from Jean if he could contact her.

Pulling on his new black leather jacket and transferring his press card into the top zipped pocket, he jumped into the Mini Cooper and headed for Jean's favourite bar. As he passed the Lower Falls Road, he saw a crowd gathering around a frail kneeling figure.

He stopped the car, grabbed his camera bag and approached slowly.

There was a pathetic sob as a girl's voice cried out for her mother.

Lizzie Tynan, like her sister before her, publicly punished for some misdemeanour.

"She's been fraternising with soldiers – the filthy slut," said one woman.

"Tar and feathers are too good for her she should be strung up," said another.

Her tears wetted the pavement more accustomed to the dark red stain of spilt blood.

Jack turned and walked away.

Chapter 5
Balls up

Jack was surprised.

Reinforcements had arrived. However, these four guys you couldn't file under "misfits". Neither were they "damaged goods". They were not even "a disgrace to their uniform". In fact, they looked like soldiers.

Real soldiers.

From their confident demeanour, they looked like Special Forces.

Again, Jack's instinct was right.

When asked, the politicians always said, "the SAS are not operating in Northern Ireland", so now some joker in the Ministry of Defence had sent in their webbed-footed cousins.

Yes, thought Jack. *The Special Boat Squadron of the Royal Marines have arrived.*

No orders or papers – they had just boarded a Hercules transport from RAF Lyneham. And here they were.

Ready for action.

Ready for anything.

These guys were just a typing error away from being the best. Not SAS – SBS.

"Pretend SAS" the boys at Hereford used to call them when their paths crossed. Those rare encounters usually started with fireworks, moved on to a marathon drinking session and ended in a singsong the quality of which would make a Glaswegian alkie sound like Mario Lanza.

"Can I help you gentlemen?" Jack interrupted their banter.

"Yep" said one of the four, "where's the war?"

Jack bristled.

There was a "Sir" or "Sergeant Major" missing in that sentence.

Then Jack realised he was in mufti. Hang on – they were too. Wrangler jeans and Barbour jackets.

Jack was carrying his camera bag. They were toting 120lb military rucksacks

Jack reached out a hand.

"Sergeant Major Jack Gillespie."

The vice-like grip of Sgt. Ken Cooke connected with Jack's equally steeley handshake.

"Pleased to meet you. I think we have a mutual friend – Johnny Mason.I did a diving course with him. He told me a lot about you."

"Good bloke Mason," said Jack.

Both Jack and Ken had a lot in common. Both had the eyes of soldiers who had seen many battles; many casualties; and many friends – too many friends – close friends, die.

The only difference was that Sgt. Cooke still had a lot to learn. That's why he and his comrades had turned up at the only shooting war in town.

The SAS were still enjoying life in their natural desert habitat of the Oman "shooting Arabs", but the SBS had not done much, apart from training exercises, since their time in Borneo in 1966.

1966? No, it was 1967, thought Jack.

Like all good Scots, he had instinctively avoided the "mortal sin" of mentioning *that year* – the year when the *Auld Enemy* won the soccer World Cup, defeating West Germany 4-2 at Wembley. How Jack had laughed when they had failed to defend the trophy two years ago in Mexico City.

Now the England team were struggling in international football. Their arch-enemies West Germany were again in the ascendancy, playing the Soviet Union in the Final of Euro '72 at the Heysel Stadium in Brussels this afternoon.

Perhaps if the 1970 England management accepted the SAS boys' offer to pop over to Mexico from their training camp in nearby Belize to provide team security, then England captain Bobby Moore wouldn't have had that bit of bother with the missing Emeralds, and without the off-field hoo-hah his team might have fared better on the pitch.

Now in the Emerald Isle, football was very handy too. It got Jack out of a few close scrapes – his cover as a Glaswegian Catholic photographer in West Belfast strengthened by an encyclopaedic knowledge of the many triumphs of Celtic FC. The Bhoys were not only the Pride of Scotland – many IRA men also held them in high esteem. Jack's tattooed left forearm bore the Shamrock emblem encircled with the words "The Celtic Football Club" and underneath "1888".

It was Celtic's Golden age.

They had won the Scottish League for the past seven years – in fact every year since 1966. This year, 1972 as with 1971, they had also won the Scottish Cup Final – the double – two years running. It doesnt' get much better than that.

Jack's distinguishing mark was the work of Dirty Dick – a part-time tattooist in Glasgow's famous Barras market. Dirty Dick worked in the back of a shop that also sold pornographic magazines in the Spoutmouth area of the market. It's this line of illicit merchandise and not that he worked under filthy conditions when tattooing that earned Dirty Dick his nickname.

Unwittingly Dirty Dick had not only created a fine piece of skin art but had also given Jack a Monopoly-style "Get out of jail free card", which had already saved his skin in West Belfast on numerous occasions.

Not many members of the British Army could produce what was such a compelling, user-friendly, identity card for enemy eyes.

Ken Cooke had a tattoo too.

It was a 9mm Browning pistol tattooed on his abdomen.

The grip was visible above his leather belt; the "barrel" hidden by the top of his jeans – disappearing tantalisingly into whatever lay beneath. No-one knew of this concealed weapon. Yet.

A 20-minute interview later and Ken's three companions were despatched to the other MRF call signs: Seven-Zero and Eight-Zero.

Only Ken would stay with Jack. They were peas from the same pod.

After lunch, Jack showed Ken the ropes: a quick tour of the inner sanctum of the MRF.

They eyeballed the rogues' gallery in the Ops room, toured the MT section and armoury, ending at about 1430 hours in the briefing room. The mess could wait until later.

Intelligence Sergeant Roy Mackay turned to greet them as they entered the room. Jack introduced Ken although the Sergeant already knew more about Ken than he did. The SBS men's arrival was no surprise to him.

"*Softly, softly* continues as the order of the day – not that it seems to mean much to you lot. Just try really hard not to kill anyone," started Sgt Mackay.

"We have intelligence reports that there is a Republican "Civil Rights" March to take place at Divis flats, in the Lower Falls Road today. Our friends at HQ Northern Ireland require some photographs of the parade, especially the people who will be leading the protest, believed to be Gerry Adams and Brendan Hughes."

He tapped two pictures which had pride of place pinned to the bottom of the operational map with a pointer.

"We know Gerry Adams is a leading member of Sinn Fein – the political wing of the IRA. Adams has stated repeatedly that he has never been a member of the provisional Irish Republican Army. However, we know that he is in fact a senior IRA figure, although we are still unsure how he fits into the chain of command. His daily activities and locations are of acute interest to the intelligence community.

"Brendan Hughes is the commander of the West Belfast Battalion of the IRA. Together these two pose a serious threat to the peace process in Northern Ireland."

Jack could detect a smile in the Sergeant's eyes, which he really was not sure about, and interpreted as MacKay purposely understating the obvious.

Mackay continued: "Under normal conditions, we would be looking for a "result" today, but in view of the press coverage that this event will attract and the large number of people in the march it would be hard to justify a definitive operation.

"Here are today's six mug shots from Adams to McGuiness."

He passed some photographs around the room.

"We need some shots of Adams, as since his release from internment aboard HMS Maidstone, he has reportedly changed his appearance. He has also disappeared from view on numerous occasions including, we believe, to make trips to the UK mainland. And we all know what that means.

"As a result, it will be a very delicate assignment. I suggest two-man patrols go in on foot and covertly take snapshots of these people. You will be armed but carry nothing which could link you with the security forces. I say that for the benefit of our new arrivals."

Jack, who would be the patrol commander, acknowledged the orders. He turned to Bert Cousins.

"Bert, we need to draw out a couple of cameras"

Pud approached them in the Op's room.

"How can I help you fellahs?"

"We need a couple of cameras with motor drives – you know, the one's that take 10 shots a second. Where we're going we don't want to be hanging around," said Jack.

Pud went to the locker and produced two new Canon SLRs with long lenses, motor drives and a handful of 35mm film.

"These little beauties will get you some very nice close ups. You can get your luppers right around the lens and move the zoom up and down like this."

He demonstrated. He'd done this before.

Jack and Bert carried their brand new booty back to the briefing room and showed them to the other member's of the team. They quickly assembled and loaded the cameras. Each fired off a couple of shots to ensure the new motor drives were working. They treated the cameras with the same respect as weapons – as if the black and white films were live ammo.

Joined by Len Smith and Bombardier Bert Cousins, the men made their way to the armoury. They each drew a 9mm Browning pistol and two spare mags, then went next door to be issued with ammunition. They filled the magazines and attached them to the weapons.

In the car park they selected their "wheels".

Len chose a Ford Consul. Ken settled on the Volvo 164. He

would drive Jack on his first time out – they considered it a soft operation.

The Ford was a common car in Belfast, so wouldn't draw any attention. The Volvo, although a little more rare, was nothing out of the ordinary. Both the cars had armour-plated door panels as well as armour plate across the whole length of the rear seats.

Len and Ken checked each car had a full tank of petrol. It was routine after each mission, whether it was night or day, for the patrols to top up their cars with fuel ready for the next crew. If you were shooting and scooting, the one thing you did not want to happen was to run out of juice.

Jack brought the four men together and told them that he and Ken would take photos of the parade as it was forming up at the Divis flats. IRA men would sometimes show themselves in a big crowd without fear of being picked up by security forces or the police, and would march with the parade for as long as they thought it was safe to do so. It was a perfect photo opportunity for the members of "Her Majesty's Press".

Bert and Len, would position themselves at the upper end of the Falls Road and photograph the parade as it was passing. Jack and Ken's role at the Divis Flats would be the crucial one, as it was possible that prominent IRA men would address the crowd before the march and then would disappear if necessary.

The two cars travelled to their positions independently. Bert and Len left first, followed 15 minutes later by Jack and Ken.

They travelled along Holywood Road onto the Newtownards Road, over the Queens Bridge, winding their way through the city towards West Belfast.

Jack and Ken – Call Sign Nine-Zero – headed for the Divis flats, while Bert and Len – Call Sign Nine-One – took a detour around the city centre, turned left up Grosvenor Road and arrived at the junction of Springfield Road and Falls Road.

They parked their car in the Victoria Hospital car park, and headed on foot to take up positions on the corner of McQuillan Street and the Falls Road.

Jack and Ken joined the crowd waiting expectantly at the Divis Flats. The two men sported their bogus NUJ Press Cards in their jacket top pockets so that just the word "PRESS" was visible.

They were happily taking crowd shots when two burly-looking heavies approached them. They demanded to see the "Pressmen's" IDs.

Jack took out his NUJ card and showed it to one of the men.

The figure dressed in a lumberjack-style check shirt barked:

"You're OK – but no more photographs."

This was significant. It told Jack someone of importance was about to join the parade.

Jack let the camera hang from its strap around his neck.

Suddenly a buzz went around and the crowd pushed and jostled the two MRF men to get a better view of what was happening nearby.

Cheers rang out.

Ken whispered to Jack that Brendan Hughes and Gerry Adams had just emerged from a house opposite the Divis flats.

Jack looked in the direction Ken indicated, and confirmed recognition of Brendan Hughes and Gerry Adams.

He quickly fired off a couple of 35mm shots.

"OK, let's go," said Jack.

He knew he had what he wanted. No one was interested in them as they extricated themselves from the melee.

All eyes were now on Gerry Adams, who was raising

a megaphone to his mouth and was about to speak. Adams spoke of peace and the word "ceasefire" echoed as the MRF men slipped away.

Adams subsequently travelled to London for secret peace talks with the British Government on July 7th.

However, Jack knew none of this.

All he knew was that the MRF were on a short leash now, due to success not failure. He did not like it one bit. Surely, very soon, the dogs of war would be let loose again, he mused.

Bert and Len, meanwhile, were waiting for the parade to appear at the top of the Falls Road, not knowing that Jack and Ken already had the snaps in the camera bag. Adams and Hughes would be near its head, surrounded by supporters, as it made its way up the traffic-less thoroughfare.

"You OK?" Bert asked Len.

He had heard that Len had had a bit of a pep talk from Jack a week or so ago.

"Suppose."

Len's finger followed the scar from the bullet that had furrowed his brow. He had unconsciously developed a habit of doing this and the other MRF boys had noticed it. He also now had beads of sweat appearing.

"No, come on tell me – really," said Bert.

"Well I've been thinking about Gilly…"

"Who is she? Your girlfriend or something?"

"Yes. She's not too happy… I suppose I shouldn't have told her about my near miss. It affected her more than me for some reason and that's really saying something.

"So I've been thinking. My leave comes up next week 'cos I've been here three months. And you know I really enjoy the buzz. So, of course, I'll see out the rest of my time.

"But, as Gilly's hurtin' like, I'll buy myself out for her sake. Settle down, have kids – you know the form. I'll never forget you boys or the unit. But £30 a week isn't really danger money is it?"

He stroked his scar again. He had not told the unit Medical Officer about the headaches and the sleepless nights and the dreams, which, when he did succumb to tiredness, brought him back to consciousness with a start.

"Good lad," said Bert

• • •

Not a single uniformed member of the security forces was to be seen anywhere on the Falls Road, but there were many faces familiar to Jack as he continued to push his way though the crowd on his way back to the car.

"It's like a ruddy MI6 and Special Branch outing," he thought.

Bert and Len did not have long to wait.

A small bugle and drum band preceded the marchers playing *The Belfast Brigade* for all they were worth. To the tune of "Glory, Glory, Halleluiah", the singers told of the hated B Specials and their fate when they under-estimated the IRA on a visit to the Falls Road in earlier times.

Bert and Len were now standing on a school wall elevated away from their original position. They too bore the shield of protection afforded by fake NUJ Press Cards.

Bert fired off countless photographs without interference.

Reload.

The motor drive was hot and running. Forty-eight frames captured rank upon rank of IRA sympathisers. Len scribbled down Bert's description of what he saw through the long lens. Names. The words on banners. Descriptions of weapons brandished with hate by men in balaclavas. There were no TV film-crews present as far as they could see.

Right then, the fruits of the pair's work were just exposures on a light sensitive emulsion – they still had to be processed into negatives and exposed on to photo paper, enlarged and dried before more educated eyes would examine them in close detail with magnifying tools.

Bert and Len went back to the Ford Consul.

Jack and Ken had reached their car some 30 minutes before. They moved away out of the immediate area. Using the microphone hidden in the Volvo's passenger sun visor, Jack pressed the foot switch, checked in with HQ on the car radio and told them they had the goods.

It was getting late.

Call Sign Nine-Zero was keen to get back to base and hand over their pictures to a runner. They'd be rushed to MI6 at Lisburn who were waiting for them like vultures hungry for their prey.

Jack took off his new leather jacket, wound down the passenger window and told Ken to put his foot down.

As they crossed the Queen's Bridge onto the Newtownards Road, unseen eyes noted their conspicuous haste on a lazy June afternoon. The colourful flash of Celtic green on Jack's Blighty-bleached forearm that rested, cooling, on the open passenger door window, heightened inquisitive awareness further still.

When Bert and Len checked in with HQ to report their successful sortie, they heard there was a change of plan.

They, too, were to proceed along the Newtownards Road and investigate a reported gathering of the Protestant paramilitary Ulster Defence Association and Ulster Volunteer Force at its junction with Susan Street.

Following a successful op, the Nine-One boys were relatively relaxed. Distracted by a crack Bert made about Jack's love life, Len accidentally jumped a set of red traffic lights. The Ford Consul braked violently and swerved to avoid a collision.

Tyres squealed and smoked.

They jerked to a halt. The engine stalled.

Unscathed the pair looked at each other and smiled with relief. That was a close call.

Apart from the occasional road traffic accident, East Belfast was a relatively safe area to drive through during The Troubles. The number of times the MRF had been challenged could be counted on a leper's stump. Jack and Sgt. Benson's experience the other day was a bit of a one off. And little wonder – as the MRF's *modus operandi* was intentionally indistinguishable from the Protestant paramilitaries, it was almost as if they were on home turf.

Nine-One could get this recce out of the way quickly and then back to the Mess for a pint… Or two… Or three.

No worries.

Len turned the ignition. The hot engine fired up first time. No harm done.

Nine-One was approaching the Susan Street junction when some men in balaclava-type masks furiously motioned the car to stop.

Still in IRA mode, Bert yelled: "Don't stop – keep going."

They passed the masked men.

A few yards later, there was a terrific bang as the Ford's windscreen caved in.

Glass shattered over the faces of both Bert and Len.

Blinded.

The car slewed out of control across the road and demolished a telephone box before embedding itself in a shop window. Len and Bert lay bloodied in the steaming wreckage as a crowd began to gather. Under the illusion that their UDA heroes had thwarted IRA raiders, the mass jeered and jibed the pair.

Slowly Bert crawled out of the wreckage and begged for help. His Lancashire accent silenced the spite of the onlookers, and they instantly turned from serpents to Samaritans. They frisked Bert down, his weapon was spirited away, and an ambulance arrived as if by magic.

Suddenly Jack appeared on the scene. He pulled Len's unconscious body from the driver's seat and onto the pavement. Petrol was now spilling from the tank but Jack ignored the danger. He retrieved Len's 9mm and stuck it in his waistband.

Len looked bad. Very bad.

The medic pushed past Jack and yanked up Len's sleeve.

To Jack's surprise there was a bandage hidden beneath the cover of his casual shirt. The medic tore it off and inserted a drip needle into his arm above the newly inked words: *For Queen and Country.* And underneath, in bold blood red Gothic script, the letters: *MRF.*

Jack held Len's limp hand as the ambulance sped towards the Victoria hospital. Even the war weary ambulance man looked shocked by the condition of this casualty. He was taken immediately to the intensive care ward where he was placed on life support.

Bert's wounds were superficial. In the casualty department, he had a few shards of windscreen glass washed out of his eyes and was treated for slight concussion. After some tidying up, and a sweet cup of tea from an over-attentive nurse, he was able to tell Jack what he remembered – which was not a lot.

Jack would need to read the initial RUC report of the incident available later that day. For obvious reasons, even that would be less than factual. The bare facts: someone from a unit that did not exist had somehow had half his skull gashed open.

Eventually a doctor came to tell Jack that Len sustained a "large wound" to his head that had allowed some brain matter to spill out. He was in "a critical condition". Jack spoke to Captain McGregor and explained the severity of Len's wounds. They agreed to contact his next of kin.

An hour or so later, a local policeman would call around to break the news to Len's family at home in Winteringham on the banks of the Humber.

Len's parents arrived in Northern Ireland late the next day. A padre from 39 Brigade, Lisburn, greeted them at Aldergrove Airport. They travelled by car to Victoria hospital with the padre and Cpl. Joe Blackmore. Jack and Ken travelled in front in the Volvo to ensure the safety of the second vehicle.

The Admin Sergeant Major from the MRF, George Gleeson, and a doctor from the hospital were waiting for them. After a short talk with army personnel, the pair were taken to the intensive care ward where their son lay. About 40 minutes later, they made the only decision available to them.

Mark and Helen Smith decided to turn off the machine, which now kept their only son alive.

At least they knew there was a child who, in a few months, could bear his name. Len's girlfriend, Gilly, had kept her condition secret from her boyfriend while he was in Northern Ireland. She planned to tell him on his next home leave and try to convince him to marry her and not to return to The Troubles.

That evening, his parents stayed at Len's bedside. A few of his comrades visited to pay their respects. When they all left the machine was turned off.

Len died in his mother's arms.

The Smiths eventually made it to the Europa Hotel and spent a few sleepless hours on their own.

Downstairs the men of the MRF were saying farewell to Len in their own way. The way he would have wanted – in the bar.

Jack had now read the interim RUC report. It stated that no weapons were fired at the car involved in the incident. The evidence seemed to point to the fact that the UDA had developed a new tactic to stop suspicious vehicles entering their territory – to throw one pound-weight lead balls at offending cars. This is what must have shattered Call Sign Nine-One's windscreen. The missile had struck Len full on the forehead.

The RAF flew Len's body and parents out of Aldergrove Airport two days later.

Jack saluted as the Hercules transport aircraft slowly left the tarmac. Dark exhaust smoke emanated from the four turbo-prop engines as they struggled to lift its cargo skywards.

His salute was lasting much longer than he intended.

Jack's bare right arm revealed a new decoration: three newly inked letters in blood red. MRF.

Even someone with half a brain would realise the UVF and the UDA were now fair game for the men of Military Reaction Force.

Chapter 6
Thompson Twins

Jean Philomena McLaughlin woke suddenly.

An explosion had just killed her brother Sean. His shattered body lay amongst the rubble of the café in Grosvenor Road. It was the place where he would always meet his Republican mates.

"The murdering Prots had used the ceasefire to hit back at her heroes!"

"Wait."

Her mind raced.

The ceasefire is not until… A dream, it was just a dream.

But so real…

She looked around the small hotel room. An empty bottle of Johnnie Walker Black Label lay on its side. Its contents were now banging on the inside of her temples.

No wonder she did not know which way was up.

The slumbering giant next to her had won the battle of the bed sheets. Now wrapped so tightly around him, their sovereignty not too easily reclaimed without a substantial skirmish as she tried in vain to cover her nakedness.

She smiled.

Next to her lay Jack.

Next to him lay…a camera!

Had they? Had he?

She couldn't even remember the night before. The evidence didn't look very good.

She quietly picked up the Canon SLR.

It was heavy and cold in her hands.

Jack gave a snort next to her.

She froze.

He stirred, turned over and resumed his slumber.

She let the breath she had trapped in her lungs go free. She opened the back of the camera. It was empty. If there was a film capturing her "night of love" for posterity then she had to find it.

Jack's camera bag laid on the floor the other side of the bed. She quietly crept over towards it. The floor creaked. She froze and held her breath again. A hand suddenly grasped her waist and threw her back on the bed. Now the roll of film was the last thing on her mind.

Ten, 20, 30, 40 minutes passed.

Jack was thinking of the 9mm Browning secreted in his camera bag. It would have taken a lot of explaining. Then there was the film, which he was looking forward to processing later. For once, it did not feature Gerry Adams.

Jack concentrated on the job in hand.

• • •

Later Jack dropped Jean off home in Andersonstown. He gunned the Mini Cooper ostentatiously as he left the kerb. If there were Republican eyes watching they would see a local girl with Jack. That was good.

But other eyes were always watching too.

MI6 officer Peter Williams had seen Jack's arrival and departure from his seat by the door of the public house near Jean's home.

Over in the nearby base at Casement Park, Army Intelligence Officers with high-powered binoculars saw the blue Mini Cooper roar away.

Above, a Wessex reconnaissance helicopter seemed to be making lazy circles in the sky.

• • •

Much later, a phone rang in the Ops room of the MRF.

An Army mobile patrol had seen a car hijacked by three armed men in the Whiterock area of Belfast.

The driver, Mr Patrick Murphy, had not offered even so much as a frown of resistance as he was unceremoniously bundled out of his much-loved motor car.

He was much too wise for that.

He would just have a change of trousers as soon as he got home.

His blue 1971 Renault was last seen travelling down the Upper Falls Road. It would be easy to spot.

Call Sign Nine-Zero was already out and about

"Nine-Zero, Nine-Zero this is Zero. Over."

The radio crackled into life.

"Zero – Nine-Zero. Over." Jack replied.

"Nine-Zero: Be aware car hijack in progress Whiterock – Blue Renault: Bravo India Alpha 5833. Three armed occupants. Over."

"Nine-Zero. Roger and out."

As if by appointment, the moment the transmission finished the blue Renault flashed past the MRF squad going in the opposite direction.

"Nine-Zero – Contact over," said Jack.

"Zero – send. Over."

"Nine-Zero reference your last: Blue Renault registration

Bravo India Alpha 5833 now proceeding down Falls Road. Over."

"Zero - Caution, these men are armed and dangerous. Out."

"Nine-Zero Roger. Out."

Without a word of command, Sgt. Ken Cooke made a sudden handbrake turn and Nine-Zero's BMW 2002ti was in hot pursuit. The roaring 120 horse-power engine made the tyres spin on the worn road surface and the back wheels swung out under the excessive demands made by the driver's right foot.

Less than minute later and Ken was right up the Renault's backside. The traffic lights at the Springfield Road junction turned red. BIA5833 stopped dead.

The hijacker in the back of the car looked out of the rear window and saw with horror Jack pointing the Thompson sub-machine gun right at him.

He screamed something at the driver. They tore away, with Jack and Ken in hot pursuit.

The Renault, just five yards ahead, suddenly turned left into the "safe haven" of the staunch Republican area of the Clonard. As Jack's BMW followed, the hijackers opened fire.

Two men with their heads and shoulders out of the Renaults side windows, as though aboard a Wild West stagecoach, were firing revolvers at the MRF squad car. The BMW's windscreen shattered.

Ken stopped the car; Jack jumped out and fired two long bursts of .45 calibre rounds from the Thompson at the fleeing Renault.

It slewed to a halt.

Two men wearing jeans and light blue shirts jumped out and dived straight into the nearest house. Jack sprinted to the Renault. One man was still inside, groaning, with gunshot wounds to the head and upper body.

He's a goner, thought Jack.

Jack reached into the car and picked up an IRA Armalite rifle and made his way quickly back to his BMW.

Ken had been busy making it "roadworthy" by punching out the remains of the front windscreen with his 9mm pistol butt.

The street was suddenly alive with local residents. Some clattered dustbin lids together. There was a hell of a racket. More began rocking the BMW.

"Stand back!" shouted Jack.

He fired the Thompson into the air.

"The next burst is for you bastards!"

The crowd fell back, frightened that this mad man would indeed shoot them all. He would have too. Capture was not an option under any circumstances.

Jack now stood tall on the sill of the front passenger's door. His weapon was held high in full sight, in case a hero was tempted to make an appearance.

But, today no such foolish a man was to be found.

Jack swung himself into the car.

"Let's get the fuck out of here."

Ken didn't need telling twice. He had instinctively put the pedal to the metal, and Jack's back hit the leather seat as the BMW flew from the madding crowd.

However, it was not over quite yet.

The rattle of another Thompson gun, this time belonging to the IRA caught them from behind as a magazine's contents thudded into the armour plating secured along the whole length of the BMW's back seat.

Life saver!

Jack radioed "Zero" and brought them up to speed on the situation.

The car entered the Falls Road.

"Jack, let's go down Grosvenor Road into the city centre and not down the Lower Falls Road. They'll have been warned, and waiting," said Ken

"Good thinking, that!"

The car made its way past the Victoria Hospital and headed for the city and base. A welcoming committee of their MRF mates greeted them on arrival at Palace Barracks.

"How the fuck did you two get away with that?" said Sgt. Peter Adams.

Jack and Ken joined the crowd who had gathered around the rear of the BMW.

The windscreen-less front looked bad enough, but the boat-like rear of the 2002 had been more than just holed below the water line. The IRA's .45 Calibre Thompson rounds had punched gaping holes through the bodywork. Each one was the size of one of the new currency – the one pence piece.

"Lucky you didn't get done for driving without lights," said Cpl. Joe Blackmore.

• • •

Back in Palace Barracks, Jack put the finishing touches to another close shave. Gone was the full beard he had grown over the last month or so. Jean would be delighted with her fresh-faced clean-shaven lover.

However, Jack was not heading for the delights of Miss McLaughlin. Tonight, he had other targets in his sights.

The Europa Hotel looked splendid with its sandbag-adorned entrance throwing shadows in the evening light. *The Longest Day minus one,* thought Jack.

He entered through the swing doors, turned left and headed

for the bar. It was quite crowded, but Jack quickly recognised a fellow snapper sitting on a barstool.

Danno Stobbart had been a freelance photographer for nearly 10 years now. A public school boy – Harrow – he was a camp follower in every sense of the word. Still in the closet, though. To his colleagues he was nothing but a macho-professional.

If there was a war then Danno was not very far away. If there was a bar then Danno was not very far away. What Danno really needed was a bar with a war in it.

Unfortunately, for Danno Stobbart, the Europa Hotel was not that bar. It was untouchable.

If you really want to influence the press, then blowing them up is not a good idea. The IRA had twigged this and you were now safer in the bar of the Europa than anywhere else in Northern Ireland. That was Danno's problem. Sometimes when he should have been at the frontline, he was back at the bar. And when he should have been in the bar, he was at the front line and the enemy were nowhere to be seen.

But, today was the day when Danno got it right.

Today he had forayed out into The Troubles, and The Troubles had delivered in spades. He couldn't claim all the credit for his perfect timing, though.

The picture desk on the *Daily Mirror* in Fleet Street had received a tip off that there were peace talks in the air and had wanted to get a definitive image of the conflict before "it was too late".

If it was good, really good, the picture would be blown up large enough to cover the front and back pages of the tabloid. The reader would then hold the newspaper up and look at the image like a Playboy centrefold.

Danno had delivered the goods for them in Vietnam a few months before. He had fired off a few test shots on a roll of 24 exposures to see if his damaged motor drive's repair had been successful. Unknown to Danno his contact strip of random test shot had accidently captured the image of an anguished girl caught up in a bomb blast in Saigon. He had dined, or rather drank, from that success ever since.

Today he had done it again – but this time it was no accident.

When Jack arrived in the Europa Hotel's bar Danno was starting his celebrations even before he had even processed his film.

The image was already perfectly fixed in his mind:

"A bearded paramilitary gunman stood amid an angry crowd firing a Thompson sub-machine gun into the air over their heads," he addressed an imaginary audience of Absinthe green fairies and their Irish Leprechaun friends. "Bullets shattered the chimney pots of the houses opposite. The terracotta cascaded down over the roof tiles and crashed onto the street below.

"The people's faces were a mixture of fear and loathing in West Belfast. Eyes bulged. Teeth bared. And there, beaming on the face of the gunman, a smile. A smile that said: 'Life is good. And this is what I was made for'."

This unborn masterpiece, Danno told the little people, was now in the breast pocket of his khaki shirt, which he patted for reassurance.

You didn't need a particularly sensitive nose to tell that shirt had travelled from South East Asia to Northern Ireland with the minimum of laundry-care.

If he were just plain stinking drunk now, soon he would be drunk as a skunk – or maybe dead drunk. Because there, sitting on the next barstool, was his new friend and fellow "photo ace" Jack Gillespie of the *Glasgow Times*, ready to share his celebrations.

"A toast!"

Danno stood up.

"To the glory of war," he said through the fog of the second half of a bottle of whisky.

From bitter experience, he knew he would be sober enough tomorrow morning to develop the precious pictures and wire them to London from the office of the *Belfast Telegraph* where the picture editor was an old school chum.

"My friend, before I join your toast, I need to know what exactly it is we are celebrating," said Jack.

Danno puffed out his chest.

"My dear, dear, good fellow. We are here together this evening celebrating excellence in our craft – nay – our art. I give you creativity!"

He raised his glass to everyone in the bar and took a large slug.

"I have today captured on celluloid the very essence of the conflict which we are here as "war artists" to record.

"May I ask you to picture the scene? I am surrounded by a braying mob. They have engulfed a gunman who, bent on destruction, has already taken one life of their precious freedom fighters of the Irish Republican Army.

"Suddenly he fires his automatic weapon at them, but due to his fear or incompetence, completely misses and in the great confusion that follows makes his escape."

"I have shot after shot of the incident here in glorious monochrome," Danno patted his chest pocket. "And on Monday his ghastly smile will be as famous as that of the Mona Lisa. It's the *Daily Mirror* front page and mayhap the back as well."

Danno lurched forward and slung an arm around Jack's shoulder.

"I have already talked to the esteemed picture editor, and

with my reputation they have taken my word for it that it is a page one splash. Hacks from the Belfast office of the *Daily Mirror* are, as we speak, rounding up some words from the Gendarmerie about the incident.

"They tell me that local people have given the RUC sworn statements that in the Clonard, a car full of innocent men returning home after visiting friends was attacked by the occupants of a following unknown car who viciously, mercilessly, opened fire. One killed, two wounded, another two escaped and sought refuge in a nearby house. It was a seminal sectarian attack."

Jack topped up Danno's glass with Johnnie Walker for a proper Scots celebration. After that, the toasts popped up like outbursts between delegates at a Tourette's Syndrome conference, and whisky flowed like water until the men's combined consumption was at least equal to the capacity of Loch Neagh.

Jack was standing long after Danno had slumped forward into the Waterford Crystal tumbler, which still held a wee dram of amber liquid.

A Black Label black out.

"Another bottle, barman. As a carry out," said Jack. "We'll continue the night in my friend's room, and I have a sneaking feeling that the wee mini bar is not going to be enough.'

Jack's accent was becoming more Glaswegian by the second.

Bottle in one hand and buffoon over his shoulder, Jack took the stairs to the fourth floor. Minutes later, he left Danno unconscious on his double bed. The door clicked quietly as Jack left the scene.

• • •

The next morning an even cleaner shaven Jack was facing a grilling from a quite irritable RUC officer who had better things to do on a Sunday morning.

However, Jack's production of the IRA Armalite, plus the fact that the RUC themselves had reported the car in yesterday's incident as being "hijacked by armed men", was enough for them to quickly lose interest.

They smiled and said to Jack: "Trouble seems to follow you around – keep up the good work!"

Forensic tests later confirmed that the fingerprints on the gun matched that of the dead man.

Across town, in the darkroom of the *Belfast Telegraph*, another good story was developing.

Technicians gathered around Danno Stobbart at the light box. They carefully surveyed strips of negatives with magnifying glasses.

Stobbart was right. The pictures were good action shots.

Maybe it was just a bit too graphic for a family newspaper like the *Daily Mirror*. In fact, it looked too raw for *Playboy* or even *Hustler*. Perhaps though, *Distillers World* would show an interest. After all, it was an unusual place to see a bottle of Black Label whisky. Even in these enlightened times. But, then it was Jean Philomena McLaughlin's party trick and it kept Jack coming back for more.

Only now Jack no longer had the pictures to prove it to the boys.

Chapter 7
Pulp Fiction

Sapper Edward "Paddy" Stuart stood frozen to the spot.

A bullet had just taken the top off the little finger of his right hand. But he felt no pain.

In the shock of being hit by a high-velocity round, for him, time was now standing still. He heard voices but not words. Saw still frames but not movement.

His 9mm Sterling sub-machine gun was falling apart in his hands. His whole world was not far behind.

The Bakelite covering of the pistol grip had shattered and the hardened plastic-like material cascaded slowly to the floor.

Whoosh!

Now it hurt.

Jack had flattened him to ground. Paddy, standing there motionless, was a sitting duck for another sniper's bullet.

Zero had dispatched the MRF to Hannahstown Road in West Belfast to investigate reports of shots fired. There was also intelligence that IRA live-firing training was taking place in the woods to the east of Hannahstown.

The plan had been to take a look-see and shoot up anyone who paraded weapons on the streets. For the MRF it was business as usual.

Call sign Nine-One was first on the scene and had

immediately come under fire. Lookouts obviously spotted them as they raced through the Republican areas. Bombardier Bert Cousins' performance behind the wheel had certainly been a bit erratic.

Selected as a driver following Len's death, he was more than a bit a bit rusty. His brake squeals and spinning wheels were a bit understandable, especially if you had been through what he had been through recently.

Nevertheless, in putting him "back on the MRF horse" as quickly as possible after the incident Jack may have been a little bit hasty. It certainly seemed that way to Paddy as he felt the pain from his right hand for the first time.

"I'm hit," he said using the time-honoured Hollywood B-Movie phrase.

"Of course you're fucking hit," said Jack. "What do you think this stuff is then – Heinz Tomato Sauce?"

A small pool of blood had formed next to the pair as they lay behind the Ford Cortina, waiting for the all clear.

"You're just lucky you are not dead."

"Behind you, Sergeant Major," shouted Peter Adams, the Nine-One Squad commander.

Raising himself up, Jack could see figures moving in a field to the rear of the car.

Grabbing Paddy's damaged SMG, Jack started to engage the IRA men who were 200 metres away across some open ground in forestry. In three-shot bursts, he emptied the magazine over the top of a hedge. Other MRF men soon joined in until there was no more "incoming" fire.

A few minutes later, the MRF men returned to their cars – Paddy in the back of Nine-Zero with Jack and a collection of wound dressings. They headed through Protestant areas toward the Royal Victoria Hospital.

Driving down Crumlin Road, Jack saw a road block ahead.

"Now what?" he said.

Both MRF squad cars stopped short of the makeshift barrier.

John Benson addressed the Ulster Defence Association men who manned the barrier in his Belfast accent.

"Security forces, British soldiers, taking a casualty to hospital. There are more soldiers in the car behind."

The UDA men quickly removed the obstruction and the cars carried on their way.

Jack looked back through the rear windscreen.

A protestant youth had an ancient revolver. He pointed at the departing vehicles pretended to shoot and then blew the imaginary smoke away like a cowboy.

"Stupid cunt," said Jack.

With Paddy patched up and the damaged SMG, complete with high-velocity tracer round wedged in the metalwork of the pistol grip, being marvelled at by armourers, the MRF men were ready for a night on the town.

Except for the MRF's skirmish, the IRA cease-fire seemed to be holding. Intelligence was convinced the patrol had simply disturbed some live-firing training.

It was Friday night and a funeral service for Paddy's fingertip was as good an excuse as any to get on the drink. Paddy knew he was going to be the butt of jokes for sometime.

"Show us your pinkie," said Pud when the boys reported back to Palace Barracks. "I've already seen what happened to your weapon. Simply hair-raising. I wouldn't know where to put my hands."

After a couple of pints in the NAAFI, the boys cremated Paddy's pinkie appropriately, and somewhat ironically, in an ashtray. Jack and Ken decided to get away from it all and pay a visit to the Strangford Arms Hotel just outside of Newtownards, where there was plenty of talent available.

What was the correct military terminology for the situation?

Oh yes – the girls were gagging for it.

The hotel was a public house with a "disco bar" that was frequented by both Protestant and Catholic girls looking for a bit of light entertainment – a welcome distraction from the reality of The Troubles.

The girls knew there was the chance of meeting people from out of town there. A passport to the mainland would be theirs if they played the "innocent Irish beauty" hard enough.

Unfortunately, small gangs of the local Newtownards lads would gather in the bar and try to discourage outsiders from interfering with "their" women. It was still a place where strangers trod carefully.

It was into this atmosphere that Jack and Ken entered on the last night of June. Strangely, this day qualified too, in its own way, as the year's longest day because an extra leap second was added to end the month for some astronomical reason or other. A longer "pip" on the BBC radio time signal.

Jack and Ken had been at the pub, the Strangford Arms, and they hoped a few girls they had met on those earlier occasions would be present so they could greet "old friends" and wouldn't have to run the gauntlet of hate and jealousy from the local lads.

They knew the corner that the women would occupy, and made their way over after ordering a couple of pints. They were both unarmed, as was usual when the boys of the MRF went out on the town, although there were a few handy items in the boot of their car "just in case". They had been in Irish bars on a number of occasions when trouble had flared. The locals would equip themselves with baseball bats and coshes retrieved from their cars. As a result, everyone in the MRF had a well-equipped toolbox.

Jack and Ken noticed a couple more of their friends from the unit arrive but they made no acknowledgment of their presence.

Twenty minutes later and things were going great. Jack and Ken had met up with a couple of familiar girls and were having a good time on the dance floor. They met some new girls too, friends of the others, a couple of right corkers. They got down to the disco beat.

Little did they know that their alleged "disco dancing" to the *Theme from Shaft* by Isaac Hayes was being observed by a jealous ex-boyfriend, who happened to be one of the local hoods, and his four mates.

"They say that cat Shaft is a baa-aad mutha...
Shut your mouth!
But I'm talkin' about Shaft!
Well, we can dig it."

The record ended and they all returned to the bar. Jack was sweating hard.

"Two pints of Guinness and two whisky chasers if you please barman," Jack gave him an English five pound note and then immediately regretted it.

Remembering his manners, he asked: "Will you be having anything tonight girls?"

"Hope so!" they chorused.

"Has anyone ever told you that you pair look just like – what's her name – Dana? Well I hope you are up for all kinds of everything," Jack laughed at his own joke and for once, other people were laughing too.

Across the dance floor, some quite obviously did not appreciate the joke.

Although Jack and Ken were oblivious to the third party interest, other MRF eyes had the best interests of "Randy and Dick", from Inchcolm on the Firth of Fife, at heart. "Randy and Dick" were, however, target-fixated on a matching pair of 38s.

It was when randy Jack went out to the toilet that Royal Marine Commando, Pete Adams, told him that he and "Dick" had some unwanted admirers. Pete was there with Les Hoskins from the Parachute Regiment.

• • •

As the evening dissipated into midnight, the time for the last dance arrived. Jack had requested *Until its Time For You to Go* by Elvis Presley, as it had a 100 per cent success rate in making the difference between a snog and grope in a doorway, and crossing over the divine threshold.

"You're not a dream,
You're not an angel,
You're a woman,
I'm not a king,
I'm just a man,
Take my hand...."

Jack was surprised that the DJ played a ballad at all. Perhaps his natural Scottish charm made all the difference. Nevertheless, it played, with a reprise, and he left with a girl on each arm. This could be interesting.

Ken followed close behind.

Hope he likes to watch, thought Jack. *Or come a close second at least.*

The fresh night air hit them as they left the smoke and sweaty heat of the bar. The foursome made their way to the MRF car. Jack was fully aware of the envious eyes that observed them as he pretended to search for his keys.

He caught sight of the other MRF boys, Pete and Les. Jack was confident that if there was trouble they could handle it.

These Protestants are getting a bit too cocky. Ungrateful bastards, thought Jack.

After all, it was the MRF doing all their dirty work. Surely, you would think they would be a bit grateful...

But of course, he rationalised, *they don't know.*

Even if they did, it might not have changed these guy's attitudes.

Jack ushered the sisters into the back seat of the Mini.

Three men approached the car armed with truncheons.

"You bastards better leave our women alone. Out of the car girls," one spat.

These guys were not only rude they were drunk.

And dangerous.

Ken quickly opened the car boot and produced two pick-axe handles, specially shortened so they fitted in the cramped space.

"Catch!"

He threw one to Jack. Just in time.

The three men advanced with their weapons held high in the striking position. Jack parried the first blow. Ken hit the second man a glancing blow to his outer left knee. At the same time, Pete and Les joined the melee. Two more of the locals joined in, but they were no match for the MRF boys.

Beaten to a pulp.

"For Len. God Rest his Soul."

The last hoodlum slumped to the ground unconscious.

Suddenly two RUC Land Rovers screeched to a halt and heavily armed officers surrounded the MRF men.

The swift production of I.D. cards satisfied the police that the four men still standing were security forces from Palace Barracks. They allowed them to go "home to bed" and took the sore-headed civilians into custody.

• • •

The next day, Sunday, as it was quiet Jack went to check on a getaway car he had "liberated" a few days previously after a botched IRA bank robbery on the Lisburn Road, which an MI6 informer had alerted the security forces to some days in advance. It was there in the car park.

"Safe and sound – long may it stay that way," said Jack.

It was important to stop the IRA's criminal activities, like bank, Post Office and payroll raids, to keep cash for the Republican cause in short supply. Unlimited cash – now that was the Spooks unique selling point! They bought people and could print the money to do it. Perfectly forged Irish money – Northern Ireland banknotes and Irish Punts – marked so their specialists could trace it as it flowed into the local economy and banking system.

Jack and the boys knew this, so any cash that fell into their hands had to be "clean" or it was not worth the paper it was printed on. The MRF had been given the bank job to sort out as MI6 needed to keep testing the IRA ceasefire, but for some reason – cock up rather than conspiracy – the Green's got there first.

The right place at the right time, or perhaps, the wrong place at the wrong time. It was always one or the other in Northern Ireland. The lucky Greens in this case were The Gunners – Jack's regiment. When Jack arrived in Nine-Zero, two of the bank robbers were being clumsily cuffed and thrown into the back of a Land Rover. The others had fled. More used to firing bloody big shells than policing the streets, the Gunnery Sergeant in charge had not a clue what to do next and was glad when he saw Jack rolling up.

"Give us a hand Jack," he pleaded. "We're very exposed here and I want to wrap it up as quickly as possible and, thinking about it, where the fuck are the RUC?"

Jack suspected he knew the answer to the last part of the question but he said nothing. Someone somewhere was hoping for more IRA blood on the streets of Belfast. That is why Jack and the boys were here instead of the police.

"Tell you what," said Jack. "You drop those two off at the RUC station at Lisburn and we'll take over the scene until the police arrive in case there are snipers. We are a lot less conspicuous than you lot."

Jack gestured to the rooftops and then to his plain-clothes unit.

Snipers were the artilleryman's worst fear. Jack had driven the IRA bank robbers' BMW 2002 getaway car back to Palace Barracks himself. He thought that it would save them the trouble of stealing yet another vehicle from the beleaguered motorists of Liverpool, as this car had probably been reported missing in Belfast. Giving it back would only confuse things.

Jack stopped daydreaming as he turned into the fortified gates of the barracks. He took a long look into his rear-view mirror to check he was not being "piggybacked" by another vehicle illegally trying to gain access to the MRF site.

The mirror Jack discovered was still adjusted for a smaller driver and, as he was setting it correctly, Jack caught a glimpse of a large canvas bag on the back seat. He was not 100 per cent certain what it contained, but he was damn sure it wasn't kittens.

He turned around and quickly shoved it in the rear foot well.

• • •

Jack drew up into the car park and got out before anyone approached. He quickly sneaked a look inside the bag, smiled, and swiftly chucked it into the boot. He popped in to see Pud in the Ops Room and asked him to put a warning notice on the windscreen:

"*Do not touch. Vehicle awaiting forensic examination. Signed WOII J Gillespie...,*" Pud typed.

Jack would have to wait to open the sack and see how much Santa had brought. The answer came three months later when Jack finally counted it on the Belfast to Liverpool ferry – £40,000! But that day all he knew was there was a bloody lot of cash in that bag. Cash that would be a nice contribution to the Gillespie Retirement Fund – if he could get away with it. He could buy a nice villa in a mountain town in Majorca. Jack liked trams, and the town he had in mind had ports blessed with one of the quirkiest narrow-gauge systems you ever will see.

The car could stay in the car park unhindered for months unless some nosey parker got suspicious.

• • •

On Monday, when Jack and Ken entered the MRF Ops Room, Pud appeared quite animated.

"Oh there you are. I was just sending one of my boys to find you. Aren't you the naughty ones then? There are some nice police officers waiting for you in the Briefing Room, Jack."

Jack's heart sank.

I've been rumbled and the bountiful bank of the BMW's boot's gone bust, he thought.

He opened the door saw two RUC officers. They greeted Jack and explained exactly why they needed to speak to him.

The civilians in Newtownards, who had their just deserts on Friday night, for the sins of their compatriots who murdered Len, were pressing charges. Some kind soul had told them their assailants were British Military and one was a Papist – Jack.

They wanted British Justice.

• • •

Two of the men pressing charges of grievous bodily harm identified Jack in the Holywood Magistrates Court straight away. A medical report presented to the court indicated that one had sustained a fractured skull the other multiple injuries including fractured ribs, a broken arm, and a ruptured spleen.

Although Jack had given the pair, as Cassius Clay would say, "a good whupping" it was definitely a fit up. Both the men looked as if they had just been freshly mauled by a lion. They had bloodstained bandages and one had a neck brace.

Jack felt a strange pride swelling up.

"All my own work, your honour," he had a sudden urge to confess.

He was glad he didn't.

Due to the severity of the injuries sustained by the two men, the magistrate said he had no option but to send the case for trial at a higher court for hearing at a later date. He allowed bail. But Jack's "brief" supplied by the Army legal service was a worried man.

"This is serious. Very serious," he whispered to Jack behind his hand.

You don't say, thought Jack.

• • •

When the date of the hearing arrived, Jack and John Benson travelled to the court in Downpatrick. The case was not being held where he had expected but then Jack didn't understand the intricacies of the Northern Ireland legal system. Who did?

If convicted he would be thrown out of the British Army … again.

It was getting embarrassing – was that the fourth or fifth time? Even Jack was losing count.

At the appointed time, the court usher came out into the lobby and shouted: "Terrence Arthur. Terrence Arthur. "

No one budged.

The only other man there looked up from his newspaper and said:

"That's you!"

"Nom de guerre," he barked when Jack remained motionless.

Jack looked the man up and down. He had seen him somewhere before. Lisburn HQ? Jack was not sure. His suit was Savile Row and he had the look of a Spook.

"Well what the hell!" said Jack. "In for a penny in for a pound. Better hung for a goose than a gander."

Cliché confetti.

"Are you Terrence Arthur of Palace Barracks, Belfast?"

"Apparently," said Jack.

"Pardon? Speak up."

"Yes. Sir."

"It is said that on Saturday the first of July 1972 in Newtownards, you did wound Alan and John Poultryman. You are charged with grievous bodily harm. How do you plead?"

Brothers in arms – that explains why they were both so stupid. They both had a go and they both fucked up, thought Jack.

"Not guilty!" he started as he suddenly remembered to answer the question.

The prosecution then outlined the case against "Terrence Arthur".

Call the first witness.

"I call Alan Poultryman."

"Alan Poultryman!"

"Alan Poultryman."

The name echoed around the court building.

"There is no reply to that name your honour," said an usher.

The prosecution counsel looked nonplussed.

"In that case I call John Poultryman."

"John Poultryman!"

"John Poultryman."

"There is no reply to that name your honour."

After a short adjournment the usher summoned, "Terrence" back into the dock.

"Mr Arthur, I am afraid that the prosecution are unable to present any evidence against you and cannot proceed any further. The case must now be dismissed," said the judge. "You are free to go."

Jack walked out to the lobby to thank his benefactor. Maybe even buy him a drink.

No one was there.

While he waited for John Benson to get the car, Jack walked up to the notice board to see who else was up before the beak.

No cases were listed for that day. Not his own, or "Terrence Arthur's" for that matter. There was only the date written up with: "Court Closed".

Chapter 8
Crime and Punishment

"Don't move a fucking muscle or I'll shoot your fucking head off!"

Sgt. John Benson of the Royal Military Police could hardly believe his ears.

The challenge, expletives included, was exactly what he would have said in this situation, but being on the receiving end was a new experience for the Belfast-born blond.

He was looking down the business end of an SLR, brandished by a naked man from his bedroom window. He stood there frozen, a set of dealer's keys in his hand.

It was 0200 hours, and he had been trying to unfasten the door lock of a Saab 96 saloon when all hell had broken loose in the quiet Protestant suburb of East Belfast.

"I am an RUC officer and a mobile unit is on its way..."

"I hear you and I'm not going to move an inch," replied Sgt. Benson in his Shankhill Road accent. He could clearly see the man's weapon.

This was a great start to his new MRF role as a motor man.

Now that Len had gone to the great scrapheap in the sky, only Joe Lock was available to scavenge for transport. Jack asked for more volunteers to help meet the MRF's insatiable demand for motors.

John Benson had surprised himself when his hand suddenly

shot up after being told there was an urgent need for a new set of wheels for call sign Nine-Zero. And now he was in shit up to his neck. Four uniformed RUC officers were pointing weapons at his person.

"Stand still – don't move," one barked.

"I am a member of the security forces from Palace Barracks," said John. "My ID is in the top left hand pocket of my shirt."

One of the RUC men ran forward and, holding a pistol to John's head, gingerly reached for the plastic wallet.

He took a step back and a quick glance at the document confirmed Benson was British Army. The RUC commander demanded an explanation.

The four green-uniformed police officers gathered around John, joined by their now dressed colleague from the bedroom above and his daughter Sandra.

At this moment Jack, who had been observing the incident from the Nine-Zero squad car, arrived on the scene. Jack and Ken had dropped Sgt. Benson off shortly before his untimely capture and he was anxious to avoid his man being the victim of some sort of instant justice.

However, when he walked up to the small group surrounding his man, his mission had evolved a new priority.

She was shivering just in front of him.

Jack wrapped his black leather bomber jacket around her shoulders. Long blonde hair slipped beneath its already warmed lining.

Sandra was beautiful.

Maybe tonight was not all bad after all, thought Jack.

"This car was reported to us as a suspect vehicle and we are just checking it out," said Jack flashing his ID.

"Checking it out with a bunch of keys?" Sandra's dad countered.

"They were on the floor by the door when we arrived," said Benson. "I had just picked them up when you appeared, waving your weapon."

Sandra giggled.

Jack smiled.

She smiled back.

"Perhaps you should go inside," said her father. Sandra nodded compliance.

Jack walked her the few yards to the door and retrieved his jacket. He recognised the powerful perfume that now pervaded its fabric: Chanel No. 5.

Expensive taste, thought Jack.

He wondered if they stocked it in the NAAFI. On the other hand, could he get it duty-free from the boys in Hereford, or maybe his mate Graham Lewis a Legionnaire in the French Foreign Legion based in Marseilles could help out.

Looking up, Jack realised he was under intense paternal observation as he pondered alone on the doorstep. As he started back down the garden path to the Saab, a Mercedes Benz Saloon broke the silence of the wee hours, manoeuvring respectfully past the RUC men standing in the roadway. The driver waved politely. Ken.

• • •

Back in Palace Barracks, Ken told Jack that the Mercedes had parked in front of the squad car just after Jack got out to go to John's aid. The driver, who appeared to be drunk, left it in a hurry when he saw the RUC men up ahead so Ken thought he would check the vehicle out.

The keys were in the ignition.

'Nuff said.

The Mercedes made up for Benson's rookie blunder in

getting himself caught in the act. There really was no margin for mistakes, as the MRF was virtually a production line operation. They had to steal at least one car every few nights to keep the flow going to REME for "hardening". Three or four squad cars would be out each weeknight, more at weekends, and invariably each week at least one incident occurred that would condemn a vehicle to a one-way trip to the scrap yard. On a bad week, sometimes two or three cars would meet their maker.

MRF men returning from leave on the mainland were encouraged to return with "hot wheels". The boss didn't have a clue what they boys were up to, but Jack did. Some who had to reach the Liverpool ferry from the other side of the UK would try two or three cars before finding one with a full tank. If they caused too much damage breaking in, before discovering the vehicle was low on fuel, they would trash the radio to make it look like local yobs nicking from cars.

Later, with the Mercedes safely delivered to REME, Jack was sitting at his desk. His fingers were in the dial of the telephone, making the first use of the number Sandra had whispered as he retrieved his jacket. Just like vital map co-ordinates, Jack had instantly memorised it.

As the chromed dial whizzed back on the last digit, there was a knock on his door.

It was Pud. The OC wanted to see Jack.

Something important had come up.

"It had better be bloody important," said Jack. "I haven't stopped all day."

He put the handset back on the receiver before the call connected. *What a waste*, thought Jack. Some proven Gillespie chat-up lines were waiting for an airing. They would have to wait until later.

Pud and Jack arrived at the Ops room. Captain Tony Case was there from G3 intelligence – Green Slime or Military Intelligence, to use its normal **non** sequitur.

Case was explaining to the boss that they had received information concerning a planned IRA ambush on British troops in Belfast. This was doubtful, Case admitted to the boss before Jack entered the room, because, apart from the Provisional IRA's "ceasefire", the intelligence community knew that the Provisional's leadership were in London at secret talks with the British Government in the Chelsea home of Minister of State Paul Channon.

However, the impeccably reliable source was adamant it was going ahead despite the ceasefire. Perhaps even to break it, in as high profile a way as possible.

The brass decided they couldn't take any chances, as many lives would be at stake. In any case, the IRA had many schisms and perhaps the attack was to embarrass those who clandestinely "supped with the devil".

As far as Jack was concerned, all that counted for nothing – "a bullet is a bullet" was his credo. When it hits you in the chest, the political or religious identity of the gunman who fired it really does not matter, just the position of the entry and, maybe, exit wound.

However, during his briefing Jack noticed the normally precise Captain Case was uncharacteristically vague as he laid out his wares.

Tony, who would meet Jack years later in Whitehall as his "interrogator", just said the situation needed the immediate attention of the MRF.

"It's come from the top and they want things done quickly!" he said. "Tonight the IRA is planning a major operation which, if successful, will leave many British soldiers dead or wounded. Our information is highly reliable. We must move right away or the IRA will have a propaganda coup at a most inappropriate time."

Jack did not fully understand the significance of the Captain's words, but any day was a bad one to die as far as he was concerned, and the Greens needed as much help as they could get.

Captain Case revealed the Royal Green Jackets were the "target for tonight".

"A Regimental mini-bus, packed with new recruits who are just out of basic training, will leave Aldergrove Airport this evening and travel to their new base in Casement Park, Andersonstown. According to the informant, an active service unit of the IRA will engage the minibus with automatic weapons. We understand the attack will take place just outside the gates to the army camp."

This location was significant, he explained, because the IRA wanted to draw soldiers from the camp into the gunfight after they had killed all those on the minibus. It would be a show of force after a relatively peaceful period. In military terms, it would be "set piece" battle.

However, the MRF would intervene to even things up by outflanking the IRA. Ambushing the ambushers.

The Royal Green Jackets' mini bus would leave the airport as planned, as the IRA would doubtless have a spotter who would confirm the soldiers were on their way. If there was anything out of the ordinary at that end then the IRA active service unit could stand down. The MRF would spring the trap.

Fingers crossed.

It was zero hour. Call sign Nine-Zero hour

Jack was paired up with Ken again. This time the SBS

man would take the back seat with an SMG, and Taff Morgan's replacement, Paratrooper Cpl. Kevin Walsh, would be driving.

Kevin had been in the 1st Battalion, the Parachute Regiment, for about four years. The MRF attachment would do his career no harm at all, as long as he managed to avoid the same fate as his predecessor.

He was 25. Red-haired with a ginger moustache, he had a round ruddy face and hailed from Yorkshire. He was a fan of the despised Leeds United AFC. Kevin had the honour of being the MRF's Ginger Nut; Carrot Top. Call it what you like, this Ginge blended in with the Celtic mix of the Northern Ireland gene pool perfectly.

He was a mongrel in a dog pound full of Micks rather than mutts.

In the MRF Jack was top dog.

"And barking mad," he smiled.

"9mm pistol," growled the Armourer bringing him back to the job at hand.

Call Sign Nine-One would be Bert Cousins, Joe Blackmore and in the driving seat new boy Bombardier Don Andrews of the Royal Artillery.

Don was from Ross-on-Wye in the beautiful border country between England and Wales. He volunteered for the MRF after seeing them in action in McGuigan's yard in March.

There was a bit of talk as the squads loaded their magazines but, more interested concentrating on the job ahead, they made their way silently to the awaiting squad cars. Usually when the MRF took to the streets, they were entering the unknown on a "seek and destroy" mission, so a fair amount of light-hearted, almost nervous, banter was present. Today, though, they knew their task: protecting the young lives of a bunch of virgin soldiers who would be dead before they even got their boots and dicks dirty on Irish soil if Jack and the boys fucked up.

There could be no surprises today.

No shoot and scoot, just a dead cert result.

No contest.

Jack asked if there were any questions and was met by silence. Apart from the new boys, who were apprehensively pale, they knew the drill and the dangers.

• • •

The squad cars made their way out of the compound and onto the streets, Jack's green Vauxhall Victor leading the way.

He wondered which Merseyside football hero had been the victim of an army requisition this time. For a few moments, the thought that it could be the Liverpool skipper entered his head. He liked Tommy Smith. A real hard man – perhaps he would meet him one day and say sorry. Buy him a few drinks.

Jack turned and looked out of the rear window to check on the other squad car. The 1600cc engine struggling under the weight of men, arms and armour plate but with a squeal, Don Andrews gunned the throttle and it pulled away in pursuit of Nine-Zero. The two cars followed Sydenham Way towards the City of Belfast, a route they knew well.

The traffic was light. A couple of teenager joy riders in faster cars overtook them and screamed off into distance. One of the kids gave Jack the finger as the Vauxhall's headlights picked him out of the back seat with his arm around a teenage girl. The MRF boys smiled at each other. With idiots like that on the loose, no one would notice the two call signs as they slipped through the streets.

After crossing over the Queens Bridge, the squad cars split up. Call sign Nine-One diverted to the Shankhill Road area, while Nine-Zero made its way towards Whiterock and Andersonstown.

When Call Sign Nine-One reached Upper Shankhill Road, it turned left onto the A55, followed it south, then swung left onto the B38, down Springfield Road to the Falls Road, and 10 minutes later turned right into the Whiterock area, where they slowed.

They were now on the precise route the IRA would expect the Army mini bus to take.

Bert asked Joe Blackmore to watch four men he could just see standing on the corner of Whiterock Drive. They were now about a mile or less from where intelligence said the ambush would take place.

"I'm not 100 per cent, but I think one of them has a rifle – do you have a clearer view?" he said.

Nine-One passed the group, Don maintaining a steady speed so as not to draw attention to the car. Joe glanced right. Two of the men, both dressed in dark clothes, had Armalites. One turned and watched Nine-One drive past.

This "eyeballing" meant Call Sign Nine-One had now lost the initiative. There was a distinct possibility that the MRF's mission was going pear shaped.

Bert radioed Jack in Nine-Zero and relayed their information to him.

"Roger. Stick around I am going in for a look-see. Nine-One, make your way to location Vixen. Out," said Jack.

"Nine-One, roger. Out."

"Get ready in the back, Ken. We may be onto something. Wind your window down," said Jack. He gestured at the glass, but Ken it was already in action.

It took Nine-Zero about five minutes to reach the corner of Whiterock Drive.

When the suspects came into view, Jack knew instantly that the gunmen had been rumbled by the first squad car. Now it was his team's turn to face the music.

The four IRA men were standing on the right hand side of the road animatedly gesturing as if arguing. Then a man with a rifle facing towards Nine-Zero raised the butt to his shoulder.

But as Nine-Zero drew alongside, the MRF men came under fire from somewhere off in front.

Ken fired a burst from the SMG and saw two men fall. At the same time, Jack fired his pistol through the open driver's window.

"Go, go, go!" shouted Jack.

Bill needed no more encouragement.

The squad car sped off under heavy fire, the hardened rear window thudding and cracking from a crystalline sheet into a blanket of snow. From their firepower, Jack realised these gunmen were, without a doubt, the IRA active service unit planning to ambush the minibus on its way from the airport.

You make your own luck in Jack's game, and the MRF's continuing run of good fortune meant their somewhat premature intervention had foiled the IRA's evil intent.

Jack radioed through to HQ that there had been a contact and that they were returning to base.

At the first report of gunfire near their destination, the Royal Green Jackets' mini bus diverted to another Security Forces location. The recruits arrived without incident at their first posting an hour later.

Back in the safety of Palace Barracks, an inspection of Jack's

Vauxhall Victor revealed five pistol bullet holes in the right hand front of the car. A combination of the engine block and door armour had stopped them dead.

The MRF men had been lucky this time.

The gunman must have been lying on the grass to the right of the car. Had his aim been a little more accurate, his two final shots would have passed through the open driver's window with deadly effect.

But that was the difference between Special Forces' combat skills and an irregular force.

Jack and the boys would spend at least two hours a day, three times a week, on their miniature firing range. If you have just one shot, it has to count. If you have time to empty a magazine, each shot must count. It was as simple as that.

It wasn't just bad aim that had ended the would-be ambushers' operation. Unprofessionalism had lead to them being caught bearing arms in an exposed position, and it had resulted in the death of one of their gunmen. The fatality meant that the RUC would now be making yet another visit to Palace Barracks.

This time they turned up in force with forensic officers in tow. They inspected the Vauxhall for evidence that the car had come under fire and recorded round entry points. Then they interviewed the members of call sign Nine-Zero. If investigations usually consist of a good cop/bad cop routine, then it seemed the good cops had stayed at home.

Inspector Eddie Robson had not had a good night's sleep the previous night. Or the night before that, for that matter. His work was non-stop. Yesterday, five Catholics, including a priest were reportedly shot dead by members of the Parachute Regiment in the Ballymurphy area of Belfast.

Then three Protestants, one of whom was a member of the

Territorial Army, were found dead in Little Distillery Street, Belfast, allegedly shot by Republican paramilitaries.

Also on the casualty list in Belfast, a Protestant man was shot dead by Republican paramilitaries, and a member of the Ulster Defence Association was killed by the IRA.

To top it off, there was the report that an innocent Catholic man was murdered in a drive-by shooting by gunmen in the Whiterock area.

Some ceasefire!

Inspector Robson's superiors had ordered him to launch an investigation into the Whiterock incident.

He had just started his initial paperwork when British Army HQ had called to report an engagement by their forces in the Whiterock area. Their men had come under fire by gunmen unknown and "responded appropriately". This was nothing out of the ordinary – but upon arrival at Palace Barracks he had lost his cool.

Normally the RUC would come into the MRF's base, listen to their explanation, give them a friendly pat on the head and leave. Of course, there were occasions that were a little trickier – like the previous week, when members of the Protestant community had complained – but that sort of thing could be smoothed out more often than not, and nothing usually got to court.

However, in this case it was not just the fact that one dead and one wounded "civilian" were left lying on the Belfast pavement by a British Army unit that was as elusive as the night. He had discovered that the boss of the men involved had disturbed his Saturday night off by trying to steal his prized Saab motorcar.

Added to this indignity, the offending Sgt. Major Jack Gillespie had taken a shine to his 18-year-old daughter and she had obviously appreciated the attention.

That was a capital offence as far as this tired and emotional RUC officer was concerned. There was no innocence at all in Palace Barracks. The whole lot of them were as guilty as hell.

Nevertheless, looking at the evidence and the squad car full of IRA bullet holes, Inspector Robson had to admit his bosses would think he had lost his marbles if he tried to make a meal out of this matter. Jack could see that the RUC man had a bee in his bonnet, and was beginning to guess the reason from the grimaces and glances he kept getting from his interrogator. Even so, he couldn't help but think of much more important things as the Inspector rattled on about Whiterock.

Legs, breasts, lips... Was she a virgin?

Yep, any relationship with Sandra was now going to have to be "strictly hush-hush and on the QT". There was also the little matter of one Jean Philomena McLaughlin.

This could be a deadly triangle indeed.

Nevertheless, with begrudging hesitancy, it became apparent that as far as the RUC investigation into Royal Green Jackets ambush incident was concerned it was case closed.

Chapter 9
Busted Flush

The shrill note of a police whistle filled the air. Then another, and another, until a countless cacophony carried across the cobbled streets of the Clonard district in Catholic West Belfast.

This is not good news, thought Jack.

Some of the boys had obviously been rumbled, but who knew what was going to happen next?

In the small of his back, he felt the reassuring pressure of the 9mm Browning Automatic pistol he had stuck down the belt of his Levis when he left his car a few minutes earlier. His camera bag was slung over his shoulder.

Jack had been walking down the Springfield Road on his way to meet Jean when he accidently stumbled upon a British Army operation in full swing.

He had stopped on the corner of Kashmir Road, camera in hand, to watch what was happening when the whistles were blown. Now the Royal Anglian Regiment soldiers were running around like headless chickens.

Someone had pulled the plug on their operation.

Earlier, Army Intelligence had received a tip off that the IRA had temporarily stored a large cache of arms in a sewer junction in the Clonard. The "Angle Irons" had been despatched to do the "dirty work".

However, no sooner had the British troops entered the sewage system, the prearranged signal of whistle blasts sent the bathwater, and worse, of a hundred Catholic homes to flush out the Army sewer rats.

Manhole covers burst into the air under the intense water pressure, but, luckily, there were no casualties, just some hurt pride and stinking bodies and clothing, as the faeces of ages were dislodged by the deluge.

More than one poor squaddie found himself covered in it from head to toe.

The IRA had now discovered its own brand of biological warfare..

"A weapon of mess disruption?" Jack smiled. "The one thing about war is that you must never lose your sense of humour."

It was a great pity that Jack was not really a newspaper photographer because the shots of the drenched and dirtied were pure gold.

Jack laughed at the mess. But as he turned around to be on his way, his face changed .There stood Jean – a human water feature.

The tears cascaded down her pretty face, joining the torrent of foul liquid that had overflowed the gutter at Jack's feet. She fell into his arms.

"What on earth is the matter, poppet?" said Jack.

Her lips moved but there was no sound.

Jack's eyes read just one word.

Sean.

As a number of British troops ran past the couple, a single shot rang out. Everyone ran for cover.

An IRA sniper was finding his range.

Swiftly taking Jean by the arm, Jack led her away from the chaos and finally into the lobby of a small hotel.

Jack had planned some afternoon manoeuvres at this map

reference, but now he sat her down at a French-style wrought iron table and ordered two coffees.

He took a paper napkin from the tray and dabbed at her eyes. It was useless. They had obviously been like this for hours.

Finally she spoke.

"Sean..."

An eternity passed.

"He's dead."

The utterance released another deluge of tears from her doe eyes.

"How?" said Jack.

"The British," she replied almost incredulously. "He was murdered in cold blood in Whiterock on Sunday. He's being buried tomorrow at Milltown with full honours. Will you come?"

Jack kissed her sweetly on the forehead.

"Of course darling. Your brother was a fighter and a true hero of the cause. It will be an honour to say farewell to a fallen comrade."

• • •

Thursday morning. The day begins 0500 hours. Quietly turning the back door key and stepping outside, he was finally free. Jack hummed a Beatles tune as he left the house.

He had kept vigil with Jean all night. She had finally succumbed to sleep just around 0300 hours. Jack had waited until it was light and now left her Aunt Molly's house. Aunt Molly was away comforting Jean's mother so it was safe for Jack to be there.

Now Jack quickly stepped forth heading for Palace Barracks and the slime. He had to clear his plans for the day with Intelligence. An IRA funeral was likely to be crawling with spooks and he had to be sure his cover was maintained at all costs.

The stakes were already too high and he was about to go all in.

Jack saw the boss, who told MI6 that his man needed to be given a wide berth.

At 0930 hours, Jack walked silently through the large black Victorian Romanesque gates into Milltown Cemetery. His camera bag hung from his right shoulder. Inside was kit any bona fide snapper would be proud of – new Canon long lenses, a couple of SLR bodies and a motordrive.

Jack's NUJ press card protruded from the top pocket of his black suit jacket as he walked up to the information office just inside the gate. The McLaughlin funeral was in an hour's time but a crowd was already gathering in the graveyard.

Jack had to be on his guard

He walked into the Republican area of the cemetery past the memorial to William Harbinson where he read the inscription: *"...who gave his life for Ireland in the cause of Fenianism in Belfast 1867."*

So this mess has been going on a bloody long time... don't suppose what we are doing will make much difference except filling this place up faster, Jack thought.

Jack looked up. He had been joined in his contemplation by a man he recognised from one of the mug shots on the Ops Room wall: Belfast IRA commander Brendan Hughes.

The two men stared at each other for a few seconds.

Hughes spoke. His two bodyguards were a few yards behind him.

"Press."

It was a statement not a question.

"*Glasgow Times*," Jack agreed.

"Been here long?"

"Just arrived."

"Where are you from?"

"My family is from Lanarkshire but I grew up in Glasgow."

"What school did you go to?"

"Notre Dame High School."

• • •

Jack slowly swung his camera bag from his shoulder onto the top of the railings that surrounded Harbinson's monument. He could sense movement from the goons behind him.

He thrust a hand inside the bag and pulled out an open pack of Polo mints. He turned to greet the pistol now held a few inches from his head. It was so close he could smell the light gun oil the weapon bore as it shook in anticipation of discharge.

"Like one?"

The red-faced gunman shook his head.

Brendan Hughes' took the packet, peeled off a sliver of the paper and popped a Polo in his mouth.

He returned the pack to Jack and walked off, the two goons in tow.

Next time we meet, thought Jack, *there will be a hole in the middle of a different kind.*

Black-clad mourners were arriving in dribs and drabs. A shaft of light broke through the overcast sky and picked out the arrival of the hearse and funeral cars entering from Falls Road. If Jack stood on his tiptoes, he could see a white mini bus laden with men arriving in the distance.

Jean stood supporting her mother at the graveside. Father Mackenzie's words disappeared into the background as Jack watched six hooded IRA men arrive stealthily at the back of the crowd.

Jack gripped the body of his Canon SLR and fired off a few

shots. A few in the crowd turned at the sound of the shutter, but said nothing. The IRA men parted the crowd and arrived at the graveside. Each man raised an Armalite to the heavens – high port position. At a command from Brendan Hughes, a volley of shots deafened the bystanders.

Jack fired back with 35mm film.

The black clad women wiped their eyes and were steered by their men away down the path to the gate as most people turned to leave.

Jack's work, however, remained unfinished.

The camera shutter clicked as the masked men moved away. It clicked when black hoods were removed. It clicked when a shaft of sunlight broke through the clouds and fell, so fortuitously, on their faces.

Jack felt a hand on his shoulder.

Shit!

He turned, fearing the worst.

It was Father Mackenzie.

"The family would be delighted if you would join them at the wake."

Ten minutes later, Jack pushed his large frame and camera bag out of the Mini Cooper and through the narrow door of the semi detached three-up two-down Catholic council home in Denewood Park.

One hand, then another thrust towards his palm, fingernails, fingertips and lifelines still bearing traces of dark graveside soil. He took the hands of Jean's brothers, Patrick and Ryan, holding them perhaps too long. Then he reached for Katherine's fragile fingers.

"I'm delighted you could come," she whispered. "Welcome to our home. Please go inside and help yourself to refreshments."

Jean's mother had already spoken these words more than two dozen times before Jack's arrival, and now there was more than a trace of the mechanical in her greeting.

Before Jack could answer, a smaller hand pulled him deeper into the home.

"Jack, there's someone I want you to meet," said Jean.

She led him into the sitting room, where another of the Ops Room wall's "most-wanted" mug shots was holding court.

The fresh, youthful face of Gerry Adams looked up straight into Jack's eyes.

"Mr Adams, I've read so much about you..." Jack started. "... tragic circumstances..."

It took Jack a moment to realise that he was talking to himself.

After a cursory nod in Jack's direction, Adams' attention had already returned to much weightier subjects, and he was now deep in half-whispered conversation with a companion.

However, Jack had attracted the attention of one of the goons from the cemetery. He casually sat down next to Jack.

"The name's Cahill Doherty. Who're you?"

"I'll have a pint of Guinness thank you very much."

The IRA man smiled at Jack's attempt at humour.

A glass of the foaming stout appeared by magic.

This guy should open a bar, thought Jack.

"How you doing?" asked the goon shaking Jack's hand.

"I'm fine."

"Friend of the family?

"Yes, I am."

"Where're you from?"

"Glasgow."

"You know Milngavie?

"Mulguy, you mean," retorted Jack, quick as a flash.

"Oh yeah, I always mispronounce that," said the interrogator.

"Some nice pubs there though…"

"So, where's your watering hole when you're at home?"

Jack gave his usual answer. The goon left his seat.

Minutes later, the telephone rang in the bar of the Springfield Vaults in Parkhead, Glasgow.

"Hi. I'm from Belfast. A few months back, I met a fine fellow called Jack Gillespie, and he said if I was ever in Glasgow to be sure to pay you a visit. What's the best way to find you? By the way do you know if Jack's in town?"

The door to the sitting room opened slowly again. The goon was back. But this time, both hands were full… with two freshly poured pints of foaming Guinness.

Maybe the guy does own a bar, thought Jack.

The goon sat down next to Jack and a broad smile cracked his face.

"You're alright, you are," he said.

They clinked pint glasses heavily and Jack joined him in banter about life, the universe, and the certainty of death.

"But for now we should celebrate life and The Struggle."

"Slainte!"

Adams looked up.

By 1900 hours, it was time to clear away. However, the drinking was far from over – it was just being transferred to another location.

Jack passed dishes to Jean at the kitchen sink. There was a tableful of best bone china to be cleaned.

"I'll wash you dry," said Jack.

"Of course, mourning will be at least a month and I suspect I will never see my mother wear a colour again," Jean said as she picked up a teatowel. "We'll all have to put our lives on hold for a while – have faith."

She squeezed Jack's hand reassuringly.

"I can wait forever for you," said Jack.

It almost sounded like he meant it.

Hey this isn't all bad. Pretty good timing in fact... As one door closes another opens, thought Jack.

At 2000 hours, Sandra Robson answered the phone.

"Hi it's Jack..."

• • •

Jack and Ken drew up at the security barrier of Belfast International Airport. Ken flashed an army ID card and, almost instantly, the crudely welded obstruction in front of the squad disappeared.

They were dropping off two of the MRF boys for the 1830 hours BEA flight to London. The pair, bound for well-earned leave, boarded the Vanguard with a little trepidation, as the airline had just suffered a major crash at Staines near Heathrow less than a month before.

Jack walked past the arrivals gate and saw photographer Danno Stobbart greeting a Granada Television film crew laden down by equipment. Each of the many aluminium flight cases carried the company's distinctive logo, the letter G with a protruding arrow pointing north.

Jack would have to clear off back to the car quickly, before he was spotted. He grabbed a discarded newspaper, held it in front of his face, and headed for the door.

No sooner than Jack had left the car to accompany the boys to the check in area, the radio crackled into life. In Jack's absence, Ken took down the orders.

"You're not going to fucking believe this but we have been tasked to take a look-see at the upper end of Springfield Road," he said when Jack got back to the Mercedes. "A security forces' Land Rover has been shot at - one man injured."

"Jesus, I thought it was back to base and a night out in the fair town of Bangor," said Jack

Jack had told Ken that his planned weekend manoeuvres included a visit to the seaside resort's Royal Hotel and the cracking South African bird that worked there.

"I'm sure she fancies me," he said aloud.

"The receptionist?" asked Ken.

Jack nodded.

"I had my sights on her too. Just my luck!" he retorted.

"Age before beauty," said Jack.

"Pearls before swine," Ken had joined in the cliché contest.

"I saw her first …

"… and that makes her mine," Jack rhymed out.

Ken laughed.

The Mercedes followed the Antrim Road back into Belfast. Jack was on the radio getting the latest gen and they took a short cut to the northern end of the Springfield Road. About 200 yard's from the Falls Road junction, a large truck pulled across the street, completely blocking the way of the MRF squad car.

Two cars, which had been parked at the side of the road behind the now stationary MRF Mercedes only moments before, now moved in to prevent any escape.

Not realising, Ken reversed and found his exit blocked.

"Out!" shouted Jack. "Follow me."

Jack abandoned the car with Ken hot on his heels.

He headed straight for the front door of the nearest terraced house. Luckily, it was unlocked.

As they entered the hallway, a woman in a greasy apron came from the back kitchen.

"In the name of Jesus, what the fucking hell is going on?" she shouted.

Behind her was an acne-faced teenage boy.

Jack brandished his gun.

"Stay where you are!" he yelled.

Jack and Ken took to the stairs.

Looking back, Jack could see a burly figure with a pistol silhouetted against the glass of the front door. Jack fired off two rounds, and he fell back into the street, dead.

By this time, there was complete uproar in the street outside of the house – shouting and screaming. Excited voices hailed a new arrival. And then *whoosh*!

A hail of automatic fire shot out the windows in the front bedrooms of the house.

The MRF pair's SAS/SBS training kicked in.

Jack and Ken threw chairs and furniture from a back bedroom down the stairs to block or hinder any pursuit from the IRA gunmen. Sub-machine gunfire was pouring in through the front bedroom windows.

It was obvious that they needed an immediate rescue.

Smoke was beginning to rise up the stairwell. Someone had set fire to the downstairs of the house with a handy can of petrol. Both men were choking in the thick smoke. Things were beginning to look desperate.

"Above you!"

• • •

Groping around in the ever-thickening smoke, Jack found a small table and placed it under the trapdoor to the loft.

He pushed the barrier upwards.

It opened.

Jack disappeared into the attic space, followed quickly by Ken.

He hoped for a series of holes in the connecting walls that

separated the lofts of the terraced houses. Some way out. Jack knew of this tactic from the IRA active service unit. When they unexpectedly encountered security forces on the street, the IRA would often force their way into the nearest house, run upstairs and disappear through a rat run of inter-connecting attics. They would then emerge 10 or more houses along the street and make their escape.

Jack's instincts had not failed him. The holes in the attic walls, acting like a network of horizontal chimneys, now sucked in the choking smoke that billowed from below.

Entering the thick smoke, the pair crawled along the attic floor. Flames were now licking through the trapdoor behind them.

They quickly scampered away from the flames through five attics. They could hear shouts from the road below, perforated by occasional gunfire.

"Burn you Prod bastards!"

"Burn!"

"Burn!"

The hysterical crowd sensed blood. They craved violence.

Ken tore away the paper roofing felt that lined the roof slates, and slid some of the tiles back.

They needed to get their bearings.

Quickly.

Jack knew the security forces would soon be on the scene, attracted by the commotion and automatic gunfire. Or perhaps a local resident, frightened that their home was next for torching, would be tempted to call for help.

But when and where would their rescuers appear?

Jack joined Ken. Their heads bobbed through the hole in the roof.

Fresh air filled his smoke-logged lungs.

The pair couldn't see the activity in the street below but they could certainly hear it. Something was obviously causing the IRA gunmen some concern. Jack could hear boots sounding loudly on cobblestones and then the noise of whining wheels.

They were coming closer and closer.

The noise reached its crescendo, and Jack could make out the welcome silhouette of a Saracen "Pig" armoured personnel carrier. It was then joined by a "command" Land Rover.

Both vehicles discharged their contents of British soldiers. They started shouting orders to the civilians on the street to stand back.

"Security Forces – return to your homes. Clear the Streets!"

Jack stuck his head up through the tiles again.

"We are British Soldiers – we need your help to get out of here!" he screamed.

A young lieutenant quickly assessed the situation, and with the prospect of possible gallantry medals flashing before his eyes, he ordered his men into the house below Jack and Ken's perilous position.

The cavalry had arrived!

Not a moment too soon.

The fresh-faced squaddies smashed down the door, terrifying the young couple that lived there. A black tomcat slinked past the soldiers as they took to the stairs like a herd of elephants. He would go to the McConnell's house – they were feeding him too.

On the landing, Jack's smiling face greeted the soldiers from the trapdoor to the attic above.

"Nice to see you, to see you... Nice," Jack imitated British comedian Bruce Forsyth, host of the new *Generation Game* that was all the rage on TV.

"Who the fuck are you – Santa Claus?" said the Squaddie. "Aren't you supposed to use the bloody chimney?"

Jack recognised the Sphinx and Egypt badge of the Royal Anglian Regiment on the beret of the young officer who had now joined his men on the landing.

"Rescued from the fires of hell by the sewer rats! I wondered what the smell was. Suppose beggars can't be choosers," said Jack, reaching out a handshake of gratitude.

A sweaty hand grasped back with a hearty grip. Jack couldn't help himself – he brought his palm to his nose when it returned to the trapdoor. Luckily, it just smelt of smoke.

The MRF pair dropped to the floor and, with jackets over their heads to disguise their features, ran to the waiting army vehicles. They were evacuated to the RUC Police Station in nearby Springfield Road. Call sign Nine-One rolled up a few minutes later.

Jack looked at his Seiko DX Automatic wristwatch.

1930 hours – a shave, a shower and still time to have some Friday night fun, he thought.

"Taxi for two to Palace Barracks, gentlemen?"

They squeezed into the back of Nine-One's Volvo 164 and Sgt. John Benson and the boys got Jack to base in time for internal debriefing before he was booted and suited and "Bangor bound". Ken took a rain check.

• • •

The blue Mini Cooper stopped at the corner of Abbey Park. A few seconds later, Sandra had jumped into the passenger seat alongside Jack. Her duffle bag flew into the back seat.

Next stop: the seaside.

"I wasn't sure you would be able to make it," said Jack.

"Nor was I but Aunty Kitty was so looking forward to my

visit. I just couldn't let her down. Could I?" she said.

"No we couldn't let pussy down," Jack agreed.

"Kitty! Cheeky!" she laughed.

Jack knew what he meant.

• • •

As the swinging sixties gave way to the sexy seventies the Royal Hotel in Bangor was the place to be. It had four stars, sea views, and was very, very discreet.

The oak-panelled reception of the hotel had seen a higher proportion of Mr and Mrs Smiths check in than any other hotel in Northern Ireland. And, more importantly, there was no sectarian divide. In fact, this was where the two sides came together between clean sheets and behind closed doors. The comings and goings were recorded religiously by South African receptionist Ann Mary Furness, who had a little secret of her own. She was a spook – and *she* didn't know it.

Jack had met her a year before on Proctor's Farm in Worcester. It was a place he would escape to from SAS HQ in Hereford whenever he needed a bit of rest and relaxation. For Jack, it was where the tough got going to when the going got a bit too tough – or simply too boring.

The day they met, Jack was with his long time SAS buddy, John Mason. John was one of the best operators in the SAS – the number one survival expert. Many SAS heroes owed their success and lives to his professionalism, dedication and expertise.

John was the leader of the famed SAS Keeny Meeny patrols, who took their name from the Swahili for the movement of a snake silently slithering through the grass as it approaches its prey. They were the forerunners of the MRF in Aden in the early sixties.

John Mason was Jack's best friend.

It was the spring of 1971 on Proctor's Farm and Jack had just returned from operations in the Oman. The Desert Song – sand, sand, sand – now thankfully replaced by the green grass of home. There was shooting and fishing, and the birds had never been known to shoot back.

A vision had appeared to Jack – a girl visiting her best friend, farmer Proctor's daughter, Cora. Her name was, Ann Mary Furness, the daughter of a South African Naval Commander. She was beautiful.

She had it all: class, style, almond-shaped eyes, and legs eternity.

But it didn't take Jack anywhere near that long.

A Proctor family dinner at Maureen McCann's Old Oak public house in nearby Peopleton, a nightcap in the farmhouse and last minute adjustments to sleeping arrangements meant mission accomplished.

A year of assignations later and Ann Mary had agreed to follow Jack to Northern Ireland. As a South African, she would be relativity safe. With the help of Special Branch, Jack got her the receptionist job at the Royal Hotel and a place to stay – a cosy flat above a shop next to the railway station in Helen's Bay.

The security forces were accommodating because this gave them covert access to the nitty gritty of who was guilty of marital, sexual and cross-sectarian misdemeanours at the hotel well known for its discretion. Special Branch and MI6 agents would loiter in the hotel lobby. A Loyalist or Republican politician would arrive at the hotel with someone who was obviously not his wife. If they checked in as "Mr and Mrs Smith" – or "Mr Smith and son" – it could be inferred that they were up to no good.

And easy prey to State blackmail.

Dirty tricks.

Dirty sheets.

Ann Mary often wondered why Jack was so interested in the hotel register. It made for rather strange pillow talk, but at least it kept him awake afterwards.

• • •

The Royal Hotel was unquestionably out of bounds for today's trip to the seaside with Sandra. Invoking Ann Mary's wrath did not worry Jack – he could soon soothe that – but the Spooks were another matter. You had to keep them sweet or some very funny things may start happening.

Instead, Jack would take Sandra to a top class restaurant (with rooms) between Helen's Bay and Bangor. The Old Inn, Crawfordsburn dated back to 1614. Its exposed beams and partial thatched roof made it look like a romantic heaven to an impressionable eighteen-year-old.

Sandra Robson, wooed, wined and dined, was swept off her feet and swiftly slipped between the clean Irish linen of Room 4. "Do not disturb" was hung on the doorknob. The finest French cognac waited on the bedside table.

Bon Appétit.

• • •

Just before 1900 hours on Sunday evening, Sandra snoozed in the passenger seat of the Mini Cooper as it headed back to Belfast. Jack switched on the car radio as DJ Alan "Fluff" Freeman introduced the number one track.

"It's Donny Osmond. Pop Pickers. It's number one. It's *Puppy Love*."

Jack's thumb stabbed the "Off" button.

Chapter 10
Super Sniper

As Jack's thumb extinguished Donny Osmond's schoolboy crooning, his rear view mirror caught a television crew filming a piece with Stormont framed in the background.

The imposition of Ulster's Direct Rule from Westminster had made the Portland-stone parliament buildings surplus to requirements. But Jack's smile was nothing to do with politics, appreciation of the architecture or the contented look of the 18-year-old slumped beside him in the passenger seat, catching up on sleep that had proved so elusive the night before.

• • •

Jack had been told that in order to camouflage Stormont during World War II, the building's Portland stone was painted with supposedly removable "paint" made of bitumen and cow manure. However, after the war, removing it proved enormously difficult, with the paint having scarred the stonework. It took seven years to remove, and the exterior facade never regained its original white colour.

"Bullshit inside and out," Jack laughed.

Sandra stirred.

Jack knew camouflage was a lifesaver. He used it all the time. In the jungles of Sarawak, he had lain unseen in enemy territory as columns of Indonesian troops filed past just inches from his position. Unseen Murut eyes, also cloaked in foliage with faces caked in barks and mud, watched the tiger insignia on the Indonesians' sleeves and slung weapons pass.

Ambush would come at a time of Jack's choosing now the enemy's unit strength and threat level had been assessed. A hundred Ghurkhas could be called in to support SAS warlord Jack's Border Scouts and slaughter would be guaranteed. The Ghurkhas' razor sharp *kukris* would leave no head on Indonesian shoulders.

Northern Ireland's war was a world away, but camouflage was still king. Jack's cover was a photographer. Other MRF men were door-to-door salesmen. One was even an RSPCA inspector's assistant.

"The unit really was going to the dogs," smiled Jack.

The IRA used camouflage, too. Ex-Special Forces personnel – paid large sums by American IRA sympathisers to impart their specialist skills – trained snipers. Urban snipers camouflaged among the seemingly endless rows of terraced homes were starting to take their toll on British forces exposed on streetscapes. One deadly IRA deception already uncovered by the MRF during operations involved roof tiles.

Often, British Army security posts were in commandeered schools or community buildings close to residential terraces. The bare slate roofs of the homes appeared to provide no cover, but the US training gave the IRA a killing solution. A single slate would be removed under cover of darkness and taken to a terrorist workshop, where it was carefully fashioned to accept the barrel and telescopic sight lens of a sniper's rifle. By the time the ruse was discovered, it was too late. Good men had already died.

• • •

Monday morning and Jack was back in the boss's office at Palace Barracks.

"So, you're back at last. Where the hell have you been? No don't tell me I don't want to know," said the Captain.

Jack remained silent.

"You've probably picked up that the Green's are in a bit of a tizzy at the moment," said the boss. "It seems that after the Republican funeral you attended last Thursday, the gloves were off. Three infanteers were taken out in separate incidents of sniper fire within a couple of days. Thing is, the spook's ballistics man thinks that the sniper fire all came from the same rifle, which means we are probably dealing with just one man.

"The Greens are calling him the "super sniper" and that sort of talk is just not on. There are people out there looking, but they are having absolutely no luck. It's our job to find who is to blame and eliminate them."

It was then that Jack remembered the single high-velocity round that had narrowly missed Jean and himself when he met her in the Clonard last Wednesday. Could it be the same shooter?

Jack scanned the briefing folder the boss had given him.

The sniper certainly hadn't missed the following day when Lance Corporal Rooney of the Royal Anglian Regiment was killed in Clonard Street in the Lower Falls or Corporal Mogg in Dunville Park, Lower Falls Road, or Corporal Meeke in Hooker Street, Ardoyne, Belfast.

All Corporals, all dead.

Sounds like a job for Hercule Poirot, thought Jack. *I have asked you all here today because all of you have a motive for killing these three men.*

But I think what clinches it, is that one of you is wearing a black balaclava and holding a bloody big gun…

Jack returned to reality.

"...so, Sergeant Major, it's up to you how you go about it. I just want results and nothing messy to clean up afterwards," concluded the Captain, who then turned, exited the room and left Jack wondering what he might have missed.

Jack entered the briefing room and read the past week's reports of the sniping incidents. None of the patrols fired on had any idea where the shots came from.

One head shot. A rifle clatters to the floor. A man drops. The echo of the discharge is left ringing from wall to wall, from rooftop to road.

Then nothing.

Eventually one of the Corporal's mates, sweating profusely, would drag his body from the road. Searches of the surrounding houses proved fruitless, and road blocks drew a blank.

This was another job for the "friends" of the MRF: the Freds.

Jack strode out of the MRF compound to the former Brigadier's "Married Quarters", which kept the Freds isolated from all other residents of Palace Barracks.

Captain Dennis answered the door. His man, another Corporal called Ginge, stood a little behind in the hallway.

"What I can do for you?" said Ginge.

"I need one of your Freds to finger someone for a lift. I need to bring in someone pretty high up who will know about operations in the Clonard and Ballymurphy areas," explained Jack.

Jack entered and the pair moved to the lounge of the house.

"Seamus," called Ginge.

A figure drinking a mug of coffee turned towards them.

Seamus Wright was a captured IRA man. MI6 gave him the choice of jail or *jam*. He chose jam.

Jail, or "internment" as it was known by political prisoners, meant being banged up without trial. If you were pessimistic, it could seem a life sentence.

Wright came from Andersonstown and was just a run-of-the-mill IRA member. Nothing special, but to the MRF he was gold dust. He knew who was who. He could also identify people from the mugshots Jack took while posing as a press photographer.

According to official record, Mr Wright had just married Mrs Wright and then just disappeared from the streets. He told his wife he was working in England, but, in reality, he was on the MRF payroll. This was common practise. Jack would often pop into the MI6 office and come away with £400 in his pocket, most of which ended up in the pocket of one Dennis Rainbow who was known by the codename Prism. He was Jack's source for intelligence about the Protestant paramilitaries known as the Vanguard Service Corps. He delivered value for money.

An MI6 organisation sent money to their wives or loved ones from England, giving the appearance they were working as building site labourers. Hundreds of miles out of harms way, hundreds of miles from The Troubles. Safe and sound.

Seamus Wright it was then.

The Wright man for the job, Jack smiled at his unspoken wit. *Fred on board*.

The trio met up with Freds' handlers at 1500 hours.

Wright said he knew a local IRA commander and could easily identify him, as he walked with a limp, the result of an earlier skirmish with the B Specials, and he took his wife everywhere.

He was also well known to the authorities. A set of photographs were produced from the wall of the MRF ops room and after taking a copy of the target, the patrol left and went back to the briefing room.

The "lift", Jimmy McNeil, a timber yard worker, was receiving a social security benefit for his disability. Wright knew that McNeil would visit a local Shamrock Club on a Monday, as his wife disliked the excesses of a Wild West Belfast Saturday night and, being a devout Catholic, could not be seen in licensed premises on a Sunday.

Time was of the essence.

Jack turned his attention to finding the MRF squad members he would need to ensure a successful kidnapping. In the past, in fact right from the start, the MRF had had some adventures and misadventures when it came to the not so subtle art of lifting unwilling people off the streets. This time it had to go right.

• • •

Sometimes Jack's style gave the impression that the boys preferred to make it up as they went along, but now he focussed on preparation.

SBS man Ken Cooke would drive. Local lad John Benson's Belfast accent would give the mission a false UVF feel, and Jack would ride shotgun.

The squad spent an hour and a half practising the actual lifting of a target from the street, with Joe Blackmore standing in as the unlucky victim until they perfected the manoeuvre.

Ken glided the car to a halt alongside the unsuspecting target. Jack and John Benson exited the car, grabbed hold of the victim, bundled him into the back seat, and handcuffed and hooded him.

While John Benson sat on him, Jack slid back into the front

seat as the car sped away. MI6 had covertly trained UVF men to use the same kidnap method so that no one could differentiate them from the MRF. Then the maps came out.

If the actual lift was as tough as Joe had been, which was unlikely, or did a runner, which was also unlikely given that he walked with a limp, then knowledge of the area and alternate routes would be vital.

There could be armed opposition, although there was no intelligence of McNeil ever having close protection or routinely carrying a gun. Nevertheless, IRA roadblocks could be set up in minutes if the alarm was raised. Alternatively, there could just be a plain and simple cock-up.

At 1900hrs, the MRF patrol met in the briefing room to run through the now familiar drill. They then armed up with a 9mm Browning pistol each, charged their magazines – some put a loaded spare mag on the side of their shoulder holsters. Jack just stuck the Browning in the belt of his jeans in the small of his back.

Experience had taught him that shoulder holsters were too bulky. Jack knew if a hand was put on your shoulder, or you received a pat on the back, the presence of the strap meant your secret was out and you were history. From undercover to six feet under.

Ken checked over the car, which was another Volvo 164 Estate. When he was satisfied with the vehicle, he beckoned to Jack. Benson extinguished his cigarette and climbed in.

The trip to the Freds' was only a short distance – a couple of hundred yards at the most. They drove it, as usual.

Wright was already waiting with his handler.

"Right, he's all yours. Good luck."

The IRA man got into the back for his ride to the RUC Station at Springfield Road. On arrival, they were admitted with little or no ceremony. Ken put the car in a position where it could leave the base again quickly.

John Benson went with Wright to the observation post. The remainder of the patrol stayed in the car ready for a quick move. Meanwhile, packed into the watchtower by protective sandbags, the Fred was keeping an eye out for the target. They saw numerous men walking past heading for the famous Fort Bar nearby in Springfield Road. Those identified as merely IRA members by Wright passed unhindered. The MRF were after a big fish tonight, the tiddlers could wait for another day.

After about an hour, now close to 2030 hours, McNeil came in sight, limping and holding onto the arm of a woman.

"Fuck – it's him!" said Benson not waiting for the Fred's nod.

"Contact let's go!" he said on his walkie-talkie.

As he bounded down the stairs, the car was already moving. He jumped in.

As the gate opened, John Benson told the squad that the target was with a woman, as intelligence had predicted. They would have to deal with the situation. The fact a woman was present was immaterial.

Pulling up behind the couple, Jack gave the go ahead and the MRF pair leapt from the car at the same time.

The woman screamed for help as the team bundled McNeil into the car. With doors slamming and the car engine racing, they made their getaway. It had been much tougher in training.

By pre-arrangement, an army foot patrol came out of the RUC station to help the civilian victims but, naturally, too late.

The soldiers took details from the now terrified woman, called the RUC, and, once the police had arrived, returned to base.

As the MRF car went unchallenged as it passed down

Grosvenor Road, Jack decided that a little "sight-seeing" trip of East Belfast was now in order. If they sped straight back to Palace Barracks, the lift might have looked a bit too smooth for the kidnappers to be UVF gunmen.

Lying on the floor in the back of the patrol car with Sgt. John Benson's big feet on him, O'Neil was crying for help. In his best Belfast accent, Benson was telling him he was the UVF and wanted some answers.

"Don't worry, you'll be treated well," Sgt. Benson told him. "You will be treated fucking well… the same way you IRA scum treated my friend, George Graham from Bangor, when you took him two months ago."

"What kind of twisted Catholic bastards are you?"

"What is this? A new Inquisition?"

"After you sadists had finished with him, after three days of pure torture, he had 96 cigarette burns on his body. His eyes had been spooned out and they lay dangling down his face. To finish him off, you murdering cowards strangled him and threw him into a river. Imagine what his poor mother went through when she saw his broken body."

"Tell me, whose is the true religion of forgiveness and compassion? If Christ was here now in Belfast preaching peace and love, it would be you bastards, not the Jews, who would be putting him up on the cross. There is not a Christian bone in your fucking body."

Benson's fist smashed into the hood. That felt better. He felt much better.

No one else in the car said a word. They were now used to such excesses.

While they may have not agreed with the religious sentiments, George Graham had been a mess when they picked him up. Animals would have been kinder with a corpse. In any case, the MRF men had no respect for their enemy as "soldiers" – the IRA men had lost any right to that professional courtesy – this was a dirty war.

Has there ever been a clean one? thought Jack.

They stopped on a hill overlooking Stormont, and Ken and Jack left the car for a few minutes before returning to further disorientate the prisoner.

Finally, the Volvo pulled into Palace Barracks.

On arrival, they dragged the kidnap victim out of the car feet first and carried him into the soundproof interrogation room that had been prepared for his arrival.

With the hood still in place, he was forced into a stress position against the wall for two hours. He was then made to sit down crossed legs, back straight, for an hour.

By now, McNeil regularly cried out for mercy, but got none.

This went on for a couple of hours.

Only when McNeil showed signs of exhaustion did Benson start the questioning.

The MI6 agents had directed the torture – Benson just had the right accent for the UVF subterfuge, which was vital if the man was to be considered for release and subsequent covert surveillance.

McNeil's resistance was strong until they took him outside and, in the half-light, made him kneel down next to a grave with a cross on it. The name on the cross was that of an IRA man who had been missing from the Whiterock area for several weeks.

The masked MI6 men took off McNeil's hood. After his eyes had become accustomed to the dark, he was able to read the name on the cross. Believing that he was an UVF prisoner, he cried out again for mercy.

The MI6 men pushed him towards a freshly dug grave close

by and forced him to kneel next to it. One shove and he would have easily toppled into it.

"Be prepared to meet your maker, you IRA filth," said Sgt. Benson.

He pulled out a 9mm Browning, cocked it, and put it against the IRA man's head.

He pushed it hard into his skull. And twisted.

That was it.

• • •

Capitulation.

McNeil broke down pleading for them not to kill him and that he would tell all.

"Good!" Benson said. "But if we do come out here again, we won't bother with the gun. We'll just bury you alive. After all, why should we waste a good bullet on a bad man? Understand?"

McNeil understood.

Back inside, but not far enough away from the smell of the fresh earth of his final resting place for any real comfort, the IRA man sang like a canary.

He did not know the "grave" next to his was empty or that its advertised occupant was now a Fred enjoying all the comforts dirty money could buy.

For all he knew, his captors would kill him anyway, but every second his pitiful existence continued was a blessing. Jimmy McNeil was sure St Peter would not be the first person he met if he did pass over and, as a better Catholic than many would have believed, he didn't want to risk not joining the sacred choir of angels.

But, boy could he sing!

He told the MI6 men things they could never have known,

While also confirming enough information already received by the security forces to give this new information great credence.

He talked of a major IRA offensive, just days away.

It could be bollocks, on the other hand it might not be. It would be interesting for all present to see if it transpired as he said.

• • •

The subsequent taped interrogation solved the disappearance of many missing civilians and soldiers, and confirmed that the IRA had indeed murdered certain people, whose bodies were found in the surrounding countryside.

McNeil told of others whose bodies would never been found. Some had simply been fed to the pigs.

He talked for an hour and a half before Jack prompted Sgt. Benson to ask the question that had been the reason for the whole escapade.

"Now, we understand that one of you bastards quite fancies himself as a bit of a shooter and has a special rifle with a trick sight on it," said Benson.

"So you know about the M40?" came the reply filled with the relief of a confession.

Jack gave Benson a thumbs up.

He knew the M40 was a sniper's rifle. Jack had come across them while jungle training US Special Forces for the Vietnam War. He recalled the foreign weapons manual:

"The US Marine Corp adopted the Remington Model 700 bolt-action target rifle and gave them the M40 designation. Most had a Redfield 3–9 power Accurange variable telescopic sight mounted."

Some, like the IRA's specimen described by McNeil, had a wooden stock. When such ordinance was exposed to the combination of heat and humidity of jungle warfare, it warped. This was something that had proved troublesome for soldiers in tropical South East Asia, but was no such problem in West Belfast. It already bore quite a few notches – each one the life of a British soldier.

A widow-maker.

McNeil said the IRA command requested it from their supporters in New York as a reaction to the success of the British Army using snipers. On one recent occasion, they had claimed the lives of three IRA youth members, he said.

So tit for tat.

"Where is he?" demanded Sgt Benson.

"Who?" stammered McNeil.

"The sniper! You fucking idiot."

McNeil froze.

What's this? thought Jack. *He's been singing like Engelbert Humperdinck all night and now he stops in his tracks.*

"He doesn't know!" Jack almost said it aloud.

McNeil spoke again.

"Now I have to be honest with you here. I don't know who your man is. He's not one of mine. He came from America with the gun. But I know where the gun is stashed – that is in my command."

"Fucking bullshit!" yelled Sgt. Benson.

"It's the God's honest truth. I am telling you. On my mother's life,"

"Life is cheap in this room. Perhaps we should get your mother in here?" barked Benson.

"You're too late. She has already departed, God rest her soul. She was a martyr to the cause!"

"Unless you tell us the truth you will see her again very soon."

The Sergeant reached across the table for his gun.

He cocked it by McNeil's face.

McNeil twisted away in his handcuffs.

"Ok, where is the M40?"

• • •

Dawn was breaking. The ashtray was full. The tape recorder spool spun aimlessly around, its full reel whipping the mechanism with a tail of green lead-in tape.

It would take an MI6 clerk a couple of days to type a transcript for London.

They took McNeil back to the soundproofed room. The MI6 men left him counting the holes in the perforated panels. They would want the correct answer when they returned. This simple chore was proven to cause hallucinations and panic attacks. Who knows, soon Jesus Christ himself may appear to the IRA man and give him absolution.

The only real choice the McNeil had left was to kill himself. He knew he had just recorded the longest suicide note in history.

However, it gave Jack just what he needed to save a few British lives.

Maybe even his own.

Jack checked his watch. It had been a long time since his head had seen a pillow. But that was not important now, not by a long shot.

He had to think straight.

He knew where the sniper's rifle was – hopefully. But there was no point in getting just the gun – he needed both the M40 and the shooter.

Should the MRF just stake out the location, deep in West Belfast, until it was collected? But how would they know that the person collecting it was the shooter and not a gofer?

His head spun.

Sleep. Sleep.

Jack snapped back.

Whatever the cost, the MRF would have to follow the rifle and catch the sniper in the act. It sounded easy. It sounded good.

The devil, as always, was in the detail.

• • •

0900 hours. Jack studied the Daily Sit Rep in the MRF Ops Room.

"Tuesday 18th July 1972.

British forces should not engage in any offensive actions today. Patrol and observe, adhere strictly to Rules of Engagement. HQ Northern Ireland."

• • •

Jack had not come across anything like that before.

It did not take a genius to work out that someone, somewhere, was up to something.

For all Jack knew the IRA could be holding peace talks with Her Majesty the Queen, or perhaps with someone a lot more ordinary.

Right let's go through this one more time. Jack went over the information again.

Normally IRA weapons were collected and delivered by "couriers" in black Catholic-operated London-style cabs. It usually happened at night, but the regular British troops know this and any cab is fair game to stop and search.

So the sniper wouldn't risk his weapon this way. And by now he would know that the ballistics file being built up by the security forces would be substantial. The only way to link him to the killings, the murders, was through the weapon, and he could not risk sharing the same location with it other than when pulling the trigger.

Nothing in this was as simple as it seemed.

Ah well we will have to suck it and see.

Jack slammed the Sitrep file shut.

• • •

Jack sat with Ken in the MRF squad car on Falls Road. He was pretending to read last weekend's *Sunday News*.

Earlier, John Benson had caught a bus along from Divis Street to Falls Road and walked into the café now watched by Jack and Ken. He ordered tea and a bacon sandwich. On the counter, an old-fashioned chrome-plated geyser hissed steam and standing somewhat incongruously against the wall behind was a grandfather clock.

It was a fine eight-day Irish mahogany long case clock. Closer inspection would reveal the dial was marked Harris, 8 Parliament Street, Dublin. Constructed around 1840, just prior to the great Irish famine, it had faithfully marked the hours, minutes and seconds in Falls Road for more than a century.

Today was no exception. Sgt. Benson checked his wrist-watch: 1100 hours precisely. Looking across the room, it was nearly 11 o' clock on Mr Harris' precision timepiece too.

The bell held on a rusty spring above the door tinkled as a couple of customers entered the café. The business would probably be welcome. Benson had sat there for a half hour without being disturbed aside from when his sandwich was grudgingly pushed across the table to join the crockery of his tea. The spouted sugar shaker, recently filled, now trailed errant crystals around its base. He crushed a few into powder with the back of his fingernails.

At the counter, pleasantries were being exchanged between the three men and the owner.

"It is indeed a terrible time. It seems there is hardly a day passes without some unfortunate soul needing your services..."

Benson's mind drifted off. He looked up again as the tinkle of the bell announced the men's departure.

He looked at his watch. 1103 hours.

He looked up at the counter. The café owner was drying a cup with a teacloth.

Then his attention turned to clock face about 10 inches above and behind the owner's bald head: 11 o'clock precisely.

He sprang across the café and pulled the unfortunate proprietor across the counter and into a crumpled heap on the floor. Benson then slid over the grimy Formica surface and stood facing the clock. A brass key remained inserted in the small keyhole in the left hand side of the large door that gave access into the case.

He pulled open the door.

Silence.

Inside the pendulum was still. However, the weights were in their fully wound position.

The doorbell tinkled. Benson spun around. The café owner had legged it.

Sgt Benson followed.

He saw the man scampering away up the street. Eyes would be looking now. He walked over to Jack's car and nonchalantly leaned through the window, a cigarette between his fingers as if asking for a light.

"Boss, the fucking gun has gone. It must of been those blokes who left a minute or so ago. They did it right in front of my eyes but I saw nothing. You must have seen something out here!"

"It's alright, I've taken the number of their car we can check it with the Ops Room," said Jack. "Now be on your way."

Benson inhaled a full breath of cigarette smoke and walked away from the car into the summer air. He smiled at a passerby. but inside he felt like he had been kicked right in the balls. He had let Jack down.

If they were lucky, the café owner could have thought he was a robbery victim. If they were very lucky. Sgt. Benson returned to the café and rifled the till to add to the cover. He walked out eating a Kunzle Cake.

Back in the MRF squad car, the radio crackled:

"Nine-Zero this is Zero. Over"

"Nine-Zero send. Over."

"Nine-Zero, your vehicle check. The registration number is of a BSA Bantam motorcycle..."

Jack's fist clenched.

"A BSA Bantam. Please tell me you are having a laugh Pud. Over."

"Negative, Nine-Zero. Over."

"Roger. Out."

"The bastards have whipped it from under our noses and gotten away with it," he barked at Ken.

Ken revved the Ford Cortina's engine and entered the traffic stream. Both Jack and Ken saw Sgt. Benson in a window seat sitting next to a young girl.

Nine-Zero took Grosvenor Road into the city centre and out over Queens Bridge towards Palace Barracks.

• • •

"On the plus side, we know that shooter and gun are now

together and sometime, somewhere today they will both see some action. The question is where and when."

The boss's analytical skills were on full speed, thought Jack.

"Boss, I suggest that all the MRF call signs get out there and see what's happening," he said.

"Ok but remember the order of the day – no confrontations," the boss said.

"Yes, sir."

Has anyone told the IRA? Jack thought.

Three call signs, including Nine-Zero, headed back to West Belfast. Jack and Ken had picked up a new vehicle from the MRF yard, as it would have been unwise to enter the Catholic areas in the same car approached for a light by Sgt. Benson.

The MRF had finally added a Saab to their stolen car tally. It slipped quietly into West Belfast. If not for the Republican graffiti, it could have been any city in Britain. People were going about their daily business.

Then came the scene that meant that made it instantly recognisable as Belfast: an Army Land Rover passed by, its windows covered by reinforced wire mesh. Its occupants, or any of the other thousands of British troops in the city, could each be a potential victim for the sniper the MRF had let slip through the net.

It won't happen twice, thought Jack.

His instincts were on full power, but this was not like looking for a needle in a haystack so much as trying to solve a mathematical equation that returned infinite answers.

Jack didn't need one of those new Sinclair pocket calculators he had read about to work out that, in reality, it would only be after the trigger of the M40 had been pulled and its 7.62 round's supersonic speed had been slowed by human tissue that the MRF would be under starter's orders.

Then the Greens would put roadblocks into place and there would be total lock down.

All the boys could do now was drive around and hope they got lucky before someone else got unlucky.

Some chance!

They did not have long to wait but, unfortunately, it was the latter scenario that predictably developed. An 18 year-old British soldier was killed by a sniper's bullet while inside the army base in the Vere Foster School in Ballymurphy. He was the 100th member of the British Forces to die in Northern Ireland since the start of The Troubles.

Her Majesty's Press were keeping count, which probably was the reason for the World in Action crew's presence in Belfast.

"This week the 100th British soldier was killed in Northern Ireland tonight on World in Action we ask the question…" It will go something like that, thought Jack.

Maybe he did have a career as a journalist. But what it really meant was that Her Majesty's Government's problems just got worse and worse. There was no "quick fix" – that was obvious to anyone on the streets of West Belfast. By deploying the MRF the British Government had pressed the "kill" button right in. Once pushed, it stayed pushed. No amount of spin would ever hide that fact.

Now someone else's number was up.

• • •

"The cunt!" said Ken.

Jack had told him the news.

"Eighteen," he shook his head.

Sgt. Benson was noticeably quiet in the back of the Saab. Soon roadblocks were everywhere. The Greens were not happy. "Miserable sods" is a good description.

Suspicious cars faced being stripped back to the bare metal in the hunt for weapons at checkpoints. No one – not even the MRF – had a description of the sniper, so the discovery of a sighted weapon would be the jackpot winner.

This action didn't make complete sense either. A courier could be being used. But that didn't matter now. Someone had to pay and that encompassed anyone who gave the Green's any lip as they went about their business.

Niceties were non-existent – the butt of a rifle soon silenced any dissent.

Call sign Nine-Zero watched from a distance.

Cleared cars trickled through. The faces of the drivers each told their own story. Catholic women swore and blasphemed in the crudest manner at soldiers young enough to be their sons. Men's faces turned as red at the nearby traffic lights as they fruitlessly blew off steam.

Then - two *smiling* faces.

Incongruously, it was the driver and front seat passenger of a hearse, waved through unhindered by the troops, who were displaying their pearly whites.

Jack watched as it sailed past complete with coffin and wreaths. "Beloved son" spelled out in yellow chrysanthemums.

"Somehow it all looks familiar…" Jack spoke his thoughts aloud.

"But don't all funerals look the same Jack," ventured Ken.

Maybe the other cars in the funeral procession were stuck back in the queue, but it seemed too late in the day for an internment of that kind in Northern Ireland.

"Fuck it! Move!" Jack thumped the dashboard and reached for his 9mm Browning.

The troops looked up. The squealing tyres scrabbled for grip as the Cortina skidded to a halt in front of the hearse a few hundred yards up the road.

The two familiar faces were not smiling now. With Jack shouting "Security Forces!" and waving a bloody big gun around, they didn't look happy at all.

"Who is that? Jack demanded, gesturing at the coffin.

"His name is on the box," the undertaker quipped. "But you will do no good shooting him, he's long dead."

"Maybe I should take a look," said Jack pulling open the back door.

Benson covered them with an SMG.

The first of the troops who had clattered up the road arrived.

"Military Reaction Force. Watch and learn," Ken told the panting Rupert who was leading from the front. The MRF exploits were becoming legendary in the Northern Ireland military establishment.

Wreaths and flowers spilled out on to the road.

"A popular man," said Jack.

"Covers the smell..." came the matter of fact reply.

"A ripe one then?" asked Jack. "How long?"

"Died this afternoon," contradicted a voice.

A local priest had joined the small gathering.

"I gave him the Last Rites myself," he crossed himself as he uttered the words. "Now be away with you all and let these good men be about their business."

Silence.

Everyone waited for Jack to reply.

Whatever he would say would have to be good or they were fucked. It was at least a couple of months since a British soldier had shot a priest and it was frowned upon anyway.

But before Jack could open his lips, a sound filled the pregnant pause.

It was a fart.

From the coffin.

"It's quite natural its just gas from the body," said the undertaker.

"The soul departs," said the priest.

"The fuck it has!" said Jack.

He leapt into back of the hearse and despite the many arms, hands and finger nails trying to claw him back and the cries of "No Jack!" from his colleagues, he fired four shots into the coffin.

There was a muffled scream.

The priest had dropped to his knees, crossing himself again and again, like a robot that had gone haywire. He was muttering skywards to an unseen force for divine intervention.

The soldiers, meanwhile, had pulled the coffin from the hearse and were hammering at the lid with their rifle butts. If the poor sod in the coffin was alive then "help" was at hand.

The lid flew off.

It was not good.

Whoever the corpse was, they should have been put six foot under long ago. The smell was overpowering.

"But how the fuck? But who the fuck?"

Jack may have been the one talking but everyone else was thinking the same thing.

He turned back to the hearse. Something was dripping onto the pavement.

It was dark red blood. Lots of it. A pool had already formed while the crowd had been distracted.

The two "undertakers" made a dash for it. They only got as far as the rifle butts of the Greens. Meanwhile, many hands and minds were looking for the source of the blood.

Suddenly a panel on the hearse opened and out fell the body of a young man, followed almost immediately by a Remington M40 sniper's rifle.

It clattered on the pavement at Jack's feet.

He picked it up and held it high above his head for all to see.

• • •

Back at Palace Barracks, the RUC had their usual batch of questions "that needed answering". But the other MRF men had some of their own too.

"How did you know that something smelt about the coffin Jack?" said Ken.

"It was a no-brainer – the undertaker told me the name of the deceased was on the coffin. He wasn't lying. It said Sean McLaughlin," said Jack.

"But he was buried last week," the pair chorused.

"The RUC are going to exhume the grave to see who, or what, was buried, but my guess is that they will find an empty box," said Jack.

At that moment, another RUC man entered the room.

"The man you killed, the man hidden in the hearse, has just been identified as Patrick McLaughlin. He was carrying a forged United States passport and a letter from his mother who is looking forward to him returning home from New York," he said.

You couldn't make it up, thought Jack.

Brothers in arms.

Chapter 11

Remember, Remember...

Sir Henry Bromley hammered on the door of Hindlip House. In his clenched fist was the warrant to search the home of Thomas Habington. Sir Henry was hot on the trail of a fugitive Catholic priest implicated in an attempted bombing.

A huge device – 36 barrels of explosive – discovered and defused. Now the conspirators were on the run and a paid informer had revealed the priest's whereabouts: Hindlip.

Behind Sir Henry were two hundred British troops, hungry for Catholic blood. It may seem like over-kill, but the stakes were sky high and the country was in uproar. This was one bomb too many, and much too close to home.

Thomas Habington, however, was not home. He was away on family business.

Troops forced down the doors and a housekeeper was callously swept aside as they poured past.

Apart from the servant, no one was home. Room after room in the mansion was empty. However, Sir Henry knew Hindlip to be a house of secrets waiting to be uncovered. He had searched it several times before, without result.

This time, however, the gloves were off. The troops began a thorough search. Furniture and ornaments flew through the air. Troops smashed in oak panelling with fire axes -–but to no avail.

Sir Henry was fuming. He had hoped for a quick result, but by the time Habington returned home hours later, they had found nothing.

Naturally, Habington denied any knowledge of the fugitive but Sir Henry was prepared to sit it out.

His patience eventually rewarded. When he finally returned to headquarters, he was able to report the finding of a number of Popish trash hid under boards in three or four places. The fugitive priest, however, was not amongst them.

The search continued but, although eleven ingenious hiding places were uncovered, some holding weapons, the priest remained at large.

By the third day, Sir Henry was more than a little perplexed and tired. He went outside to gather fresh air and inspiration. His eyes wandered to the skyline. His methodical mind automatically started to count the brick-built chimneys that spiralled skywards from the Tudor-built pile.

"Nine, ten, eleven," he enumerated.

Yes, eleven multi-potted stacks adorned the tiled roof but there were none emanating from the south side of the house that surprisingly did have a drawing room, which he knew to boast an ornate fireplace

He should have realised much sooner. When first inspected, Sir Henry remembered that, despite the coals and dry tinder set in the grate, the fireplace was so clean it could never have seen a flame.

Now he raced back inside and, with the help of a couple of soldiers, tore into the false chimneybreast.

Two Catholic priests were uncovered in a closet hidden behind the false chimney. The place was so low that neither of them had been able to stretch their legs, which were swollen from lack of movement, and they suffered continual pain as they were roughed up by their rejoicing captors.

The fugitive Father Henry Garnet and as a bonus another "conspirator" Father Edward Oldcorne were in the bag.

Garnet's namesake, Sir Henry, now had to get them back to London where justice was waiting.

Jack yawned.

"That was on Thursday, 23rd January 1606, and now we use the very same space where that room once stood as the force armoury," said Sgt. John Davies of the West Mercia Constabulary.

He had been waxing lyrical – historically hysterical, more like – for the past 10 minutes in the canteen at the Police HQ, Hindlip Hall, while Jack and Regimental Sergeant Major Bill Morriston gazed anesthetised out of the window.

When they weren't watching the antics of the squirrel population and feigning intense historical interest, they sipped from the mugs of tea, which had been supplied together with a fluttering of eyelashes from the well proportioned canteen lady.

Sarah Cartwright, watching them from behind her counter, had a "thing" about men in uniform. And their handcuffs.

The two military specimens now on offer in her canteen, looked an extra tasty treat. She particularly fancied the one with the blue SAS wings on the top of his uniform's right arm.

Sarah often suspected that it was Hereford's finest she saw enjoying nights out in the Diglis House Hotel set on the banks of the River Severn in Worcester. Owner Greville Edwards used to ensure the SAS boys got special treatment, and some of the parties had been of epic proportions. Now Sarah wished she had joined up with the elite band of brothers.

Perhaps it was not too late.

"Haven't I seen you somewhere before, lovely?" she said to Jack as she cleared the crockery away from the table when the three men rose to leave.

"If you have, it's probably better for you if you forget me," said Jack.

His deep voice sent shivers down Sarah's spine.

"Yes every inch of the Constabulary's headquarters 40-acre estate is seeped in history," droned Sergeant Davies. "Around 1820, the original house was demolished to make way for the present Georgian hall built by Lord Southwell as a gift for his new bride.

"The death of Lord Southwell marked the end of a long line of Catholic owners. Henry Allsop, a wealthy brewer from Burton on Trent, then bought the property and continued to modernise the house and estate.

"During World War II, the hall was taken over by the Ministry of Works. At the end of hostilities, the Ministry had no further use for the hall, and the County Council eventually purchased it. The land was set aside for future use as a college and the house turned into the headquarters of the County Police.

"Five years ago on 1st October 1967, with the amalgamation of the constituent forces of Worcestershire, Herefordshire and Shropshire and Worcester City, the Hall became the headquarters of West Mercia Constabulary."

"What happened to Father Garnet?" asked Jack who was in danger of becoming a cop killer if this man did not shut up about his blasted HQ.

"Oh? Well Henry Garnet was tried and sentenced to death for treason. He was the priest who took confession from the six Gunpowder Plot conspirators and, despite disapproving of the plan to blow up the Houses of Parliament, he felt the confidentiality of the confessional prevented him from informing the authorities about the outrage he knew was about to happen."

"Guy Fawkes?" exclaimed Jack.

"Precisely!" said Sgt. Davies triumphantly. "Father Garnet was his confessor.""It's really quite interesting you see. Garnet's last words before they led him to the scaffold were:

'I pray to God the Catholics may not fare the worse for my sake, and I exhort them all to take heed they enter not into any treasons, rebellions or insurrections against the King.'"

"So he was hanged?" Jack was interested now. He was a supporter of capital punishment. After all he had seen, after all he had done, Jack felt he knew all about life and death. The bottom line was that some people were simply so evil they did not deserve to walk God's Earth.

"He was hung, drawn and quartered. His body was hacked apart with an axe, his intestines burnt on a fire and his heart ripped out and shown to the crowd outside St Paul's Churchyard," the police officer continued. "Fortunately, he was dead at the time, which was not always the case!"

Jack raised an eyebrow.

"Yes it is all perfectly true I can assure you. It is well known that the executioners at the time often became somewhat impatient and did not always let their prisoner hang long enough to die.

"However, as Garnet was a Catholic Priest, some in the crowd surged forward and hung on to the end of his legs to ensure he died on the scaffold and not in agony while being rent apart."

"Thus this holy man passed to his eternal reward on the 3rd May 1606, aged 51," quoted Sergeant Davies as if he *completeth* the first lesson.

"I have some sympathy with the executioners," said Jack, remembering his last encounter with the Catholic clergy in Belfast. "That reminds me – I must sharpen my axe!"

Jack laughed.

Sergeant Davies did not have a sense of humour.

That certainly endeth the history lesson, thought Jack.

The trio move to their next destination in silence.

Opening an unmarked door, they went into the basement that had, in a different age, provided refuge for the Catholic Priests. They faced a green steel door with padlocks, dead locks and a stencilled label: *Armoury.*

• • •

The police officer switched on the fluorescent lights. Around the walls, there were racks of bolt-action .303 rifles for police marksmen, and, in the middle, a wooden table full of light weapons. There was everything from sub-machine guns to service revolvers. Each bore a handwritten brown label attached by string to the trigger guard.

This was the reason Jack and RSM Morriston were here: to survey an Aladdin's cave of previously "illegally-held" weapons. Some confiscated from old soldiers' "collections" and some surrendered in the recent gun amnesty. On the table lay the cream of the crop.

Ostensibly, the Army Special Forces needed them for "Foreign Weapon Familiarisation".

In covert operations, you needed to be an expert in not only your own weaponry, but also the enemy's ordinance. Jack needed to be able to ID a weapon use it instantly if his own gun was out of ammunition, damaged beyond use, or lost.

However, Jack's presence today had a sinister ulterior motive.

One of the problems the MRF found in operating *shoot*

and scoot in Northern Ireland was that on certain occasions the man just killed may not have been armed. It made it look a lot fairer if they were carrying weapons, and stopped the RUC in their tracks if they were asking too many questions.

This stronghold was the source of many "IRA" weapons, even though the terrorists had never even seen, let alone touched, them until they were "gripped" by the cold fingers of a corpse on a mortuary slab.

They also proved useful for the occasions when the crowd had spirited away genuine IRA weapons from corpses in the moments between when the MRF had scooted and the RUC and security forces had arrived on the scene. These weapons could also be planted in suspect addresses.

A Thompson sub-machine gun quickly caught Jack's eye.

"Where did this little beauty come from?" he said.

"It came from some US Army base. Some mad yank got tanked up and decided to wake up sleepy England. The sign outside the Plough and Harrow, Peopleton, was sheered right off as he shot the moon."

"Right, we'll certainly take this one," said Jack.

Shame I can't breed them, he thought.

Jack now had a matching pair.

Sgt. Davies snipped off the label and recorded the gun's departure in a register.

An English Lanchester sub-machine gun – a type normally issued to the Royal Navy, immediately followed the American Thompson. Then a German Schmeisser sub-machine gun, a Mauser pistol, two Webly .455 calibre revolvers Mk 2, a 7.62mmx17mm FN-Browning M1900, three 9mm Walther P 38s, and a 1937 mint condition Luger pistol.

The Luger had a German eagle stamped on the left hand side of the body. Its claws held a swastika and underneath stood the letters *SS*. It must have been a Nazi officer's, and the subsequent collector's, pride and joy. At least now it was going to a good home with Jack, rather than under the police steamroller or the cutting flame of an oxyacetylene burner.

Ten weapons would accompany Jack and RSM Morriston to an armoury in Salisbury for servicing, each "processed" to conceal their identity.

• • •

It had been a rough crossing.

Jack drove the 1966 Wolseley 6/110 MkII saloon off the Liverpool–Belfast Ferry. The rear wheels squealed as its 120hp straight-six cylinder engine powered it off the "up" ramp. Safe in the boot was the valise with the pick of the new weapons cache. Now clear of the steel structure of the ship, his finger stubbed the car radio "On" button.

"Good Morning everyone. It's Radio One from the BBC. Friday July 21st 1972. It is eight o'clock it's the Tony Blackburn Show..."

A new song from Rod Stewart filled the car:

"Angel came down from heaven yesterday
Stayed with me long enough to rescue me
And she told me a story yesterday
About the sweet love between the moon and the deep blue sea
Then she spread her wings high over me
She said she's goin' now, come back tomorrow
And I said, fly on my sweet angel, fly on through the sky
Fly on my sweet angel tomorrow I'm gonna be by your side
Fly away, high away, fly away
Sure enough this morning came unto me
Silver wings silhouetted against a child's sunrise

And my angel she said unto me
Today's the day for you to rise..."

• • •

"Cheerful bastard," Jack said aloud.

Jack threaded his way from Donegal Quay through Corporation Square, then Victoria Street and on to the Queen Elizabeth Bridge crossing into East Belfast. He then headed towards Palace Barracks.

Children were on their way to school. Was it the last day of the summer term? Ulster Bus vehicles belched diesel fumes as they delivered their precious packages.

Tony Blackburn interjected:

"How about that Rod Stewart? Will his sore throat ever get better? I know *I'll* send him some lozenges. That was "Angel" from his new LP *Never a Dull Moment*. Really is a knockout! A song written, of course, by the late, great Jimi Hendrix..."

• • •

"*Never a Dull Moment*... must have been thinking of here," Jack smiled.

He drove through the double gates in the 20ft corrugated iron fence of Palace Barracks and into the MRF compound. Taking the valise from the boot of the Wolseley, he deposited the weapons in the unit armoury and walked over to the Ops Room to report in.

"There's some mail for you here," said Pud holding one envelope aloft. "Perfumed .... Avon Field Flowers if I'm not mistaken."

"Pam," reasoned Jack. He remembered the Fragrance and Frills gift set he had purchased for her birthday in March. Four 1 1/2oz size Lavender-fragrance soaps in a lavender plastic box with, in the centre, an 1/8 oz bottle of "Dazzling" perfume in "Field Flowers" Scent.

"Not a bad night for ten bob," remembered Jack. "How the hell did you pick the scent?"

"My mother's an Avon Lady. Avon calling…," Pud mimicked.

Jack bristled and pocketed the letters for later.

"What's been happening while I've been away?"

Pud tossed a clipboard carelessly towards Jack. Jack studied the Sitreps intently.

Nope, nothing worth bothering about.

He walked into the Sergeant's mess where Ken looked up from a copy of the *Daily Telegraph*. Premier Anwar el-Sadat of Egypt had expelled all Soviet military advisers from his country.

"Light the blue touchpaper…" said Jack.

"And retire?" queried Ken.

"No, no, those Egyptian Infantry Battalions are pretty hot stuff at the moment. I can't see them sitting on the banks of the Suez Canal for much longer," said Jack.

Jack joined Ken. He sat down in an adjacent brown leather armchair. A mess waiter brought over a cup of tea and some digestive biscuits.

Jack sipped his tea and took out his mail. He opened a buff envelope. It was a note in Pud's handwriting.

The priest who had challenged Jack in the hearse incident on Wednesday had made an official complaint to the RUC, but the Army had been unable to help them identify the personnel involved in the incident.

"Good!" said Jack with a smile. "No need to find an axe then."

Ken looked up.

"What did you say?"

Jack didn't reply, and Ken pointed to the letter.

"What's that?"

"Nothing much," said Jack. "It's just some reassurance that we're all still on the same side."

Ken returned to his newspaper.

Half an hour later Jack jumped into his Mini Cooper and, camera bag stashed on the passenger seat, headed into town. He had rung Jean's mother who had told him she was out shopping. Perhaps they would bump into each other at lunchtime.

Perhaps not.

There was no reply from Sandra's house.

Jack parked on a reserved strip by the Europa Hotel. The concierge, Joseph McMullen, was used to keeping an eye on Jack's car when he was in town.

Jack went through the revolving doors into the hotel and entered the restaurant. He had hoped Jean might be there, but she was nowhere to be seen. He had a spot of fish and chips for lunch, hoping she might materialise.

She did not.

• • •

Jack left the hotel at 1400 hours and headed off along Howard Street towards the City Hall.

In the distance, he could hear a police siren. A chill wind seemed to rise beside him and then fall.

Jack pushed his way through the busy Friday shoppers until the clock on the City Hall loomed into view.

1410 hours.

Suddenly, a muffled explosion was heard in the distance.

Shoppers stopped momentarily and scattered to safety.

More sirens.

Jack headed for a red phone box.

He dug into his pocket for a two-penny piece.

He dialled 66787.

Pud answered.

"It's Jack. What the fuck is happening?"

"The balloon's gone up," said Pud. "The RUC have had 20 bomb warnings from the Samaritans…"

"Twenty?!" exclaimed Jack. "When? Where?"

"There were so many I could hardly take them all down. Where are you Jack?"

"Just outside the City Hall."

"City Hall? Right, well the first explosion has already been reported in the Smithfield Bus Station. Now looking down the list the other bus depot in Oxford Street is also in the firing line, and the train station.

"But there are loads of others. So many, the RUC are running round like headless chickens. We've been asked to help.

"Call sign Seven-Zero is heading for York Road Railway Station as they were patrolling nearby. There are reports of a suspicious suitcase on a platform."

"Suggest you RV."

"Roger!"

Jack sprinted from the telephone kiosk, leaving the black receiver a pendulum swinging on its wire, with incessant, insatiable pips demanding more coins inserted immediately.

The railway station was about five minutes away at a flat out run. Jack dodged round shoppers who had clustered in mutual confusion After some close shaves with dopey drivers, he turned the corner into York Road.

Another distant thud!

Jack could see that call sign Seven-Zero were already about their business. Their Ford Cortina was parked at a crazy angle outside the station entrance.

Jack pushed his way inside.

He could see MRF man, Sergeant Jim McKinley, gingerly approaching a young woman who seemed frozen by fear, unable to move away from a suitcase just in front of her on the platform.

He grabbed the sleeve of her raincoat and dragged her towards the station entrance.

Jack lent a hand as they started to pull and frog march her around the corner.

Whoosh!

The blast from the suitcase bomb blew the trio off their feet. Chunks of debris rained down on the MRF men as they shielded their female companion.

Clouds of dust, and then silence.

Then ringing in the ears, and disorientation.

Nausea.

A RUC inspector who had witnessed the whole episode came over to the pair who were dusting themselves down and took the woman away.

Ambulances arrived.

The MRF left.

Jack jumped in the back of the Cortina with McKinley.

"That was an incredibly brave thing to do," said Jack.

"And incredibly stupid," said Jim.

"I just couldn't leave her to her fate. Someone had to do something and I was the first to move. I am sure someone else would have if it wasn't my turn."

"Where next?" said Jack.

"The other bus station?"

"Just the ticket!"

"Right let's move!"

Unfortunately, the traffic was now at a standstill and, despite their best efforts, a huge blast told the MRF men they were too late.

They were greeted by a scene of complete carnage.

Body parts of more than one British soldier were scattered around the area. The remains of a car bomb smoked nearby. Buses blazed.

An Ulster Bus peaked cap was upside down in the gutter. People with blood streaming down their faces were aimlessly wandering in a daze. Some were looking for something, or someone, to tend them. Children sobbed. Women with prams screamed names.

Then Jack heard a woman's voice screaming.

"Jack!"

Her voice seemed to come from two directions at once.

An echo? Maybe, Jack's ears were still ringing.

It was Jean.

"My brother Ryan just gave me a lift to town and ..."

The other MRF men distanced themselves from Jack and disappeared into the crowds.

Jack took his camera out of his bag and fired off a few shots.

One would appear in the next day's papers.

He gave his film to Danno Stobbart at the Europa Hotel, where he had taken Jean to escape the insanity.

They stayed there until the madness and mayhem had subsided and then, to calm her further, Jack drove down the Antrim Road to the Chimney Corner Hotel whose restaurant had become one of his favourites. The owner, Philippe, greeted them at the door.

"*Oh bon ! Bien venue Monsieur Jacque. Mon plaisir.* "

"Two?"

"Bien. "

Jack and Jean sat opposite each other with just a tricolour of carnations between them. Where Jean was now, mentally, was anyone's guess. It was tough enough for a hardened veteran of the battlefield to witness such things as they had seen together, let alone a young girl.

Perhaps there was more to it that that.

Was it a coincidence that she was at the bus station with her brother?

Were the pieces of a giant jigsaw finally falling into place? These were too many questions for the time of day.

After coffee Jack popped the question that was on his mind: "Would you like to come upstairs for a fuck?"

Each sought solace in each other.

• • •

The next morning, in the Sergeants' Mess, they scanned the newspapers.

"Massacre!" screamed the *Daily Mirror*.

"Murder Friday!" clamoured the *Daily Express*.

Over in the Ops Room, Pud pirouetted around the room. His dancing partner was the front page of the Belfast broadsheet, the Catholic-favoured paper, *The News Letter*.

"Bloody Friday – or Day of Infamy" it read.

"Infamy, infamy they've all got it in for me," he mimicked Kenneth Williams' carry-on voice, which Jack suddenly realised was not too far removed from Pud's own. Pud held out the newspaper.

THE FOLLOWING STATEMENT WAS MADE BY THE SECRETARY OF STATE FOR NORTHERN IRELAND, MR. WILLIAM WHITELAW, IN THE HOUSE OF COMMONS, 24 JULY 1972:

"As the House will know, the city and people of Belfast suffered a murderous sequence of explosions last Friday. Most of the 27 explosions in Belfast that day occurred within a three and a half hour period in the afternoon – at a time when, and at places where, high civilian casualties must have been expected and intended.

No adequate warnings were given.

Seven civilians and two soldiers were killed and at least 130 civilians injured, many gravely. I hardly need point out that all sections of the community are indiscriminately affected by these outrages. Of the dead, two were Roman Catholics. Of the 130 injured at least 40 were Roman Catholics. 53 were men and boys, 77 women and children.

I am sure the whole House will wish to join with me in expressing sympathy to the families of all those involved in this wanton attack on innocent men, women and children.

After the appallingly bloodthirsty and criminal events of last Friday, there cannot be any remaining shred of support for the men who perpetrate them. Even those sectors of Roman Catholic opinion throughout the world that have traditionally identified themselves with, and perhaps given the benefit of the doubt, to any group of men who claimed to speak for the Irish Republican movement can surely no longer continue to uphold the men who were responsible for Friday's horrible catalogue of slaughter.

Supporters of the Republican movement in this country, in Northern Ireland, in the United States and elsewhere, will no doubt notice the revulsion in some circles in the Irish Republic.

Since Parliament at the end of March entrusted the Government with complete responsibility for all administration in Northern Ireland, we have made the most patient and reasoned effort to secure the end of violence.

No one can deny that Her Majesty's Government have now an absolutely unchallengeable right to ask this House, this country, and indeed the whole world for their support in an absolute determination to destroy the capacity of the IRA for further acts of inhumanity.

They have degraded the human race, and it must now be clear to all that their sole object is to promote their aims by violence and by violence alone."

"So this is where we come in, Gentlemen..."

Jack put down the *Daily Telegraph*, which he had just quoted at length. His ears were still ringing from Friday's brush with death at the bus station. Now he was on the war path.

"Talk about gunpowder plots. According to the powers that be, this was the biggest bomb attack on the Crown in peacetime since Guy Fawkes. Needless to say the gloves are off!

"There is talk about a big army push happening soon, and our orders are to keep the pressure on the IRA until the big move happens.

"Now, Intelligence informs us that there is a gathering of armed men at a bus stop in Glenn Road, a notorious meeting place for the Divis Flats/Falls Road fraternity of taxi drivers.

"Basically, they transport IRA men, weapons, and contraband between these two places. We allow them to operate relatively unhindered for intelligence reasons, as they have for a long time been infiltrated by the spooks. But today the cocky bastards are parading with automatic weapons and rifles in plain view of the local population, which is something we simply cannot allow especially after the bombings.

"Call signs Eight-Zero and Eight-One will proceed to the area and take the necessary action."

The door opened and the boss of the MRF, Captain Hamish McGregor, entered the room. He was keen to lead his men on this one.

Based on previous experience Jack was keen that the boss never be let out alone.

Jack continued:

"As I was saying... Call sign Eight-Zero with myself and Captain McGregor on board will execute any necessary engagement. Eight-One will recce the area before we move in."

The boss, Jack and Taff Watkins – the Royal Military Police Sergeant who commanded call sign Eight-Zero – made their way to the armoury. The boss drew a 9mm Browning as did Jack. Sgt. Watkins, who was a good steady soldier, used to taking the fight to the enemy, chose the unit's new Thompson sub-machine gun with the 50 round magazine.

"The choice of kings and IRA hoodlums," said Jack.

Everyone laughed.

The Republican link to the Thompson sub-machine gun always caused confusion when it was the hands of the MRF. There were so many schisms in the IRA they could never really be sure that they were not under attack by even their own side.

In any case, Jack felt safer with the extra firepower on board.

They climbed into a green Cortina and tested the radio. Then the two cars left the compound, with Eight-One in a Morris Oxford Estate leading the way.

Jack was in the back of Eight-Zero, sitting directly behind the boss, who was in the front passenger seat with the radio transmit foot switch. Taff Watkins was seated next to Jack, behind the driver Sgt. Greg Allen – one of the SBS boys who arrived with Sgt. Ken Cooke in June.

The MRF usually operated with three aboard to mimic the UVF, but today they were being cautious. It always seemed that things went pear shaped whenever the boss was about. Perhaps it was just bad luck.

The four were a formidable force on the loose and the even number felt better to Jack – it was the same number of men on a standard SAS patrol.

They headed down a sunny Holywood Road, onto the Newtownards Road, then across Queens Bridge into the built-up area of Belfast. The trip up to Andersonstown Road and the Glen Road area went without incident.

As call sign Eight-One approached the Glen Road bus terminus – a turning point at the end of the bus route – they could see a small crowd in the distance. They spotted several taxis across the road from the men as they passed. Eight-One identified the crowd as the taxi drivers highlighted in the briefing, as more than one of them was armed.

They radioed Eight-Zero that the area was "hot".

Sgt. Allen drove slowly along the road, when they were side on to the men a shout came from the boss: "They have guns!"

At almost the moment, shots were fired at Eight-Zero from many weapons. Instantly, the Thompson opened up as the car started to accelerate away from the incoming fire. A long single burst from Taff Watkins' sub-machine gun and two or three of the gunmen fell to the ground screaming.

Eight-Zero was still under fire from an unknown location. The Cortina's rear window shattered as they escaped. A second burst from Taff, which emptied the Thompson's magazine, silenced the hidden shooter.

Jack was acutely aware that the taxi drivers might now be in pursuit of the MRF men. If they didn't get out quickly, there would be time for IRA gunmen to ambush them before they left the Glen Road. A hasty retreat was in order for the MRF boys.

Eight-One radioed, offering assistance, but Eight-Zero declined. The contact had ended.

There was a buzz in the Cortina as Sgt. Greg Allen tore off down the road.

Smiles and anxiety blended into a heady mixture, like a fine Scotch single malt whiskey. The aroma was testosterone, the body was violence and the aftertaste was success. They had been under heavy fire and yet they escaped without a scratch. Given the number of rounds fired in their direction, that amounted to a "bloody miracle".

"Maybe they were firing blanks," joked Jack." Or rubber bullets.

He wiped pellets of shattered window glass off his now nicely aging leather jacket.

Yet again, REME's armour plate had done its job, as they would soon discover.

Eight-Zero's driver, Greg, was an SBS Sergeant, no orders need be barked at him. He could handle a situation like this with ease. Even if there had been casualties, there wouldn't have been a different reaction from him. His driving would always be swift and surefooted. He was refrigerator cool.

• • •

If a gunman had jumped in front of the car as the MRF crew made their scoot, on the odds were that Greg and his companions would have magically eluded harm.

As the car slowed down, ready to take the turning into

Kennedy Way, Jack, who was acting as "tail end Charlie" kept an eye open out of the punched-out rear window, in case the gunmen were in pursuit

It was all clear.

The MRF men made themselves comfortable in the car. Their weapons were still at the ready and they travelled down Kennedy Way, aware of not to drawing attention to themselves.

They negotiated the roundabout at the end of the road and made their way down Stockman's Lane. The safest route back to Palace Barracks was to take the Lisburn Road into Belfast City centre. A half a mile down Lisburn Road, Taff spotted an RUC roadblock.

The MRF weapons disappeared in a manner that conjurer David Nixon would have applauded. Perhaps he would admit Jack and the MRF men into the Magic Circle. Taff and Jack put the Thompson, its barrel was still warm from discharging 50 .45 calibre round under their feet with a car rug on top, There were still the bloody big bullet holes from the driver's door to the tail light and across the boot lid to contend with.

The RUC were suspicious to put it lightly.

"Who are you boys?" asked the first RUC man.

A companion covered him with a Sterling sub-machine gun from a few yards distant.

"Security Forces," said Sgt. Allen as he flipped out his military ID card.

The officer took it and examined it closely.

"OK, pull up over there."

There were another four RUC officers waiting for them. Greg manoeuvred the car between the *chicane* of the roadblock and pulled up.

"Out of the car please, gentlemen!"

The MRF men climbed out and stood together like a NASA crew who had just finished an Apollo mission.

"Who is in charge?" asked the RUC Sergeant.

This was not immediately obvious because at least three of the men ranged in front of him looked like leaders rather than followers. And, of course, all were in plain clothes. Taff had a black beard and all their haircuts weren't anywhere near regulation length.

In fact, from their appearance they might as well have been super group Crosby, Stills, Nash and Young. Sergeant Ian McCallum of the RUC, a fan since 1969, wouldn't have been surprised if they had burst into a quick chorus of *Teach your Children*. The anti-war anthem would have gone down well with him after the past few days of The Troubles.

"Him."

Taff was pointing at Jack.

"I'm the senior officer," interjected the boss. "Captain Hamish McGregor, Parachute Regiment. These are my men."

Greg smiled.

The RUC men insisted on seeing each of the MRF men's ID cards and made a careful note of them.

"Are you carrying weapons?" asked Sgt. McCallum.

The roadblock, already informed of the Glen Road gunfire by radio, had anticipated the MRF men's arrival. The RUC hadn't known exactly who to expect but, as the Cortina halted and the men stayed in the car, the situation seemed under control.

Had Jack and the boys not stopped, or had attempted to escape, they would have undoubtedly come under fire from the RUC.

And they were good shots.

"Yes. They're in the car," replied the boss.

"Can we get them out of the car, Sir?" asked McCallum.

"Feel free."

Two RUC men moved forwards and a short search of the perforated Cortina retrieved the weapons.

"What the fuck is this?" said McCallum, holding aloft the Thompson sub-machine gun passed to him by a colleague. "Is this a legal weapon, Captain?"

"Yes. It's official Army issue, as are the Browning pistols. Can we be on our way, Sergeant?"

Sergeant McCallum's body language showed some reluctance but vocally he acceded to the request. He had all the necessary information he needed, and, after all, they were all on the same side no matter how unorthodox the fight and the fighters had become. After Friday afternoon's carnage, the RUC needed all the help they could get.

"What was that all about?" asked Jack.

He was used to a friendly wave on after a quick flash of an ID card and a swift chorus of "Security Forces". It seemed that perhaps Friday's glut of bombs had changed things.

"He must have got out of the wrong side of the bed this morning," laughed Greg.

Twenty-five minutes later, they were back at base. The boss led the crew to the Ops room for a "debrief".

Pud appeared and told them that Captain Tony Case, the intelligence officer from Lisburn HQ, was on his way, and asked them to wait for him. The RUC had also been on the phone to say they would shortly be joining them, too.

"Captain Case says that under no circumstances are you to talk to the RUC until he has personally debriefed you," said Pud.

The boss, Jack and the men waited in the rest room for the arrival of their interrogators.

Taff lit up.

Over a hot cup of tea, they checked that their recollections of the action were the same. This was not collusion, but a standard practice as occasionally, in the heat of battle, there can be confusion. For instance, if you were firing an automatic weapon, you may not have heard or seen all of what was happening around you, whereas, your comrades may have had a better view. This evidence may not be good to parade in front of the RUC.

It was certain that witnesses in Glen Road would be doing the same thing as they shared their recollections of the shocking events brought on by the IRA gunmen.

Captain Case arrived at Palace Barracks and, after talking to the team, seemed satisfied and left. His interest was unusual but at the time felt positive and welcome.

The RUC arrived.

Three other officers, one more senior, now accompanied Sgt. McCallum.

It was Sandra's father.

Jack smiled at him. Inspector Eddie Robson returned the expression, accompanied by a dark frown that said much more than just: "Not you again!"

The MRF men each had an individual verbal interview followed by written statements. The RUC men then talked for a time together out of earshot in a huddle.

This is dragging on a bit, thought Jack.

He began to tap his fingers on the table. First one hand and then the other took turns to break the silence. The boss was the first to loose his patience.

"Now, Inspector, what exactly is this all about?"

"The problem I have, Captain McGregor, is that I have four wounded civilians – one of whom was asleep in bed when his room was hit by a hail of bullets, two ending up lodged in his leg – and a bus queue of unarmed people who claim to have been mown down by you and your men!

"Added to that, your weaponry seems to be suspect to say the least. However lawless Belfast has become, it is not Chicago and there can be no excuse for discharging, quite recklessly, an automatic weapon when so many civilians were in the proximity.

"An initial inspection has shown that there are more than 20 rounds embedded in the walls of surrounding houses...."

"There are more than that embedded in our car..."Jack interrupted.

Inspector Robson thundered: "You are just lucky that no-one was killed or we might take a much more serious view of events. Take this as a warning: there is no place for your kind here no matter how desperate the situation has become. Should our investigation show that there has been wrong-doing, you will find that there is no hiding place. Not even your uniform..." He looked Jack up and down with evident disgust." ...if you have one, will protect you from justice."

Before Jack could react to the slur, Inspector Robson had turned, and, with his entourage, departed. As the door closed behind them, Taff stubbed his cigarette out in the ashtray that was now full to overflowing.

Jack looked at his Welsh comrade and shook his head. He felt that this was not the end of things as far as this RUC officer was concerned.

For some reason or other, just like Sir Henry Bromley centuries before, Inspector Robson was not going to give up until he had his man.

Chapter 12

On the Road to Bruin

Jean Philomena McLaughlin watched through a gap in the net curtains as khaki truck after khaki truck of British soldiers poured into West Belfast.

She looked down to her hand resting on the gloss-painted windowsill at the expensive wristwatch that Jack had given her a few weeks ago on that romantic night in Crawfordsburn. The hotel staff seemed to know Jack so well and were so attentive, tending to her every need and desire. Just like Jack that night.

She sighed.

She playfully rotated her wrist to make the gems that adorned the watch's face and strap flash and sparkle in the early morning light. The minute and hour hands pointed to five o'clock. 0500 hours.

"South African diamonds and 14 carat white gold," Jack had told her.

It was the most precious thing she had ever been given.

The watch didn't exactly look brand new, and it did not come in a box as one might expect for such lavish a gift. Just a local jeweller's reference tag on a white piece of string had been attached to the clasp. However, it was she who had spoiled the surprise by discovering the watch while rummaging in Jack's bag, hunting for her cigarette lighter again.

The lack of silk ribbons and bows didn't really matter, of course, because men are absolutely rubbish when it comes to gift-wrapping, as her American friend, Sarah-Beth, would say. She had even seen Jack have trouble with cellotape. He could never find the end on the roll and would whip out a pocket magnifying glass, which he kept for "looking at photographic negatives on a light box", to help him.

She went over the moment when he had given her the watch again in her mind again.

"That's for you, Poppet," Jack had exclaimed when she waved the gift in front of his nose in the hotel bathroom. He had looked somewhat surprised at its sudden appearance, as if a conjuror had produced it from a hat.

"I was just waiting for the right moment to whip it out and surprise you," he laughed. "Look, give it here, let me put it on you. It's a 21-jewel Hamilton automatic – you just have to shake it to wind it up…"

Now she would shake it religiously everyday but it still stopped unless she wound it with the winder as well. Perhaps she wasn't doing it right.

She stopped her daydreaming and looked out of the window again. Now the three-bedroom semi shook from the weight of passing military traffic, rocking the foundations of her Denewood Park family home.

Her mother stood motionless in tears as the trucks thundered by.

Her only brother, Ryan, had initially been itching to go outside when the army trucks first made their appearance but, after a brief phone call, he now seemed resigned to staying at home.

That dried his mother's tears. For now.

It had been more than a week since "Bloody Friday" and

Katherine McLaughlin had barely slept a wink. That was why she was wide-awake when the thousands of British "invaders" had arrived on her doorstep shortly after 4am.

She had roused her son and daughter, convinced they were about to be slaughtered as they slept in their beds. The British would surely want revenge for the IRA bombings, which had shaken her already heartbroken world 10 days ago, she reasoned.

But no, she was mistaken. The convoy of heavy trucks had passed by, and their now disgorged contents had taken up positions at each and every street corner.

The next-door neighbour, Mrs O'Reilly, had taken Tootsie, her 12-month-old Yorkshire terrier bitch, for a long morning walk. On her return to Denewood Park she had reported that the barricades, which had been manned continually by the IRA over the past months, had been smashed through and were being dismantled by scores of British troops.

"It seems like the whole of the British Army has turned up to torment us, Mrs M," she gossiped. "Our boys are nowhere to be seen. I thought we were well passed the days of IRA. standing for 'I Run Away'..."

"Now hush your tongue, Bernadette and don't talk so disrespectfully," Mrs McLaughlin thundered.

In the haste of her gossip, Mrs O'Reilly had momentarily forgotten the huge sacrifice her neighbour had made for the cause.

Jean pushed a steaming cup of sweet tea into her mother's hands. The teaspoon clinked and then nestled tightly between cup and saucer.

As the early hours wore on, Jean sat listening to her mother's grief filled sighs as the troubled woman slept in fits and starts in a green coloured armchair. Jean twisted the watchband around and around her small wrist.

"He loves me. He loves me not… He loves me …he loves me not..."

She realised that the bejewelled watch was not going to give her the answer she so desired, and stopped her rhyme abruptly.

At the same time, a heavy knock on the front door brought her back to reality. Her heart began to race.

Her mother stirred but did not wake.

Jean reached the door before another knock hit home.

The outstretched fist of a woman greeted her. It withdrew suddenly, as its intended target disappeared out of reach.

"Sorry love, I was just about to knock again."

The smiling face of a dark-haired Catholic woman greeted Jean.

"Now what it is… is that we are starting a new home-delivery laundry service, and dry cleaning, if you will."

Sue Brennan – fragrant, fresh-faced, attractive, and with a lovely bubbly personality that well equipped her with the ability to sell door to door. She was so good at it that her boss, Bob Dennis, said she could have sold the Sphinx to the Arabs.

Just like the Egyptian icon, Sue's exquisite smile also hid a secret.

"Sue" was in fact, Lance Corporal Sarah Jane Warke of the Royal Military Police and her boss "Bob" was Captain Robert Dennis of the Royal Engineers. They, and their "Four Square Laundry", operated under the protection of the MRF as part of the intelligence-gathering community.

Sgt. Major Jack Gillespie and the boys provided them with covert cover. Sue's "van driver", Sapper Edward Stuart – known in the MRF as "Paddy: our man from Strabane" – took part in many front line MRF operations before his transfer to "laundry duties".

Paddy was now in the same safe hands as the fugitive Freds: MI6.

The Four Square Laundry was the ingenious idea of Spooks based at 39 Brigade HQ, Lisburn. For many years, forensic experts had been able to tell whether an individual had discharged firearms, simply by testing their clothing for residues of certain chemicals produced by combustion. A single shot from a pistol could send a fine spray of the burnt propellant, a cocktail of cordite and lead molecules, over the arms and torso of a gunman. It would remain on their clothing, visible to science, until thoroughly cleaned.

Those "terrorists" who handled explosives also harboured telltale chemicals.

The hard bit, as far as the men of the British Secret Intelligence Service were concerned, was getting the suspects to take their clothes off and voluntarily give them up for testing, and then stay put in their homes waiting for the results to come in.

However, a bit of lateral thinking from the very best brains that the Public Schools and Red Brick Universities of England could produce did the trick. The solution from the brilliant minds was the Four Square Laundry in which the IRA would be "taken to the cleaners" and "hung out to dry".

After a couple weeks of instruction from the Spooks, Sue and Paddy had started leafleting the Republican areas of West Belfast. It had been tough, at first, to drive around in the fake laundry van due to the IRA roadblocks and harassment from criminal elements wanting protection money.

However, one of the dividends from this morning's massive military operation was that it would, without doubt, assure the success of the Four Square Laundry. The military operation, which the Catholic Community thought was a direct response to Bloody Friday, *was* massive. Known as Operation Motorman it was the British Government's biggest troop movement since the Suez Crisis.

Almost 22,000 soldiers, 27 infantry and two armoured battalions, poured in to West Belfast and Republican "Derry". Included among the armoured vehicles were several Centurion AVRE demolition tanks, which were a specialised derivative of the Centurion – the British Army's main battle tank of the immediate post war period.

These were the only heavy tanks deployed operationally by the British Army in Northern Ireland during The Troubles. The tanks, transported to Northern Ireland on board the landing craft assault ship HMS Fearless, operated with their demolition guns covered by tarpaulins and pointed to the rear.

That day the British employed an overwhelming military force, roughly four per cent of the whole British Army. By the end of July 31st 1972, there were no more "no-go" urban areas in Northern Ireland.

The Provisional and Official IRAs did not attempt to hold their ground – they lacked the necessary armaments and numbers for a direct confrontation with the British. In West Belfast, just 50 IRA "regulars" faced more than 8,000 British troops. Remarkably, no actual killing took place.

Now the British "ruled the roost" in Republican areas, the British might have just as well set up IRA recruiting offices on every street in West Belfast. The Four Square Laundry ruse, however, would work like a dream.

By making the service dirt cheap, MI6 would make the people of West Belfast a laundry and dry cleaning "offer they could not refuse".

Through an intermediary, MI6 operatives negotiated a bulk

laundry and dry cleaning contract with a Protestant-owned company in East Belfast. This meant the MRF service could massively undercut high street cleaners and offered a complimentary home collection and delivery service too.

Sarah and Paddy would visit all the homes in a street where a single address had been pinpointed by the Freds, and others, as the homes of IRA members or active sympathisers. Sarah would half-heartedly spell out the laundry's price list to the neighbours and save the "hard sell" for the house of interest.

They would then take the suspect's clothing to a prearranged rendezvous with MI6 agents. The Spooks would transport it to the forensic scientists at Castle Reagh Police Station.

After stringent testing, any evidence of weapons use or munitions handling would be logged and then the clothes would be put back into the system, professionally cleaned and returned by "Sue and Paddy" to their rightful owners.

All in all, it was a first-class service – every single speck of dirt accounted for.

The end results could be spectacular. Many IRA men had their collars felt in early morning raids that resulted in their internment, or worse. Not for one minute during the summer of 1972 did Brendan Hughes and his fellow members in the IRA high command suspect that their dirty secrets were being washed in public.

Back in Denewood Park, Sarah's visit to the McLaughlin household was, as you would suspect, no accident. Ryan McLaughlin's mug shot gazed down on Jack from both the McLaughlin living room mantelpiece and the wall of the MRF Ops Room.

Ryan was now top of the MI6 washing wish list.

• • •

Sarah departed the McLaughlin residence, clutching Ryan McLaughlin's muddied black woollen overcoat in a plastic bag tight to her chest. Jean had remembered how her brother had absentmindedly wiped his hand on his coat after throwing soil on his brother's coffin.

"Because of that dirty mark, I will be reminded of your brother every time I see you in that blasted coat," anguished his mother ten days previous.

Being a thrifty Catholic girl, Jean thought the overcoat much too good to leave in the cupboard, and took advantage of the Four Square's "special introductory offer".

"I'll have it back on Thursday no trouble," Sarah had said in her broad Belfast accent, waving goodbye.

Jean smiled at her efficiency – her brother would never know the overcoat had even left his bedroom. She could tell him she scrubbed the dirt off with a nailbrush.

It seemed no sooner had she closed the door on Sarah than Jack appeared. She was about to tell him of the bargain offer she had just taken advantage of but thought better of it. After all, what would a grown man want to do with dry cleaning. That was woman's work.

"About that Friday – the one with all the bombs…," Jack started but was interrupted.

"Did your editor like your pictures? I saw them all over the front pages of the British press. You could even see the sleeve of my coat in one of them!" exclaimed Jean. "Wasn't it just so terrible…? But to think that when the whole world was ending around us, we were together…"

"Yes, poppet, they came out fine. I just thought I would come by to see how you and your mum are bearing up," hushed Jack.

Mrs McLaughlin was still snoozing in the wing chair. From

time to time, a snort and snuffle, accompanied by a few indistinguishable syllables, would emanate from her general direction.

Jack's presence at the McLaughlin residence was, of course, no coincidence. He would often photograph the collection or delivery of dry cleaning by the Four Square Laundry team. This was not the first occasion since Bloody Friday.

Legend would have it that two MRF men would be ensconced in the roof of the white Morris laundry van, covertly capturing the faces of those who had been taken to the cleaners – forensically – but this was rubbish. It was just Sarah and Paddy in the van, with Jack and the other MRF men usually, but not always, somewhere in the surrounding areas.

Jack noticed Jean twirling the watch around her wrist.

He still hadn't recovered from the shock of his "impromptu" generosity to her. Now a certain South African hotel receptionist was asking him when her watch would be back from being repaired.

They don't teach you how to get out of that sort of scrape in the SAS, he mused.

In his heart he knew he didn't have to worry. Things always worked out for Lucky Jack and, of course, it was just a matter of time before Jean would discover she had "lost" the timepiece while out shopping.

Jack hadn't worked out the fine detail yet, but as a draft plan it had potential.

In the end it would all turn out happily ever after for Jack. It always did.

"I do like you without your beard, Jack," cooed Jean.

"Well don't get used to it. I feel a new one coming on again soon."

Her face fell.

"Do you fancy a trip to the seaside this weekend?" he attempted to reverse her frown without success.

To Jean, Jack's shaving habits seemed to be linked with the cycle of the moon or seasons in the Sahara – anything other than fashion or logic. Sometimes she almost didn't recognise him when he approached her in the street. Especially on the occasions after he had returned home to Glasgow for a few weeks' break. It was obviously hard work being a photojournalist, up all hours of the day and night, she reasoned.

She, of course, looked forward to the day she would meet Jack's mother. What was her name? Did he say? Yes, of course.

Jean!

Jack strode out of Jean's house. He waved his hand in acknowledgment of the IRA Youth Movement members who were messing about outside.

Jean was too busy with her mum's problems to be available for seaside fun and frolics in sunny Bangor. Who was next in the Black Book?

Jack's Black Books were legendary in the MRF.

There was the Black Book that contained the names, addresses, telephone numbers, car registrations, holiday homes, relative's homes, and siblings of all the main sectarian terrorists in East and West Belfast. It was better than any card index system and a lot more portable.

As an aide-memoire, it was invaluable and, at first glance, remarkably like a journalist's contacts book. National Union of Journalists membership was a lifesaver for Jack, but the mystique of the profession and the way in which the IRA gave him almost unhindered access to Republican areas and events was beginning to surprise even him.

In fact, he could have walked up to, and assassinated, Gerry Adams or any of the IRA members in West Belfast almost any time he liked. Jack was just surprised no-one had ordered it. In fact, he often got the impression, in Adams' case, that it was being actively discouraged.

A for Adams. He was on top of the MRF's target tree, but, whoever in Intelligence handed the six "most wanted" mug shots to the patrols seemed to almost compulsively leave his ugly mug out. That had been the case all summer long. Until now, after the bombs of Friday 21st of July.

Now he was there on the front page of the wanted booklet, and, surprise, surprise, Adams was nowhere to be found around Lower Falls Road, or anywhere else for that matter.

Maybe his black suit and beret will soon need a dry clean, mused Jack. *Anyway, is he really so important? He's only 23 for Christ's sake!*

Today's Black Book was not that Black Book.

This Black Book was one that would have made Hugh Hefner green with envy. Inside were the contact details of some of the world's most beautiful women, as pneumatic and curvy as Playboy bunnies but with brains to match. Grey matter was important to Jack, but sometimes in the line of duty you had to lower your sights.

Perhaps today was one of those occasions. S is for Sandra.

Jack thumbed through the pages and read 58526. The dial whizzed and whirred until the tone turned to ringing.

Jack waited. He knew it was the right time to call her, the coast was probably clear, but there was no need to take unnecessary risks even in this kind of engagement.

Sandra spoke.

"Hello?"

"Hi, it's Jack," he replied.

Silence.

His ear strained for clues from the background noises that

hissed at him down the telephone. Jack was momentarily uneasy. Was her father in the hallway nearby?

No, she would have just pretended to be talking to an ex-school friend, like last time that had happened, and he would take the hint and ring off. But this time there was just silence, although he thought he could perhaps detect a sigh or even a "harrumph!" type of noise.

Then the explosion shook his ears with a piecing scream.

"You piece of ignorant shite! How could you?! It's bad enough that you were two-timing me with another woman, but a Catholic? I ask you, was I that bad a lover that you had to sleep with a piece of taig?"

Sandra at last took a breath and wailed.

"You made me feel so dirty... so used! I thought when I saw you in the bus station that you were my knight in shining armour, come to rescue me from the horrors of hell. I called your name, but you just headed to that slip of a Papist prostitute! I gave you my innocence and my heart and you crushed it like a fragile flower with your fist... I've followed you every day since... what kind of creature are you? How could you do that to me? You..."

"Just one question," interrupted Jack. "Have you told your Father about this, about us?"

"Is the Pope a Catholic? You bastard!" she slammed the phone hard into the receiver.

Jack gingerly replaced his, as if the venom of her words was still dripping from the receiver.

How the fuck did that happen? he wondered. *What are the chances?*

A sign in Jack's brain lit up "tilt", as if it was a pinball machine abused by someone playing too rough, forlornly calling for help from a dozy attendant in an amusement arcade. There was no-one to rescue Jack on this occasion, either. No attic door appeared in his cranium to allow him escape from the mental anguish of this cruel twist of fate.

Was this the day when Lucky Jack's luck ran out?

"Never mind," he said aloud to himself. "Worse things have happened at sea and there are plenty more fishes in it."

He was kidding no-one – not even himself. Damage crontol was now the order of the day.

No wonder the RUC were so interested in the Glen Road incident, thought Jack.

Jack realised that he and his companions on that day were not going to get an easy ride due to his multifaceted love life. Had the MRF lost their "Get out of Jail Free" card?

Time after time, they had been able to slide effortlessly away from the red tape came with the civilian authorities playing by the book. For the MRF in Northern Ireland, that book invariably seemed to have been ripped up and the pages consigned to the wind. Jack felt that unwritten assurance gave him and the MRF boys the *carte blanche* needed for success.

Not only that, but if one of the Freds stepped out of line, the same rules seemed to apply to them. The MRF had friends in very high places. Jack's friends seemed to stretch all the way to the top of the judiciary too. So maybe Inspector Robson was just a gnat on an elephant's back.

"Carpe Diem!"

Jack put his feet up on his desk and began to read the *Daily Telegraph*.

"Thousands of British dockers have begun an official strike to safeguard jobs. No cargo will be handled by the country's 42,000 registered dockers, but roll-on roll-off ferries will still pass through railway ports like Dover and Folkestone..."

A knock on the door diverted his attention from the mundane tales of 1970's industrial strife.

"Jack! How do you feel like a visit to a massage parlour?"

It was MI6 calling.

Ginge to be precise – the custodian of the Freds.

The MRF were going to operate another bright covert monitoring idea thought up by the London Spooks. Not content with collecting the IRA's dirty laundry, the MRF were now to eavesdrop on the terrorists' "pillow talk" in a bogus massage parlour in the Antrim Road.

It was an old industrial unit, extensively refurbished to be fully equipped for pleasure with the added bonus of being wired for sound, Super 8 cine and still photographs by MI6.

"We've been working on this for weeks now. It's time for you lot to have a look-see," said Ginge. "The boss says we should check the layout in case things ever turn nasty and you need to go in or come out guns blazing."

Using an ageing Ford Cortina so not to attract any attention, the pair arrived at the Gemini Parlour and climbed the staircase to a small office on the first floor. From there they went into an attic space.

Inside there was a table and two chairs. A reel-to-reel tape recorder was set up and ready to run. A notebook and pen lay nearby waiting for a scribe. There was a door leading to a fire escape that the MRF operatives would use to access the monitoring station when the new Madame would start letting the punters in next week. Downstairs, there were six private rooms in the establishment, each with its own theme: Caribbean, Arctic, Jungle, Spanish, Desert and Dungeon.

All places where the SAS excel, thought Jack.

• • •

For obvious reasons, Jack could never meet the Madame, Kitty O'Neill, in his true identity but as Jack Gillespie photographer, he would get quite friendly with some of her girls. They were all lookers and were recruited from within Northern Ireland and as far away as Dublin – tempted by inflated salaries.

The "working" girls were completely ignorant of the true activities taking place on the premises and the existence of those who were upstairs listening to their clients' small talk. Not so Kitty, a Belfast Catholic. She was a "sleeping" agent of the British.

She had been working in New York's seedy nightclub scene for the last three years and, as The Troubles worsened, had been coming home on increasingly regular short visits for the past 12 months or so with a view to returning home permanently. By the time the Gemini opened its doors for business, Kitty had been back for some time.

She had gotten to know the leaders and members of the Belfast 3rd Battalion of the IRA "intimately". Kitty put "her" proposition of opening a massage parlour to them, and suggested paying them 50 percent of the net takings to allow her to operate unhindered.

The IRA agreed, and at the end of the refurbishment, the place was the finest brothel in Belfast, used exclusively by the men of the local Republican areas.

Within weeks, the Gemini girls' skills were producing useful intelligence as the IRA men boasted of their importance in the organisation. A number of IRA operations were completely compromised in this way, and IRA commanders were obsessed with the idea that there was a British agent in their inner circle.

Meanwhile, the cash given to the IRA by Kitty as their share of the spoils really was dirty money. The notes were marked to enable MI6 to trace it if the IRA paid it into legitimate bank accounts or changed it for US Dollars. Ironically, bearing in mind its source, Jack thought greedy Republicans probably hid most of it under mattresses and kept it for their own purposes, rather than, as originally agreed, feeding into the terrorist organisation's coffers.

Each morning a courier collected the films and tapes from the MI6 brothel and delivered them to their section at Army HQ at Lisburn. Jack was called in on a number of occasions to listen to the tapes when the photographic evidence was inconclusive in the hope he might recognise the voices.

One such voice was Ryan McLaughlin.

Just as one of the girls was taking him through the gravy strokes, Ryan cried out for his mother, or someone's mother. Jack's recognition thus linked the McLaughlin brother with Gerry Adams, as earlier on the tape he had boasted the IRA leader as a personal comrade in the struggle.

Ryan was certainly in the thick of it. The lab report on his overcoat would cause some consternation.

"Your girlfriend's brother has so much C4 on his coat that if he put a detonator in his pocket he would blow his balls off!" was a fair assessment.

Jack's take on the safety of the MRF people operating the monitoring station at the Gemini, weren't too safe either. Sitting ducks, watching fucks.

"Not a bad way to earn a living, though," said Ginge.

• • •

The days before the weekend dragged by.

Apart from the visit to the Gemini, call sign Nine-Zero, or any of the MRF boys, didn't get out much that week. In

Belfast, you could not move without tripping over a Squaddie of some description or other and there was "peace" on the streets.

Finally, it was Friday and the happy campers of the MRF were off on a trip to the seaside.

Ken Cooke and John Benson joined Jack in a soft-skinned Morris Oxford Estate that, along with the Mini Cooper used for Jack's "press" jobs, were the MRF's recreational vehicles.

Portavogie in County Down – the unromantic sounding "harbour of the bog" – was the final destination of the boys' trip. A somewhat incongruous choice, as Portavogie was a village without any pubs.

It did, however, do a good trade in supplying the Loyalists with guns from Scotland. MI6 were on top of that one, so the boys could just party on the sands. Thanks to John Benson, some Protestant girls from the Shankhill would arrive on Saturday. *Maybe twins again*, hoped Jack.

The boys stocked up with supplies of beer in Bangor, and stop off for a swim on the beach at Donaghadee. As Ken loaded the pint bottles of beer into the back of the Morris Oxford Estate, Jack popped into the reception of the Royal Hotel.

Ann Mary Furness was on duty. Her face beamed as she saw Jack enter.

She was one of those women whose smiles could fill a dull room with sunshine and lift the hearts of the world-weary. Number one in the world-weary charts on Friday 4th August was one Sergeant Major Jack Gillespie and the smile worked for him.

"Hi, turtle," he returned her smile.

"Hello stranger, long time no see," she said.

"You OK for an RV later? I've got to see the boys bivouacked, but then I can extract myself under cover of darkness."

"It will have to be a dawn raid, soldier, because I am working late tonight. A little advance warning wouldn't go amiss," she said.

"I didn't expect I would be able to get away, but there are a lot of Green's on the streets and not much elbow room left for us to operate in. Too much chance of killing each other instead of the enemy," Jack said, only half in jest.

Some newly-arrived Greens had already fired on an MRF call sign but no-one was hurt. Just some Rupert's pride and chances of promotion.

"Ok. I'll see you at home whatever time you can get there..." Ann Mary broke off.

A man approached the reception desk.

"Hello Mr Dolman, welcome to the Royal. How can I help you?" she beamed.

In Jack's Black Book, Mike Dolman, a chartered accountant by profession, had a secret life as a UDA weapons instructor

Jack was out of there. He didn't like taking work home with him. In any case, Billy Rainey of Special Branch would not be very far behind if Mike Dolman was out and about.

In fact, more than one pair of eyes watched Jack as he left.

Jack rejoined the boys outside in the car. It was brimful of booze, apart from a large black teddy bear occupying the front seat where Jack's backside was headed.

Both parties looked at each, puzzled .

"I said beers not bears, you idiots," joked Jack.

"Isn't it yours?" they asked. "We thought it had something to do with the tales of B Squadron SAS in Malaya you keep boring us with. You know, the mascot."

"The bear was there in the car when we came back with the beers. Some people wear commemorative cufflinks, you carry a stuffed one," Ken laughed and shrugged his shoulders.

Jack carefully removed the bear from its seat and carefully placed it on a wall in the car park. They sped out of town.

At Donaghadee, the sandy beach soon bore the footprints of the MRF boys. SBS man Ken was way out offshore, swimming back strongly against the tide. Jack and John were paddling along the low water mark discussing this and that.

"I hear your social life is a little complicated," said John. "Blood runs thicker than water here and you can't just kiss and run. Folk have long memories and do not take kindly to outsiders messing around with their women. It's not like swinging London."

"Probably for the best then that it's over," said Jack. "Just a few hurt feelings..."

He didn't say whose.

A cloud covered the sun. The temperature dropped a few degrees and the pair headed back to the car to wait for the MRF's "Mark Spitz" to finish his Olympic training.

Errant sheep blocked he road through Ballyhalbert, which after a few minutes were worked away by a black-and-white Irish collie. Finally, the trio reached a camping field by the beach about two miles before Portavogie.

The tents went up and Jack flicked the bottle tops off the beers with a spoon. They watched the sun slip below the distant hills and toasted each other. "Women", "Missing friends", "The Gunners" – the football club as well as the Regiment – other Army units and finally "Irish Beer", which would soon be in short supply. Empty bottles were strewn around the campfire.

Jack took command.

"Right! Ballyhalbert has an off-licence. I am just going outside and may be some time."

Despite being a little worse for wear, Jack drove the four

or so miles to where the sheep dog had worked a few hours previous. He parked in the oblong car park and walked into the village shop.

A bell tinkled as he entered.

There were a few people about the village, but the shop stood deserted, except for an elderly woman.

"A bottle of your finest Bushmill's Black Bush," said Jack noticing his native Scotch was absent from the shelves behind the counter. "And some beers. Harp will do."

Loaded up, Jack headed back into the car park. He put his purchases on the passenger seat and started the Morris Oxford.

He hummed *Maybe I'm Amazed* by Paul McCartney to himself and thought of Ann Mary. He would soon be with her. He would dump the drink off at the camp and skedaddle.

Now in the mood for music, Jack reached for the "on" switch of the radio. It wasn't there. He groped some more, keeping his eyes on the road. The whole radio was gone! There was just a blank piece of metal in the dashboard.

"What the fuck? Some dirty Irish bastard has stolen the car radio from right under my nose!" he exploded.

Jack looked in the rear view mirror. A pair of eyes glowed back at him from the darkness. The headlights reflected against a dry stone wall and flashed onto the intruder.

The brakes squealed in an emergency stop and the precious booze flew into the foot well. Jack swung around and grabbed the neck of… a big black teddy bear.

"What the fuck!"

As his vocabulary failed him again, Jack looked about the vehicle.

He could not for the life of him remember any of the MRF boys packing a baby food sterilisation unit or a pushchair, never mind rubber rings for swimming and a whole bunch of beach towels.

In fact, the only thing he did recognise in the car was the beer, which was now forming a small lake in the foot well the other side of the gear stick.

He was in the wrong car!

He pulled the car keys out of the ignition. They were his all right. There was no doubt about that. The leather fob with the gold Springbok that Ann Mary had given him was reassuringly present.

Quickly putting the car into reverse, he headed back to the village. He parked up again and exited the vehicle. If someone had gone off in the "company" car, it wouldn't be the end of the world – there were no weapons, maps, or anything incriminating on board. There would just be so much egg on Jack's face that not even an Auntie's hanky, moistened with a good mouthful of spit, would ever get it off.

And then, there was the bear. Don't mention the bear. Jack would never hear the end of it.

"On the road to Bruin – that's for sure," laughed Ann Mary after Jack had re-lived the tale. "You're my big bear, give me a hug."

Jack obeyed that order.

Across the country in the Europa Hotel photographer Danno Stobbart was introducing a man from Grenada Television to one of his best contacts.

"Inspector Robson, Royal Ulster Constabulary, this is Brian. He works for *World in Action*."

Chapter 13

Hanging by a Fred

"Driving in a car down the Falls Road, one IRA man says to the other: 'Tell me Michael what will happen if this bomb goes off early, like all the others did?' 'Don't worry, Patrick, we've got a spare one in the boot'."

The MRF mess erupted into laughter at Jack's joke.

August had not been the IRA's month. Their bombs seemed to be going off prematurely, taking the terrorists to an early grave.

Doing the MRF boys' job for them. There were even gaps on the Ops Room wall where the IRA casualties were outpacing the Intelligence Officer's "replacements".

Since the "success" of the Bloody Friday bombings, the IRA master bomb-maker had seemed to lose his touch. Quite why that should be the case was a mystery to Jack, but the MI6 boys did seem to have very self-satisfied smiles whenever he saw them.

MI6's own charges – the three Freds – were proving their worth, too.

Their intelligence was spot on. The Fred's pinpointed the homes, and even temporary addresses, of IRA personnel to the Four Square Laundry team of Sue and Teddy and the results were positive.

Yes, August 1972 was a great month for the Security Services – everything they touched seemed to turn to gold. Their good fortune continued into September.

But, just like King Midas, this golden touch was fatally flawed.

The Freds were getting cocky and homesick. They were getting to be like nitro-glycerine – something that needed to be handled with the utmost care.

Top of the list were the Freds Seamus Wright and Kevin McKee. Wright was a newlywed when the MI6 cash had turned his head. His new bride was now pregnant and giving him an ear bashing on the phone.

McKee was a gun fetishist. He liked to wear a shoulder holster with a 9mm Browning on board at all times. Ginge, the keeper of the Freds, used to humour him and allow it, although it made Jack and the boys jumpy, even though they knew there were no rounds in the mag as the MRF boys never carried personal weapons in their compound.

Jack found something truly distateful about the Freds. No real soldier likes a traitor, a turncoat, an apostate. Yes, apostate was the perfect word to describe Wright, McKee and the third member of MI6's Holy Trinity, Lewis Hammond, in Northern Ireland's Holy War. Jack believed Northern Ireland was awash with religion but lacked any "Christianity".

The MRF were the conflict's heretics. They were anti-establishment, anti-authoritarian, and pretty well out of control.

Official doctrines such as the Yellow Card – the Rules of Engagement for shooting on the streets of Belfast – and the DCI – District Council Instructions – otherwise known as the Army "Bible" were jettisoned. The MRF even wrote their own SOP – Standard Operational Procedures – so they could virtually make it up as they went along.

It was a dirty war and the so-called un-badged "SAS" – the MRF – were fighting dirty.

As for the Freds "apostates" was definitely the right description for this trio of likely lads. Jack thought it would be probably better for all concerned if one day the prodigal pair of McKee and Wright were added to the conflict's ever-increasing casualty list.

As usual, Jack was right.

Wright was getting used to the large sums of money, £500-£600 ,– when the the average weekly wage of the time was about £20 – in return for each piece of accurate information on the IRA supplied to MI6 at Lisburn. Nine times out of ten, it checked out.

He gave details of the IRA command structure in West Belfast and had private screenings of newsreels, freeze-framed so that he could put names to faces. He even informed on childhood friends who were Republican sympathizers.

He was also correct in his estimates on the strength of both wings of the IRA in West Belfast. Many of the mugshots on the MRF Ops Room wall were there simply because he had fingered them and would bear responsibility for many of their deaths. Had Wright ever seen the Ops Room, wall he would have realised the enormity of his treachery.

He never did, though. It was the Holy of Holies – the MRF's inner sanctum. Instead, he radiated the naive invincibility displayed by many young men in their early 20's. Too young to know any better and intoxicated by the whiff of espionage, he was used by the cruel and cynical men of MI6, who knew he could never come back in from the cold and return to his old life.

He was an accident waiting to happen, but these were heady days, and he agreed to travel to England for intensive training in the MI6 spy school just outside London.

This was to be his downfall. He missed his pregnant wife back in Andersonstown. She thought her husband worked on building sites in the UK. To support the cover story, MI6 always posted his "pay check" home from a London address.

Wright phoned her many times, both from England and Palace Barracks. The calls were routed via the military phone network to avoid tracing. This was a precaution in case the IRA were smart enough to have anyone working in Post Office Telecommunications – unlikely in Northern Ireland because the telephone workers were almost exclusively Protestant.

It was during one of the telephone calls from London that Wright's wife asked him to come back home. However, because he was a member of the IRA, and did not have "permission" to go away to work in the first place, he was worried about the reaction of the West Belfast IRA boss, Brendan Hughes, if he just suddenly arrived back on the scene.

He agreed to come back home on the condition that his wife contacted Hughes and cleared the way for his return. She got in touch with the IRA commander, who was also known by the nickname "Darkie". He told her a man wanting to look after his pregnant wife was understandable and "all would be forgiven". He said that they looked forward to having Seamus "back in the fold".

Wright contacted Kevin McKee, back in Palace Barracks and told him the "good news". Both decided to go back home.

Their handlers warned them that this course of action would be extremely dangerous, but the Freds had made up their minds and were not to be dissuaded.

Wright arrived back in Belfast with a handler and, after reportedly having a night of passion with his wife, met up with McKee. The pair reported to Brendan Hughes.

It was a trap. IRA interrogators quickly elicited the truth

– that the pair worked for the British. They also gave up the identity of the third Fred, Louis Hammond, who had been listed as "missing in action" by the IRA.

The pair compromised the MRF's undercover operations, the Four Square Laundry and the Gemini massage parlour, and revealed the location of the Laundry Offices at College Square East in central Belfast.

After five days of interrogation the IRA did not impose a sentence of summary execution. Instead, they ingeniously put Wright and McKee back into Palace Barracks as if nothing had happened, with a remit to spy for them. Wright may have naively felt some security in being a "double agent".

At this point, Jack and the MRF were not even aware that MI6 had let the Freds out. The MI6 kept this information close to their chest as they realised the two men had probably been "turned" and planned to feed false information back to the IRA through them.

Had MI6 had been out-bluffed by the extent of the pair's treachery? Perhaps not. Perhaps they just gambled on what was to happen next. Had MI6 scrapped the Four Square operation there and then, the IRA would have known the game was up.

The clock was now ticking not only on the MRF covert operations but also on the lives of Wright and McKee and every one else involved. Had Jack or Ken realised what was going on they would have pulled their people out. As it was, the pendulum had swung fully in the IRA's favour – they now had the initiative and the element of surprise.

MI6 had hung the MRF out to dry.

• • •

Jack slid back the driver's window of the Mini Cooper. It was getting stuffy in there. The time was only 1100 hours but, for an October day, it was pretty warm. He looked up as Sue and Ted passed by in the laundry van.

L/Cpl. Sarah Warkes made eye contact with Jack for a split second and was gone as the pair drove the Morris van into the Twinbrook Estate in West Belfast. They had just had a snack, "elevensies", picking up some takeaway food in the Whiterock area and stopping to eat in a lay-by.

Ted, "Teddy Bear" as the kids on the Catholic Estates called him – Sapper Edward Stuart – was on top form when he met Jack later. Jack had just finished photographing a "laundry" delivery using a telephoto lens earlier that morning.

Ted was full of mirth and banter passed between the pair as they discussed the next delivery run. Jack had to keep tabs on the Four Square pair and keep HQ informed of their progress.

Had they been together in the mess, Jack would have happily downed a few pints with Ted, but he decided to turn down the offer of joining the covert team for some food at the roadside as he did not want his vehicle to be linked with the laundry van. You never know who might drive by and see them drinking cuppas from the same Thermos flask.

The rest of the delivery round looked pretty routine – legitimate laundry business rather than the dirty stuff MI6 was interested in – so Jack continued to practice his aimless driving around the West Belfast area. His Mini was a familiar sight and as a news-hungry photojournalist, he was often seen to be out "ambulance chasing".

It was then he heard the unmistakeable sound of automatic gunfire.

Jack stopped the car.

He squeezed out of the cramped confines of the blue BMC Mini and stood upright.

More shots. The unmistakable sound of a Thompson sub-machine gun.

"HQ this is Nine-Zero. Gun shots heard from the direction of Twinbrook Estate. I am going into investigate. Please keep me advised. Over."

"Roger Nine-Zero. Be careful. Out."

Jack knew the other Nine-Zero call signs would have heard the transmissions and now knew of his intentions.

He quickly headed towards Twinbrook. It took him a full 20 minutes.

His worst fears greeted him.

The Four Square van stood riddled with bullets and the RUC was on the scene. Camera in hand, Jack advanced, not knowing if the attackers had fled or were still in the vicinity.

The RUC men were on edge. Guns drawn, they scanned the nearby houses. Jack could see that there was a casualty in the van. Ted.

Suddenly, the front door of a nearby house opened and a RUC officer brought out an ashen-faced Sarah Warkes. Jack had seen all he needed.

He made as if to take some pictures of the scene, then jumped back in to the Mini and was on the road out of Twinbrook. Jack was just about to press the transmit foot switch when the radio crackled into life.

"All stations. All stations. RTB, RTB. Out."

"Nine-Zero. Roger. Out."

Jack heard the other Nine-Zero calls signs comply with the order to RTB – return to base.

Back at Palace Barracks, the full extent of MI6's reckless gamble lay for all to see exposed in the cruel light of day. There was no hiding place for the Spooks.

Their hands were seeped in blood.

As well as the delivery van, the MRF's operations at the Gemini massage parlour, and the Four Square Laundry offices in College Square East had been hit in a well planned and executed IRA operation.

At 1500 hours, Captain Hamish McGregor called the 30 men of the MRF into the briefing room.

"Gentlemen, I have some bad news. One of our chaps – Sapper Edward Stuart – who, as I think you all know, has been operating with the Freds, was murdered this morning by an active service unit of the 1st Battalion of the Irish Republican Army in the Twinbrook Estate.

"Sapper Stuart was operating undercover as a laundry van driver when he and Lance Corporal Sarah Warke, of the Women's Royal Army Corps, came under concerted attack by gunmen using automatic weapons.

"Sapper Stuart was unarmed, as was of course the Lance Corporal, in an area that was busy with ordinary people going about their everyday lives. The MRF mission was an unarmed intelligence gathering operation on behalf of the security services and posed no threat to the law abiding civilian population. This was a particularly cowardly attack, and quite frankly what we have lately come to expect from an enemy who have no regard for the rules of war, common decency or human life.

"Fortunately, Lance Corporal Warkes had the presence of mind to take action to preserve her life and, with the help of local people, survived the savage attack. No other personnel were involved. You can be assured I have conveyed all our condolences to Stuart's family and next of kin.

"I am sure this setback will only stiffen your resolve to bring these criminals to justice. Let's get the IRA bastards!"

A cheer greeted his rallying call.

There was a buzz in the room as the MRF men filed out. They would soon be saying their own traditional farewell to their fallen comrade.

Jack headed for the Ops Room where he greeted Pud.

"How bad is it exactly?"

"Hi, Jack. It is bad, but better than it sounds," he said clasping a ream of papers. "The IRA is claiming to have killed a total of five undercover British Agents. The truth, as you might expect, is somewhat different. Through luck, rather than judgement, we lost just the one. But the chief has gone through the roof and is demanding to know who cocked up."

The chief was Brigadier General (Sir) Harry Tuzo, who Jack had known for many years. They fought together in Sarawak, Borneo, in the early sixties.

Jack's SAS patrols, operating deep behind the lines in Kalamantan, would call Tuzo's Ghurkha Battalions in to interdict Indonesian troops illegally crossing into the British protectorate.

Pud started to read the official record of events:

"At 1115 hours, there were simultaneous attacks on the Four Square Laundry van at the Twinbrook Estate, the Laundry's Offices in College Square East and the Gemini Massage Parlour in Antrim Road.

"In a sustained attack at Juniper Park, the laundry van took multiple rounds of automatic fire from two assailants, leading investigators to believe that the IRA suspected it might have contained concealed personnel. It did not. The attackers fled before security forces arrived.

"Another IRA Active Service Unit arrived at the laundry office building with the intention of killing the occupants. In their haste, an automatic weapon was accidently discharged in the stairwell. Armed MRF personnel situated on the third floor heard the shot and prepared to repel the attack. In their panic, the attackers abandoned their mission at the sound of movement above and fled. They subsequently evaded capture.

"At the Gemini Massage Parlour, two cars pulled up in the car park. Four armed men from the first car entered the building and started to clear it of clients. The girls were also told to leave.

"Two armed men from the second car entered the office of the Madame, Kitty O'Neill. No MRF personnel were on the premises at the time. Discovering this, the IRA team began a systematic search of the premises, during which they uncovered surveillance equipment. The Madame is now missing, believed to be in the hands of the IRA."

Pud put down the carbon copy of the report and waited for Jack to respond.

"So who's to blame for this fucking mess then?" asked Jack.

"It doesn't take a genius to work that out!" Pud pirouetted as he replied.

In his hand now was another piece of paper informing the MRF that the two Fred's Wright and McKee were "missing."

"We need to get to them before the IRA do," said Jack with a vicious gleam in his eye.

"You might find that a bit difficult. They've probably been fed to the pigs by now," said Pud.

Jack nodded but he wasn't convinced. His SAS training had taught him never to accept that someone was dead until you had seen the body. Jack's instinct was to get out on the streets and have a look-see.

In West Belfast, it was always revealing to visit the Republican haunts in the hours after a major incident. Some chose to lay low, other's would be as bold as brass out on the streets.

The Mini's tyres squealed as he left the Palace Barracks compound and headed west towards Jean's house in Andersonstown. There were more Army and RUC roadblocks than normal. It seemed the world and his wife were looking for the fugitive Freds.

Things had cooled down with Jean during September. She had paid a surprise visit to "Jack's" flat in Helen's Bay during late August. Earlier in the year, Jack had made the mistake of taking her to "his" flat while the full-time occupant, Ann Mary, was away visiting her parents in Cape Town.

He had been desperate for a shag and it was cheaper than a hotel room. As Jean didn't have a car it was, unlikely she would ever return without him, Jack had reasoned. However, on August Bank Holiday Sunday, Jack discovered the element of surprise can be just as devastating in love as in war.

He had answered the doorbell of the flat in Bridge Road opposite the railway station at about 1000 hours in his boxer shorts. God knows who he thought would be calling, but Jean was the last person he expected to see on the doorstep.

The last person Jean expected to see behind Jack at the top of the stairs, wearing nothing but a smile, was Ann Mary. Fortunately for all present, Jean fainted on the spot.

When she finally came to, Jack's "sister" was now on her way to board a ship back to Liverpool and then catch the train North to Glasgow.

She had just been "getting dressed" when Jean had called.

"How long had I been out?" asked Jean.

"Long enough to scare the living daylights out of me," said Jack. "My sister helped me carry you upstairs before she had to dash for the train. She sends you her best wishes by the way. In the end it was my magical kisses which brought you back to life."

"Just like Sleeping Beauty and Prince Charming?" asked Jean.

"Yes, poppet."

Jack then pulled back the bedclothes and used all his powers of persuasion to quell any lingering doubts.

"Just so long as she never visits the Royal Hotel we will be OK," Jack had confided to Ann Mary in Bangor later.

Ann Mary lived in the real world. She was a sophisticated woman of the 1970's and understood that the "other girls" were just part of Jack's job.

"Just like James Bond 007 – but more believable," she often reassured herself, twirling the precious watch, a present from Jack, around her wrist, "and much better looking than Sean Connery in *Diamonds are Forever*."

Now it was Jack's turn to knock on Jean's door. While he waited for an answer, Jack turned and surveyed the panorama. The leaves of the trees nearby had their autumn colours. Just up the road, a blue Ford Cortina stood parked facing the house. Two men were sitting in it; one was reading the paper the other smoking a cigarette.

Jack made a mental note of the registration number – he would check it out when he got back to base. Hopefully it would not be a 175cc BSA Bantam.

The door opened.

"Yes," said Jean.

Jack stretched out his arms. Jean took a step back. She was breathless. Jack liked that he had this effect he had on women.

She moved forwards and held him on the doorstep for a few seconds.

"You had better come in," she said finally and ushered him into the lounge.

Her brother, Ryan, was sitting watching television. He

half-turned towards Jack and gave a casual sign of recognition and welcome with his hand.

The children's TV programme *Fingerbobs* was on the BBC. Fingermouse, a mouse consisting of a grey paper cone head with paper ears, whiskers and a grey cotton glove for the body, made his entrance.

"Fingermouse, Fingermouse, I am a sort of wonder mouse," he sang.

For a second, Jack thought the IRA man was actually going to join in.

"Have you seen this? It's funny!" Ryan said to his sister.

She shook her head seemingly in pity and went off into the kitchen to get some tea. Jack stood silently for a moment. He smelt a distinctive odour in the room he recognised, but its presence in the current domestic setting was incongruous. He couldn't put his finger on what it was.

The awkward silence in the room continued.

Then Gulliver, a seagull with a head made from a white ping-pong ball placed over a thumb, joined the on-screen finger-puppet menagerie. Enough was enough.

Jack followed Jean into the kitchen and placed his hands around her slender waist. She took his fingers in her hands and firmly removed them.

"What's the matter, poppet?" asked Jack.

"Nothing," she replied and turned her attention to making tea.

Something was up. Jean usually greeted such amorous advances with enthusiasm.

"I'll just use the loo if that's OK," he said, puzzled by the rebuff, and climbed the stairs. Jack needed time to think.

On the penultimate step before the landing, something glistened metallic-bronze.

It was a single bullet.

Jack looked down, picked it up and then looked upward. Directly above him was the attic trapdoor.

He quietly stood on the blanket box on the landing, displaced the trapdoor and groped into the darkness.

His hands immediately felt the unmistakeable cold of gunmetal. Then wood. Then he felt a round magazine.

Jack put the trapdoor back and quickly went to the toilet. He sat there with his jeans around his ankles and turned the stubby .45 calibre bullet around in his fingertips.

Well, that explained why a grown man was to be found spending his afternoon viewing *Watch with Mother* on the television, usually the domain of the under-fives. He had obviously been cleaning a Thompson sub-machine gun on the dining room table when Jack had rung the doorbell.

The men outside in the car were now worried Jack greatly. Potentially outnumbered, and with the killings earlier in the day still in the front of his mind, Jack the Hack was going to have to make his excuses and leave.

"Poppet, how do you feel like a trip out tonight?"

Jack was gambling on getting a negative response.

"Sorry, Jack. Ryan and I have promised mother we would stay in tonight and keep her company. Well, you know she isn't herself, don't you?"

Jack was in the starting blocks. A quick peck on the cheek and he was out of the front door. Ten seconds later, he was behind the wheel and driving past the blue Cortina.

Back at Palace Barracks, Jack quickly checked the suspect vehicle's registration. The Cortina belonged to none other than one Mr Daniel Stobbart, photographer extraordinaire.

Jack thought he recognised it from somewhere – he had seen Joseph the concierge at the Europa Hotel valet parking it. But it hadn't been Stobbart at the wheel or in the passenger seat.

Jack rewound in his mind to the few moments he had seen both the men's faces.

He had certainly seen one of the faces before. But where? Jack would have to sleep on it.

Jack always slept well after a passionate encounter with Ann Mary so perhaps this was a good excuse to see her. Not that he needed an excuse – she was always on his mind.

The way The Troubles were turning out, Jack sometimes wondered whether he had done the right thing by bringing her over to Northern Ireland. Sometimes he wondered whether he had done the right thing coming to the Province. The number of casualties was soaring as the year progressed. Hardly a night passed without multiple killings.

He rang the Royal Hotel.

The receptionist answered but it was not Ann Mary. It was Janet. She was a young Protestant girl who shared duties on the front desk.

She liked Jack too.

"Jack, it's good to hear from you. How can I help you?"

"I just wanted to get a message to Ann Mary to say I will be down tonight. Has she left already?"

It was getting late now. Jack assumed that she had already signed out or maybe it was her night off.

"Ann Mary? We havn't seen her since Friday. But she left a message in case you rang."

"What was it?" asked Jack.

"Nothing special. She just wanted to thank you for the teddy bear," said Janet.

"The what?"

"The teddy bear. Is it some kind of lover's code?" she said excitedly.

"The bear. Oh yes, I understand," said Jack.

Understand? Did he fuck! Jack didn't have a clue. He was out into the car park and on the road in a few seconds. Something was up. Ann Mary would, without fail, contact him if she was going to take a few days off or was feeling unwell. If she had so much as a sniffle Jack knew all about it. Pity any pedestrian between here and Helens Bay.

There was, of course, the multitude of roadblocks. As darkness gathered, trigger-happy Greens viewed any speeding car as a legitimate target.

Shoot first, ask questions later.

A further 25 minutes and Jack turned into the car park outside Helens Bay railway station in Bridge Road. He slammed the car door and sprinted the 20 yards to the flat.

It was ajar. Not wide open – there was just a gap of a few inches between the door and the frame. This was unusual, but as this first door only gave access to the building, which consisted of two flats, it wasn't decisive in concluding there was anything wrong.

Still, with his instincts telling him all was not well, Jack wasn't going to take any chances.

He pushed the door gently inwards. The number 22 in black passed his line of sight and then he had a clear view of the hall stairs. Twenty-two was the same number as the Regiment – he hadn't really thought about it until that moment. Another coincidence or did he subconsciously chose the flat because of that common denominator?

Jack drew his 9mm automatic and inched his way up the stairs, listening for any sound that would betray the presence of an intruder, or preferably, the best-case scenario: lovely Ann Mary.

Outside Flat 2, he stopped and put his ear to the door.

Nothing.

He took the Yale key from his leather jacket, silently slid it into the lock, and gently turned it to the left.

Click.

It opened. Jack pushed the door gently and it swung into the hallway.

"Ann Mary, are you home?"

Silence.

Jack moved into the empty kitchen. A lone coffee cup stood sentry on the Formica worktop. The milk bottle keeping it company was displaying a green hue, suggesting it was on the turn.

Jack didn't need Hercules Poirot to tell him that if this was a crime scene then there was already evidence that it, whatever *it* was, had happened some days ago.

Jack's mind raced: this could be an "unhappy ending".

Jack's long-term intentions for himself and Ann Mary were the traditional fairytale ending: happily ever after. It appeared the bottom could be about to drop out of the world of Jack Gillespie.

The lounge was clear.

The bathroom, too.

That just left the bedrooms.

The guestroom was cold and musty.

Next the passion palace.

In his mind, Jack saw option one: Ann Mary spread sideways across divan breathlessly awaiting his entrance.

And option two: blood everywhere.

What he did not expect was a bloody big black brute of a teddy bear sitting on top of his pillows with a note pinned to its chest.

He grabbed the piece of paper.

It bore just the imprint of a scarlet kiss in expensive lipstick.

He scrunched it up into a ball and batted it away with one clenched fist hitting the other. Realising that he had just unconsciously repeated his farewell ritual, Jack hastily retrieved the paper and carefully uncrumpled it.

On the back of the scrap that bore the lipstick missive, he could just make out the imprint of a telephone number from the sheet of paper that had once been above this one on a notepad.

So Poirot is on board this mission, he smiled to himself.

Jack opened the wardrobe. Ann Mary's cases were still there. He opened her knicker drawer. The Janet Reger lingerie he had so expensively purchased was all present and correct. Jack stood to attention.

"Where the fuck is she?"

His investigation switched to the dressing table drawers, scattering the contents on the bed, floor and padded stool.

Then it fell out.

Her South Africa passport was still here!

Jack heard footsteps on the stairs.

Ann Mary, he prayed.

Instead, the face, which confronted Jack, was of a nervous RUC officer – nervous because Jack was still holding his weapon.

"Security Forces," said Jack.

"Thank God," replied the RUC man as he collapsed, cap in hand, into a lounge chair. "B'Jesus! I thought my time had come! Now tell me what's going on here. We had a report of something suspicious happening so I came straight over from Bangor."

"I wish I knew. I have only just arrived myself," said Jack. "Who made the report?"

"It was a woman, young, from the sound of her voice – she didn't leave a name."

"Did she sound South African?" Jack asked.

"No she was from here. Perhaps Belfast, I would say."

Despite the mess, Jack reassured the RUC man that all was hunky dory.

Nothing could be further than the truth.

Jack locked up the flat and headed back to the car. Several heads turned towards him and his ursine friend as he walked across the car park.

• • •

"It's a Steiff," said Pud who knew a thing or two about bears.

"I know its dead, I just want to know what kind of fucking teddy bear it is," fumed Jack.

"A Steiff is a very rare and valuable stuffed bear produced in Germany since the end of the 19th Century. This, unless I am very much mistaken, is a very rare one indeed. It's black, and many believe that Steiff's black bear was only created in 1912 to commemorate the loss of life on the Titanic, which, of course, was built here in Belfast at Harland and Wolfe. But, a very small number of bears have turned up that possibly pre-date this. These bears are even more rare, although there are no records of when they were actually produced. This bear is possibly worth thousands of pounds to a collector. Can I keep it?"

"No you fucking can't. It's the property of the MRF and, in any case, it's me who it keeps following around," thundered Jack.

"It usually has a button just on its left ear but this one has one on its right one as well. It has a name written on it," Pud continued.

He picked up a magnifying glass off the counter.

"Chieftain', I think. The writing's tiny."

Jack went silent, grabbed the bear and left.
He had been rumbled.

Chapter 14
One Final Foray

It was the early 1970s and Jack was on the scrapheap. His last covert operation was a balls-up from beginning to end, and the SAS Warlord was employed as an instructor at the Royal Artillery Junior Leader's Regiment at Nuneaton in Warwickshire, England. Teaching the kids how to kill. Well, at least how to shoot. Killing was something different.

Instead of battle hardened SAS patrols, boys between sixteen and seventeen-and-a-half now hung on Jack's every word. He was a man who had killed – hundreds of times – and they were still pulling the legs off flies. When their fingers were not stuck up their noses or other more unsavoury places, that is.

For Jack, this was a punishment detail. He was better than this. He knew it, the Brass knew it, but how else did you bring someone who had learnt how to walk guided only by the stars down to earth with a bump?

There were bits that Jack liked at Nuneaton. Sorting out the bullies that have always plagued British Army training centres was one of them. He playfully "reformed" them with his fists. In battle, you need men who are properly motivated alongside you, not those who fear you. Leadership should be formed by example not by coercion was Jack's belief. Also bullies begat bullies. Jack begat soldiers.

It was January 1972 and it was freezing on the live-firing ranges. A hundred young soldiers had accompanied Jack to Hythe Ranges in the county of Kent for their first taste of weapons firing at Lydd Training Camp.

Winter sunshine bathed the Skill at Arms Camp behind the groynes and sea defences of the shingle beach looking out over the Straits of Dover. However, incongruously for a Jungle Range, there was ice on the trees and frost on the cinder track.

Sergeant Jack Gillespie was instructing on the use of the Sterling Mark III sub-machine gun, the main ambush weapon of the British Army since the early 1960's.

Each of the youngsters who, up until now, had only handled guns in the classroom walked along a marked out path firing at targets as they appeared without warning. Jack stood at the end of the facility known as the "Close Quarter Battle Range" providing detailed supervision of the firer.

"Two rounds at each target!" Jack screamed at some idiot who had mistakenly switched his weapon to automatic fire and had half-emptied his magazine into a Figure 11 target that had popped up startlingly in his path.

Suddenly Jack heard the range warden shout that there had been an accident in the brick-built hut behind the firing point at the start of the range.

He sprinted back and found Junior Gunner Les Fowler lying on the floor bleeding to death from eight bullet wounds in the upper part of both legs. Jack guessed that a main artery in one leg had severed, and that Fowler had already lost too much blood to have much of a fighting chance.

Some stupid boy soldier had stolen a full magazine of 9mm rounds and gone into the toilets with his SMG. He had loaded the weapon and somehow accidently pulled the trigger, scything down Fowler who was standing at a urinal.

Most of those at the scene had not even seen a drop of blood spilled before, never mind a bucketful, but Jack had been in the thick of it since Malaya in the fifties and knew exactly what to do.

He ripped off the boy's trousers and saw that one of the rounds had gone from the right leg into the lower groin. By applying force to a pressure point in Fowler's lower stomach, Jack managed to stop any further loss of blood. He then applied shell dressings to all the bullet entry points and administered morphine to ease the shocked youngster's pain.

Jack continued his battle to save Fowler's life in the ambulance as it raced the six miles towards Folkestone and the waiting operating theatre. The ambulance crew had no experience in dealing with bullet wounds. He was on his own.

Thanks to Jack's efforts, and despite losing pints of blood, Fowler was still alive on arrival at the Royal Victoria Hospital.

When the hospital's casualty team finally took over in the emergency unit, Jack was exhausted, but he remained at the hospital throughout the night, keeping vigil as surgeons fought valiantly to save the life of the 16-year-old.

By a sheer stroke of luck, some of the United Kingdom's top surgeons were present at the hospital attending a conference. Their expertise and intervention doubtlessly saved a desperate situation, helping their Kent colleagues pull off a remarkable feat of modern medicine.

Fowler remained on the "very seriously ill list" for some weeks, and it would be months and a series of operations before he finally walked out of the hospital and out of the army for good.

Jack never saw him again.

The incident put Jack back in the army's good books and

with a citation and a promotion to Sergeant Major. He knew it would not be long before he would be on the move again.

He was right.

When the call came from the Ministry of Defence, it was a surprise. It was not another foray into the jungles of the Far East or detachment to the deserts of Oman. It was almost a home posting just a few miles "doon the watter" from Glasgow.

OK, it was way doon the watter – Belfast

The calls to arms had come right from the top. Jack had worked for Brigadier Frank Kitson in Malaya and General Harry Tuzo in Borneo before, and his Special Forces record ticked all the right boxes for this unique assignment. More importantly, as a Sergeant Major he could now "command" a unit of Sergeants and Corporals – the signature make-up of an elite fighting force.

"There will be a junior officer attached to you for appearances' sake and to liaise with other units, but we want you to follow your instinct. It will be like Borneo 'but with fewer trees'," they told him.

It was "Top Secret".

It was the Military Reaction Force.

The Brass described it as a "plain clothes under-cover unit set up to counter Irish Republican Army raids on innocent targets in Belfast".

During the next few days, Jack was de-kitted. His army uniform and equipment was taken from him. He went to the office of the Royal Army Pay Corp and collected £200 to purchase civilian clothes and generally prepare for his new mission. He then shopped in the John Collier store in Nuneaton for some clobber.

Jack knew that there were no SAS units operating in Northern Ireland. The British Government's new idea, they explained to him, was that a force of "ex-SAS" would operate with a free hand on the streets of Belfast and "clean up the terrorists".

Jack took the midnight ferry from Liverpool to Belfast. Being March, the boat was half-empty and there was lots of room in the usually packed bar.

He had just a few drinks, most of a bottle of Johnny Walker Black Label, "no water, no ice", and then retired to his cabin.

That night the Irish Sea was at its most ferocious. It tossed the ferry around like a cork. Jack didn't get much sleep and when he did, he dreamt he was swimming in a sea of blood. Suddenly, a giant tidal wave swept an avalanche of dismembered legs, arms, torsos and entrails down on him. He woke shaking and sweating. The rest of the night passed slowly.

He was glad when morning came.

Tomato juice and Worcestershire Sauce accompanied his cooked breakfast, and he went up on deck to a bright sunny day. The outline of Belfast was visible on the horizon.

Jack wondered what the future would bring.

He went down below to get his bag. He opened a buff envelope containing the paraphernalia of his new identity. He put a National Union of Journalists Press Card in his top pocket and walked down the gangplank, putting his feet on Irish soil for the first time.

In the small car park, Jack hesitated. A tall well-dressed man approached him and stood facing away from him as if watching the disembarking passengers.

"Penguin," he hissed to no one in particular.

"Dolphin," answered Jack.

The pair walked towards a waiting car. Jack got in the back and was joined by his new companion. The man sat stiffly and pulled down the central armrest so that it formed a barrier between them.

The driver set off en route to Palace Barracks. The conversation was nothing special but Jack had noticed that a green and white Morris Oxford Estate had been on their tail since the ferry terminal.

He alerted "Mr Penguin" to their presence.

Both turned to look out the rear window. Penguin waved his hand.

"Sergeant Major, meet your new men."

• • •

Jack's career had certainly been a rollercoaster ride.

Now, more than a year later, life had turned full circle again. His Belfast cover was blown and Jack was as useful as a chocolate teapot.

But when Ann Mary had joined the ranks of the many "disappeared" in Northern Ireland, he stopped caring much about anything else.

The Spooks had him "pay a visit" to their department at 39 Brigade HQ at Lisburn and told him they were using their "inside" men to find out "what the hell was happening".

Jack one of a few key covert Army personnel known to the Freds, and one theory was that they had given him up under torture along with the Four Square Laundry and the Gemini Massage Parlour. That was the best MI6 had so far – or so they said.

Meanwhile, bored stiff and confined to his quarters in Palace Barracks, Jack just wanted to know where Ann Mary was.

If she were alive, she would have contacted him somehow.

There had been nothing, not a word, since the bear had made its third and final appearance with its lipstick kiss goodbye.

The significance of the bear was now what the US Special Forces called a "no brainer". Jack had been standing so close to such a big clue that even when it stared him in the face he hadn't seen it.

Someone, somewhere, was dropping an unsubtle hint that the game was up and had been doing it for quite a while.

But, who and why?

The black Honey Bear was the mascot of B Squadron SAS in Malaya. Jack was a key member of that elite force. The unanswered question was how his past had caught up with him here in Northern Ireland – a war theatre where his uniform was a leather jacket and jeans?

• • •

A couple of weeks later, Jack was still none the wiser but things had changed. He now had a desk job. He was the liaison officer between the Army in Northern Ireland and the SAS in Hereford.

The MRF were continuing to operate successfully without him with Ken and the SBS boys playing leading roles, although it had become more of a reconnaissance force since he had left.

Shoot and scoot seemed to have gone out of the window for the time being.

The RUC pressure was still on the boys for the Glen Road incident, although Jack seemed to no longer to have "been there" at all.

Meanwhile, the television companies seemed to have discovered the Northern Ireland conflict in a major way. The media hysteria was such that film crews were even filming other film crews filming soldiers firing plastic bullets at stone throwing mobs of youths.

Many foreign film crews were making regular appearances

on the streets of Belfast. Cash often changed hands between unscrupulous overseas producers on a tight deadline and teenage rioters.

"Rent-a-mob" was born.

Maybe if the TV film cameras hadn't been there, the streets would have been calm. However, every minute on the TV news or *World in Action* or *Panorama* made the IRA out to be a bigger force and bigger threat than they actually were.

United States' TV appearances showing British injustice boosted fundraising there no end.

Jack knew what all that Republican pandering to the media was about. He had seen the how the IRA operated that side of things. Look at the way they respected his press card, which wasn't even worth the paper it was printed on.

Just like Vietnam, Northern Ireland's "Troubles" was becoming more and more a TV war.

All the time, sadly but inevitably, the death toll and casualties kept on rising. Bomb followed bomb. Shooting followed shooting. Sectarian funeral followed sectarian funeral.

Jack was no longer there to record the mourners, but, ostensibly, the only place he was missed was in the bar of the Europa Hotel where the story circulated that he had been recalled by his picture editor to Glasgow.

Even the leader of the Protestant Democratic Unionist Party, the Reverend Ian Paisley, asked Danno Stobbart about Jack Gillespie's whereabouts.

The reality of the Northern Ireland situation now was that the British Army, one of the best armies in the world, was being given the run-around by a raggle-taggle bunch of idealists playing soldiers and commanded by a young man, who would have been a second-lieutenant in Her Majesty's finest at best.

By June 1973, with all the British pieces on a game board

constantly rocked by shootings and explosions, it seemed a bloody political stalemate. Even the secret peace talks had stalled.

Meanwhile, British politicians, especially those in Her Majesty's Opposition, the Labour Party, were making questionable statements out of a mixture of frustration and desperation about the future of Northern Ireland, threatening the status quo.

The ruling Conservative Government's inability to resolve The Troubles quickly was damaging their popularity on the mainland. People were fed up with a sectarian dispute they did not understand and the prospect of a General Election was looming. The time had now come for a decisive move.

A wild "endgame" from the MI6 Grandmasters – perhaps even as high as "C" himself.

It was a real Berserker.

• • •

Jack had not been in Palace Barracks for some time. He was busy shuttling back and forth between Northern Ireland, SAS HQ in Hereford, and a top-secret training base at Newark, Nottinghamshire, in England.

In Newark, he was preparing SAS instructors for the inevitable call to take a leading "surveillance role" in the Northern Ireland conflict as it escalated out of control.

Due to the IRA's October 1972 success in attacking the MRF's covert operations, the top Brass immediately decided to phase out the now compromised three call sign ad-hoc set up of one officer and 30 men. It was impossible to deploy regular SAS troopers in Northern Ireland at that moment, as the Ministry Of Defence would obviously have preferred, because of political restraints.

In fact, there was a bizarre rule against employing such elite personnel until some two or three years after their SAS service had ended. There was a list of such available ex-members of the Regiment kept by the MOD.

Quite perversely, this rule did not apply to SBS members – a loophole fully exploited by the MRF. For example, when Jack put in a request for the urgent services of the SAS close quarter battle-weapon instructor, Alexander Prentice, to fine-tune his call signs in early 1972, it was refused. Instead, the MOD sent Jack both a top SBS instructor, and another four SBS men arrived, out of the blue, to beef up the MRF's firepower.

Because of these constraints, the Brass planned a longer-term solution.

In late 1973, they would replace what remained of the MRF with a new crack unit of highly-skilled volunteers known as the 14th Intelligence Company or the DET. It would be open to all members of the armed services and to both sexes. For the first time, women would be able to enlist in a British Army Special Forces unit.

A specially-created Training Wing of the 22nd SAS would prepare its handpicked members for Northern Ireland. Jack was fully involved in this process.

The intensive surveillance and combat training course would take a full nine months to complete. Specialist training for the volunteers and their SAS officers would be vital, as this kind of urban conflict was brand new to the Regiment. The fact that it was on home turf and involved UK subjects meant there were new psychological and practical difficulties facing covert troops.

In years to come, it would be compulsory for all SAS personnel to attend this new concept in training and subsequently hone their newly won skills from active service in Northern

Ireland. If they refused to do either, they would have to leave the Regiment immediately: RTU, which stood for "Return to Unit", was what the "unfortunate" knew it as.

Jack's knowledge and front line experience was vital in this transitional period, and the SAS instructors hung on his every word.

Initially, Jack introduced a mixture of 10 officers, NCOs and privates, including some women, to the tactics successfully employed by the MRF.

The courses would continue throughout the summer and into autumn. However, sitting in the classroom was beginning to cramp Jack's style.

Then in early June 1973, the order came for Jack to return to Palace Barracks, Belfast, and report to the officer commanding the Military Reaction Force.

When Jack arrived in the boss's office, a world-weary looking Hamish McGregor looked up from his desk and said, "I have got someone here who wants to see you Jack."

He left the room and returned with Captain Arthur Watches. Jack could almost hear the James Bond Theme playing as Watches entered the room. He was the officer responsible for overseeing the formation of the MRF in early 1972 and had offered Jack "command" of the unit.

Jack suspected Captain Watches had been pretty close to the Spooks then, but now, with the boss edging slowly towards the door frame, there was no doubt about it – Watches was definitely an MI6 "operative".

"You two know each other," said McGregor. "I'll let you talk in peace."

He closed the door silently behind him.

Captain Watches turned to Jack.

"I have been tasked to set up a very sensitive operation. You must listen carefully and tell me if you think we can do it."

Watches was talking slowly, almost mechanically, as if he was a ham actor struggling with the memory of a script, or perhaps a schoolboy with a half-learnt, half-forgotten poem in Prep school.

"Fire away," said Jack, trying to speed things up.

"I don't need to tell you we live in extremely delicate times." Watches continued.

"A Provisional IRA leader, Gerard Adams, has been having meetings with the British Secret Service representing Her Majesty's Government for some time, but recently "relations" have gone cold.

"All kind of things are happening that appear beyond our control. You see, there are elections here in Northern Ireland soon that we need to ensure go off without a hitch, even if they are a waste of time and of little significance to the bigger picture. Politicians just like to see the people putting a cross on a piece of paper. God knows why."

He stopped babbling and hesitated, as if he had wandered from his prepared text.

"Reliable MI6 sources tell us that on the afternoon of the 23rd June a meeting is planned that will include senior figures of the IRA. Gerry Adams is scheduled to attend, along with, amongst others, the local IRA commander in Andersonstown, Brendan Hughes. You need to challenge the known IRA members and, in the ensuing fight, ensure our man is shot and killed. With a bit of luck, they will think you are a UVF team out to assassinate Adams."

"Jesus Christ, boss!" said Jack. "Assassinate in broad daylight! Are they serious?"

"Deadly serious, Jack. What do you think?"

"It can be done, of course, but it will take some planning.

With a lot of luck, we should be able to carry it out and escape without revealing our true colours," said Jack.

"Good, so you'll do it? Start work and keep me informed of your progress. Good luck!"

With that, Watches left the room.

Jack felt a shudder of anticipation run down his spine.

Excitement – that was the feeling.

Jack was actually looking forward to being target practice for a bunch of Catholic amateur gunmen again. It's incredible how driving a desk for a few months can make you lose that zest for life which comes when you live from second to second as part of a crack team.

Now alone in the boss's office, he looked at the 1973 calendar on the wall. The black Chinagraph pencil crosses, which had already totally obliterated May, were beginning to spread like decay across June.

Jack counted forward to the 23rd.

"Two weeks and counting...," he spoke as he made a mental note.

As he left the room, he noticed the 28th circled in red Chinagraph.

The 28th of June was Ann Mary's birthday. For the last one, Jack had given her the diamond watch. He wondered if she still had it. He wondered if she still had the need to know the time. Was she still alive? He liked to think so. He *needed* to think so in order to keep going. No-one had turned up with her head in a sack yet, so in jungle terms all was not lost. He lived in hope.

Jack went to the briefing room to think. He knew this project was his baby and his baby alone. McGregor had left the room and played no part in the discussions. It was probably for the best. There was no room for passengers.

He started to plan. The mission was unusual to say the least – even in Jack's chequered history of global shenanigans. It wasn't very often that a unit's CO introduced you to a senior office you suspected – no make that *knew* – to be a member of MI6, who then asked you to go and assassinate the leader of the enemy forces.

"Just like that," Jack impersonated Tommy Cooper.

It was no joking matter.

And Jack had a funny feeling that with no written orders, the difficult thing about this attack was not carrying out of the dirty deed but surviving the aftermath, the fallout, of this explosion of violence and death. Whatever that might be.

The MRF escaping alive would be a start. Keeping out of the clutches of the RUC would be good. Not spending the rest of the century behind bars would be even better. If this was a "piratical venture" then the traditional punishment for such piracy was hanging.

If it was ever leaked that this was an officially sanctioned assassination by the British Army, they would never hear the end of it. It would even make Bloody Sunday seem like manslaughter.

Jack imagined a huge nest of hornets being disturbed as he pulled the trigger of the Thompson. It sent them flying with a hail of bullets towards a crowd of IRA men who, for a fraction of a second, stood frozen to the spot and then fell silently to the ground. The dark cloud of insects swarmed above the scene and then descended into hell with the souls of the departed.

Jack closed his eyes tight. His thought processes started to roll.

Right, here we go. The assault will be in broad daylight and, unlike the early days of the MRF, Belfast is now crawling with trigger-happy

Greens. There are no "No Go" areas. So, somehow, the team need co-operation from all branches of security forces on the ground to or there is a danger of a fight breaking out with our own side during the escape.

Two or three cars packed full of armed men scootin' away from a shootin' will make a mouth-watering target for some Rupert fresh from Sandhurst, unless he has it in writing that a plain clothes operation is underway.

OK. The MRF will tell the Greens they plan an outing, even though there is the risk of compromising the whole operation. The local army Brass will not know exactly what we are up to but they will know we are "out and about" and looking for trouble – possibly on their patch. We might even require back up if necessary.

"Heaven forefend!" Jack mimicked a "Rupert" as he

left the briefing room and walked briskly across the compound. He could hear digging. Intrigued, he followed the noise and came across a couple of MRF men with shovels next to a rectangular hole about six feet by three feet behind one of the buildings. It was about four feet deep.

"What goes on fellahs?" Jack said.

One of the pair wiped the sweat from his forehead, looked up, recognised Jack and said, "Just preparing another nice surprise for a kidnap victim."

Next to the hole was a rectangular piece of ground, again about six feet by three feet. It was covered by small white stone chips. At one end was a cross, which had on it the words: "Rest in Peace".

Yet another fake grave.

Jack grunted the old chestnut "Carry on, Macbeth", as a note of approval and was gone.

• • •

A few days later, the MRF call sign Nine-Zero "top team" stood in the briefing room, looking at quite a sophisticated model of the community hall, and surrounding streets of Andersonstown, where the IRA meeting was due to take place on June 23rd.

Pud said that, according to Benson, it had arrived from a "closet friend".

The target location was on a main road – Andersonstown Road, at the junction of Slemish Way – which would make the job a lot easier.

"The plan will involve surprise, aggression, and speed."

SAS – Jack liked saying those letters.

The enemy would be engaged and destroyed before they realised the MRF were there.

Three squad cars, the call signs Nine-Zero, Nine-One, and Nine-Two, would be parked up staggered at intervals along the road. The nearest, call sign Nine-Zero, would be barely 50 yards from the target, ready for immediate action. At such short range and with overwhelming firepower, there was no question. The attack would be devastating.

The briefing was short and to the point. Then it was down to the 30-metre miniature target range in another Army barracks just outside Holywood.

They also practised defensive tactical shooting, using hardened cars as cover, in case the whole thing was a set up and the engagement turned into an ugly shoot out from which shoot and scoot, or even retreat, would not be an option. The MRF would have to wait for the cavalry to arrive, and there was no guarantee that they would. Perhaps they should carry extra ammunition.

On the morning of the mission, MI6 at Lisburn informed Jack that the party "including Gerry Adams" would be arriving at the meeting at precisely 1400 hours.

In the briefing room, Jack ran over the plans again, and again with Peter Adams and John Benson.

After a while, the rest of the patrol members joined them. Jack took the cover off the model and pointed to Slemish Way where it meets Andersonstown Road. He indicated the exact location of the meeting place and the surrounding buildings. He then went through the plan of attack.

When each individual call sign was confident with their precise role, Jack ordered the men to fall out. Most went back to their billets to relax. Read the papers. Some wrote letters.

They would meet again at the armoury at 1230 hours.

For Jack, the safety of his men was of paramount importance. He went to the MRF Ops room to get the latest intelligence coming in from call sign Seven-Zero and Eight-Zero patrol cars on "routine" patrols. They knew call sign Nine-Zero had a "big op", but no clue as to what exactly it was.

The only reports of any interest were of small groups of people gathering on some street corners in Andersonstown.

Possibly lookouts, thought Jack. *Not unusual at all.*

If the operation was successful, and word of the assassination spread, there would be thousands of people on the streets of Belfast rioting and worse. It would be a night to remember.

"Bloody Saturday!"

"Remember me handsome?"

Pud popped his head up from below a counter when he had been rummaging around in a basket.

"Can I interest you in some unusual pictures, young man?"

Pud unfastened the seal of an envelope marked RESTRICTED and pulled out a sheaf of black and white prints. He shoved them underneath Jack's nose on the worktop.

"Where the hell did you get these?" Jack demanded.

"They were in the internal mail a few months ago. They

spilt out of an envelope onto the floor," Pud winked. "I copied them in the darkroom and sent the originals safely on their way. I hadn't seen you around for a while then, so I just hung on to them. What ever happened to you, Jack? You just disappeared all of a sudden. Poof! You never called, you never wrote... You could have been dead for all I knew."

"Can I have them?" Jack said tersely. He was not really in the mood for chitchat – not even with Pud, whom he had a soft spot for.

He already had a lot on his mind and needed a distraction like a hole in the head. And now this.

"Can't see why not," Pud called out as Jack left the room without waiting for an answer.

Back in his quarters in the nearby Sergeant's mess, Jack laid out the photographs on the green candlewick bedspread.

One black and white print showed Ryan McLaughlin with Danno Stobbart and another man standing by a parked car in Denewood Park, Andersonstown, Belfast.

Another showed McLaughlin outside the Royal Hotel in Bangor. More pictures showed McLaughlin with other men, most of whom Jack did not recognise.

"Wait a minute, that's that bastard Seamus Wright," Jack said aloud.

He turned the photo over to see if was dated.

It wasn't.

Jack quickly sifted through the other pictures until the last one appeared.

It was a long-range telephoto shot.

It showed Ryan McLaughlin pretending to look into the window of a village shop as a woman walked by. Although his body was parallel to the shop window, McLaughlin's eyes were fixed on the woman.

Jack's fist hit the wall.

A trickle of blood from his hand left a dark smudge on the green gloss paint that reached halfway up the wall by his bunk.

It was Helens Bay.

The woman was Ann Mary.

• • •

The MRF men met at the armoury as arranged and began the process of drawing out weapons.

Call sign Nine-Two: rear seat: Cpl. Bill "Ginge" Barnard, Parachute Regiment, Thompson sub-machine gun; driver: Cpl. Nigel Shrivers, Welsh Guards, 9mm pistol; squad commander: Sgt. Peter Adams, Royal Marine Commandos, SMG.

Call sign Nine-One: rear seat: Cpl. Jacky Battrick, RAF Regiment, SMG; driver: Cpl. Joe Blackmore, Royal Engineers, 9mm pistol; squad commander: Sgt. John Benson, Royal Military Police, 9mm pistol.

It was call sign Nine-Zero's turn next. Rear seat: Sgt. Ken Cooke, Special Boat Service, SMG; driver: Les Hoskins, Parachute Regiment, 9mm pistol; Patrol Commander: Sgt. Maj. Jack Gillespie, Thompson sub-machine gun.

Tooled up, the team drew their ammo and headed for the cars.

Jack had chosen a 1970 blue Rover 3500S. Its V8 184-horsepower engine would be powerful enough for all eventualities.

The Rover 3500S had a car body composed of non-structural steel panels. They could all be unbolted and removed from an underlying monocoque structure. This meant it was easier to armour the car with composite panels, and offered the best protection of any of the MRF cars modified so far.

Rover designers had originally dreamed of installing a revolutionary gas turbine engine in the model, hence the unusual design features. A prototype was made but the jet power programme soon abandoned. The traditional internal combustion engine lived to fight another day.

This conventional Rover was stolen from the car park of the Europa Hotel especially for the mission and, apart from a test drive, today was to be its only outing before being sent to swim with the fishes in Belfast Loch.

As standard equipment, the MRF's top of the range Rover also had what the boys called a "penguin detector" – an Ice Alert warning device, factory-installed to sense humidity and warn the driver as outside air temperatures dropped. It was not a lot of use in June but a good talking point for the nervous amongst those on board.

The second car was yet another trusty Morris Oxford Estate – not a car to own in Northern Ireland. The REME boys, who armoured the vehicles, said they preferred it as it was the easiest to harden in a hurry but the model became increasingly difficult to find and lift. The final vehicle was a white Ford Cortina – another sturdy MRF workhorse.

"OK, chaps, this is it. You all know the drill, but any questions before we go?" asked Jack.

There were none; the boys just wanted to get on with it, get it over with, and then enjoy a night of celebration in the mess.

At 1250 hours, the three call signs left the base and headed for Belfast. The drivers maintained variable distances between the cars – a tactic that concealed their true purpose quite well. It did not look like a convoy of like-minded individuals heading for the same destination or, more to the point, a military raiding party armed to the teeth. They were just some nice young blokes sharing a ride into town.

Everything was strangely calm in Jack's car. There was none of the banter that usually disguised the nerves of the team on a patrol when they did not know what would happen next. Les hummed an unrecognisable tune as he drove. It could have been Z Cars. It could have been Tchaikovsky's Violin Concerto, which was Jack's favourite and now filled his head as they drove.

Today they knew exactly what they were going to do:

Assassinate the leadership of the IRA.

Tomorrow morning, Gerry Adams' picture would have disappeared from the most-wanted wall of the MRF Ops Room and instead be seen splashed on front pages of the Sunday newspapers.

"IRA Gunned Down in Sectarian Murder."

Or even: "Mass Murder".

By then the boys would be sleeping it off in bed and Jack would be safely back in Hereford.

The Rover 3500S took the Holywood Road, then Newtownards Road into Belfast. Les turned left over the bridge through a few side streets until they came to Grosvenor Road and they turned right. Nine-Zero then drove until they reached the junction with the Falls Road and turned left.

Nine-Zero went along the Falls Road for a couple of miles then turned left at the fork in the road, which then became Andersonstown Road.

Jack called the other cars with his location and ordered them to close in.

There was to be an interval of 10 minutes between the first and the last cars taking up their assigned positions. They were then to maintain visual contact with each other at all times.

As Nine-Zero pulled into its starting position, the time was 1340 hours – not long to wait. Jack saw the other two cars pull into their designated spots.

1400 hours. Adrenalin was surging through their bodies. They checked their weapons on their laps.

Suddenly, there was a lot of activity going on outside the meeting place. In the distance, Jack could see several cars travelling along the road towards the hall.

Jack pressed the transmit stud in the passenger foot well.

"Get ready! The Eagle is about to land. Over."

"Nine-One. Roger. Out"

"Nine-Two. Roger. Out!"

The MRF men cocked their weapons.

A man with a pistol held close to his side got out of the first car to pull up outside the meeting place. Two more cars pulled in. He looked up and down the pavement, oblivious to the danger no more than 80 yards away.

Another two men quickly joined him. They then walked to the second vehicle, one opened the door and Gerry Adams appeared.

Jack cradled the Thompson in his hands. His foot felt the presence of the waiting radio transmit stud. His lips parted slightly, sucked in breath, ready to exhale "Go!"

Instead, Jack stopped dead as the car speaker crackled:

"Zero to all units ABORT! ABORT! RTB, ASP. Over"

Jack pressed the transmit stud again. This time successfully.

"Nine-Zero Abort! RTB. Roger. Out."

Jack heard the other two cars acknowledge Zero's transmission.

"Nine-One Abort. Roger. Out."

"Nine-Two Abort. Roger. Out."

Jack then transmitted: "Nine-One Nine-Two. This is Nine-Zero move out now. Out"

Les put the Rover into gear and, as if in slow motion, Jack's team glided silently the few yards towards Gerry Adams and his companions now surrounded by a reception committee.

Suddenly, Ryan McLaughlin turned around and looked straight through the windscreen at Jack. He blew him a kiss.

Goodbye.

Jack's hand tightened on the Thompson and then Nine-Zero was gone.

Jack turned and watched the others follow unhindered.

Then emptiness.

Just like the Grand Old Duke of York, Jack had marched them up to the top of the hill and then down again. Everyone looked at each other and shrugged. Never in all Jack's years of undercover and regular army operations had someone called off the ball when the shot was about to be taken.

Were they watching? Was someone watching?

• • •

The blatant truth – as clear as day to all in Nine-Zero – was that if one tenth of a second had clicked by, then Gerry Adams and everyone surrounding him in the street and in the cars would have been dead. Cut down in a hail of a hundred rounds of annihilation from the .45 Calibre Thompson twins at point blank range.

Gerry Adams was a very lucky man that day.

A lucky man indeed.

Chapter 15

The Mything Force

It was 0230 hours, Jack was down on his hands and knees looking at the underside of the Mercedes with a small torch. The dim beam was woefully inadequate for the task but it was all he had on hand.

An hour or so earlier, he had received a call revealing his cover had been broken.

"You had better watch your back Jack, because an active service unit of the IRA could be on your case," warned the caller. That was why he was now down on the ground searching for an explosive device on the underside of his car.

A new Government agency had published his location for all to see. All that work, all the form filling, wasted. Bank accounts, insurance policies, social security number, pensions – the lot.

Was it a cock up or conspiracy? With this new Labour Government, you could never be sure which.

Jack liked to be tucked up in bed by 2230 hours, or 2300 hours at the latest, but tonight he would not have a wink of sleep.

As the dawn broke, he breathed a sign of relief. The world was coming to life. He could slip into the streams of busy commuter traffic passing the small estate and escape again into anonymity.

He would have to rent yet another house or flat, of course. Go through all the bother of yet another new identity and, let's face it, he was getting far to old for all this kind of caper.

He had even "died" once in his quest to leave the past well and truly buried! He was reported to have been on a Chinook helicopter that went down on a lonely Scottish mountainside, killing crew and passengers.

Now he answered to anything. Even "Hey Jimmy".

Perhaps he had been wrong to decide to tell the truth. What did Mr Ferguson say in school?

"Truth will out, Jack. Truth will out."

Or was it: "Murder will out. Murder will out."

Well, that was the Scottish schools system for you. You were so scared of the teachers and the "tawse" – a leather strap used for corporal punishment – that you hung to every word they said. You did not listen exactly, but, for self-preservation, most kids in the class evolved a sub-conscious "last 10 second recall" which they could replay inside their heads to order when challenged: "Gillespie, please will you so kind as to tell the class what I just said."

A half-dozing Jack could comply faultlessly.

Anyway, whichever of the two homilies it was, they were equally as relevant as the other.

The truth *was* out.

It spread over three pages of a British newspaper, including the front page. A Google internet search of the name used in the paper revealed Jack's exact whereabouts thanks to a link to a Government website.

Unbelievable!

"Britain's 'secret plot to kill Gerry Adams" the newspaper headline roared.

"A FORMER soldier has claimed he was a member of a

secret British Army squad ordered to kill Sinn Féin president Gerry Adams.

"In the early 1970s, Jack Gillespie says he belonged to an Army unit unacknowledged at the time called the Military Reaction Force (MRF).

"According to Gillespie – not his real name – the squad operated a shoot-to-kill policy in Northern Ireland aimed at eliminating IRA volunteers.

"The book he is writing, with Welsh ghostwriter Tom Siegriste, reveals previously unpublished details about MRF's operations, including an aborted bid to assassinate the leading Sinn Fein figure in Belfast in 1973.

"Siegriste told the *Western Mail*: 'In late June 1973, a high-ranking MI6 agent turned up at Palace Barracks in Northern Ireland. He suggested to Jack Gillespie that it was time Gerry Adams was dealt with. Obviously, Mr Adams' photograph had been on the wall of the operations room since the beginning of the MRF's operations.

"The agent suggested he had intelligence that Gerry Adams would be attending a meeting at a community centre in Andersonstown, Belfast, and that perhaps the MRF should do a drive-by shooting to assassinate him.

"This method of operation would make it look like it was the UVF (the loyalist paramilitary Ulster Volunteer Force) who were trying to assassinate Adams anyway.

"The operation was then put into place quickly. A couple of MRF units were involved. They went out, got into position and, as Adams drew up in a car, they were ready to attack. The second before they were going to drive past with guns blazing, the words 'abort, abort' came over the radio, and they drove straight past without opening fire.

"After that, Adams, who was on the run, was picked up in

July without any kind of violence. The rest is history. I don't suppose Mr Adams knows of this narrow escape he had.

"Siegriste added: 'Hopefully someone will read this account and publish this book, or make a film from the book or a TV series. We're under pressure from the military and the secret service not to write this book for their own reasons. But it is nearly 36 years ago, so what harm could it possibly do?'

"The existence of the MRF was eventually admitted by Conservative Defence Minister Jeremy Hanley in a written parliamentary answer to Labour MP Chris Mullin in 1994. Mr Hanley's statement said: 'The MRF was a small military unit which, during the period 1971 to 1973, was responsible for carrying out essential surveillance tasks in Northern Ireland in those circumstances where soldiers in uniform and with Army vehicles would be too easily recognised.'

"In 2001, the highly respected journalist and documentary maker, Peter Taylor, who has written about Northern Ireland for more than 35 years, published a book called *Brits: The War Against the IRA*.

"Taylor's book tells how the MRF was a special unit within Military Intelligence based at Palace Barracks, Holywood, County Down.

"The unit, consisting of soldiers seconded from the SAS and other elite regiments, was involved in a number of controversial incidents where Catholic civilians were killed."

Jack tossed the newspaper on the floor and then picked it up again, gripped it tightly in his fists and ripped it apart.

"Now I know why they call them ghost writers – it's because we all end up dead," he snarled.

Jack, or whoever he was, now questioned his decision to employ Siegriste. Nevertheless, his pride had been hurt.

He certainly regretted the day he went into Waterstone's to shelter from the rain. He could never remember if it was them or the other one that had the coffee shop inside every branch. Or both?

He never found out. He got as far as a book display offering some deal on a book called *Brits – The War Against the IRA* by someone whose name sounded familiar – Peter Taylor.

"Wasn't he something to do with Brian Clough?"

Jack read the dust jacket. No, this Peter Taylor was a well-respected journalist and author. He flicked thorough the hard-back's copious pages.

Jack liked military history books and had a fine collection at home. Many of Jack's friends in the Sportsmen's Club said he should write his autobiography but, like many other ex-SAS men, Jack had pledged never to write about his or the Regiment's exploits.

That was for one very good reason. He did not want to risk the operational integrity of the brave men who today wore the blue wings by giving away any small clue to how they might operate on active service. The basics never change.

He also did not want to risk losing the right to come to Hereford Camp and have a good piss-up with mates, old and new. The reunions in the Sergeants' mess were legendary.

Jack knew that those who had decided to write their memoirs now included the odd General and some fantasists who he doubted had ever been in the Regiment. Or if they had, it wasn't them who did the daring deeds that now bore their names in the paperback racks.

"There must have been 3,000 SAS men at the Iranian Embassy at the last count," was SAS survival expert Lofty Wiseman's favourite saying.

For Jack, the bottom line was that if the boys could make

some money by giving some gullible publishers a load of tosh then good luck to them.

However, Peter Taylor's book did not come into this category. The rain was still coming down in cats and dogs and Jack had managed to have a good free read of the chapters as he waited for it to stop. *Brits* seemed authoritative and accurate. It was good stuff.

Moreover, as far as Jack knew, Peter was never in the SAS so that was OK, too.

Then Jack had turned to page 127 "Piratical Ventures".

It had hit him straight between the eyes.

"What? What!" he spluttered.

Heads turned to see who had broken the relative calm of the bookshop.

The secret Jack had kept for more than 35 years was out – well, sort of out. Until that moment he had never seen a book that included his exploits in the MRF.

According to Taylor, the military authorities wrote off the MRF as a "learning curve". In addition, they said that the unit was wound up immediately after the Four Square Laundry incident.

Jack now had a new mission.

If this was all the world knew about his unit then he would make sure they knew the whole truth. The bravery, the good times, the foul ups, the successes and most of all, the story of those who obeyed orders and died for their country without any kind of recognition.

Or even worse – official denial.

And there was a bonus. As the MRF was not an SAS unit, he would not be exiled from the Hereford family. Unlike Chris Ryan, Andy McNab and General Sir Peter de la Billiere.

So drinks all round!

• • •

Jack sat on the balcony overlooking the sleepy Spanish village. The finca below consisted of three houses dating from the Muslim period grouped around a new, quite large, swimming pool, which reflected the azure of the sky. The orange groves seemed to stretch from here to eternity.

He had already made a cracking start reliving his adventures. Half an A4 ream of closely-written handwriting was neatly stacked underneath a partially quaffed bottle of the finest Rioja.

A lone cloud appeared above the mountains and almost evaporated, like the others did then they hit the warm air captured by the ring of peaks that made the settlement a virtual Shangri-La.

Although there was a twisting and tedious mountain pass to the village, a long modern tunnel now connected it quickly with the outside world. However, as you emerged from the concrete structure, time sweetly slipped backwards like honey returning to the jar from a too generous heaped spoonful.

But this cloud was made of sterner stuff.

Like a black jungle scorpion, it still had a death throes reflex even though the machete of the mountains had sliced its being in two.

A zephyr first, and then a squall of icy fingers, gripped the citrus trees and whipped the blossoms into a frenzy. Sacrificial petals filled the air and Jack watched as the white spectre approached him with a wicked rasping whisper.

No sooner than it had arrived, the vortex was gone, and so was the fruit of six months scribbling, now being scattered over tens of acres of flowering trees like a paper trail of confetti.

"Fuck this for a game of cowboys and Indians," said Jack.

He stomped off inside the villa.

Here there was no nubile Portuguese housekeeper willing to dive into the distant ocean of foliage and retrieve his wondrous words. This was reality not a Richard Curtis screenplay.

Anyway, he was back off to Blighty tomorrow and his mate John Davies had mentioned he knew a ghostwriter who could knock the memoirs into shape. He would be the man to rewrite Gillespie history accurately and eloquently. He would start from scratch.

• • •

It wasn't until sixteen months later that Jack was back on the same balcony.

The immature oranges and lemons now adorned the citrus branches and the summer heat lay heavily on the Spanish marble of the patio next to the small plunge pool.

A lot had happened in those months. A new name was the least of the adjustments Jack was living with. There was a new order.

Research undertaken to complete the book had thrown up a lot of material that those involved at the time were unaware of, as it was happening around them unseen as part of a much bigger picture.

The Public Records Office, now known as the National Archives at Kew in London, England, was only one place where the cupboard was completely bare. There was no material relating directly to the activities of the Military Reaction Force dated in the period 1972-73. Nothing even released after 30 years of gathering dust.

The files in the Northern Ireland Office were almost equally empty. There was just a short note saying the papers once kept were duplicates of those in London and been removed and destroyed. There were no details as to what those papers were.

In the United States of America, Pentagon papers on fighting terrorism mention the MRF but quoted *Brits* by Peter Taylor as their source.

These things are certain:

The MRF were not wound up after the IRA attack on the Four Square Laundry, as the authorities would want you to believe. The unit did some sterling work patrolling on the streets for months afterwards. This included the aborted assassination attempt on Adams and his IRA commanders in June 1973.

Shortly after this MRF operation, it is understood, covert talks between the IRA and the British Government restarted. At the end of that long dialogue, Northern Ireland today enjoys relative peace.

What finished the MRF were not the IRA gunmen but publicity. The broadcast of a television programme on the 10th September 1973, namely *World in Action: A Question of Intelligence,* revealed the MRF's tactics and some alleged errors. The programme dealt with events in 1972 but took so long to come to British TV screens due to British Government interference via the Independent Broadcasting Authority.

Even presenters David Boulton and Sue Woodford admitted, on the programme, that the MRF did some "valuable work", but, at the time, the Government were in denial about condoning such aggressive tactics.

For the Brass, it was the last straw. The politicians were asking too many questions. Just three days after the programme was aired, on the 13th September 1973, the Ministry of Defence officially disbanded the MRF and the remaining soldiers returned to their parent units. And history, as we have seen, was rewritten.

Jack Gillespie went back to the Oman with the SAS.

In January 1974, the volunteer replacement force for the MRF Jack helped train, the 14th Intelligence Unit otherwise known at the DET, formed. Commanded by SAS officers, but not SAS-badged, its official SAS status came a year or so later in 1975.

For their part, it seems MI6 filled the time gap between the two units by pretending the MRF still existed. Men in hoods appeared in Palace Barracks identified to Protestant paramilitaries as MRF men. None of Jack's men ever wore a hood – that was an MI6 thing.

Any action attributed to the MRF during this period, or later, certainly needs to be viewed with that knowledge in mind.

One good way to manipulate the past is to blur the identity of the MRF. In various documents available to researchers, the letter "R" erroneously translates as "Reconnaissance" and the "M" to "Mobile".

It seems clear that when it comes to any variant of the *Military Reaction* Force, Jack's contemporaneously recorded "Black Book" is the definite source of the truth.

For example: more than a year before the aborted assassination attempt, on Tuesday 20th June 1972, again following a direct order, Jack spent many hours watching and waiting for Gerry Adams outside 23 Servia Street, Newtownards, where his parents lived. Another MRF unit was at Elm Grove, Portaferry, where Adam's brother George lived and a further unit watched the summer cottage at 29 Ballyblack Road, Portaferry.

If Adams had appeared, he would have been killed.

However, "Top Secret" papers released on 1st January in 2003 under the 30-year national security rules reveal the security services knew exactly where Adams was located on that date.

He was meeting two British Government representatives at 3pm in a house on the Donegal border. One, Frank Steele, was a member of MI6. The Secretary of State for Northern Ireland, William Whitelaw, knew of the meeting and so did the British Prime Minister, Edward Heath.

Who ordered such an unnecessary surveillance operation, and why, is anyone's guess.

One thing is certain about all this: it all happened a long, long time ago. In three decades, things have changed. For a start, Gerry Adams is now President of Sinn Féin, and a member of the Northern Ireland Assembly, his party settled in a power-sharing executive with the Protestant majority.

Perhaps to consign this story to the history books and move on is the best for everyone.

Jack has.

• • •

The Midday sun beat down on the terracotta tiles of the villa roof. Heidi, Jack's prize pooch, had retreated to a cool spot in the citrus groves. Somewhere distant, the village's canine population volubly marked the start of siesta time. Then silence and sizzle.

Tom Siegriste joined Jack by the pool, and a bottle of Cava popped open. As they raised their glasses, the chimes of the doorbell joined the celebratory clink of crystal.

"No-one knows we are back," said Jack. "Perhaps it's next door keeping an eye on the property and seeing that everything is alright."

The two men gingerly opened the door as a panting Heidi prepared a slobbering welcome for friend or foe.

A fine young man in his mid-thirties stood before them. He looked at a dog-eared black-and-white photograph and held out a hand.

"Hello my name is Jack. I am told you are my father."

The End

Epilogue

Jack Gillespie watched as Prime Minister Harold Wilson stood with both hands in the pockets of his double-breasted suit jacket, uncomfortably posing for photographs with members of his Cabinet at a "meet the press" on the lawn at 10 Downing Street.

If Wilson's trademark pipe was in one of those deep pockets, he did not reveal its presence to the press. To mark his return to Government, artist Ruskin Spear was to paint him as "the man and his pipe". In reality, the briar was a just a political prop ideal for a 1960's man of the people – Harold preferred more plutocratic cigars.

In the sixties, times were a-changing. In the seventies, society had changed, evolving rapidly, erratically, and the media now had new priorities.

It was April 4 1974, exactly a month since the Labour Party took power from the Conservatives who had failed to find a willing partner for a coalition government.

Although now surrounded by the many male members of his minority Government, the more enlightened members of the press were keen to picture Wilson standing with Shirley Williams, Secretary of State for Prices and Consumer Protection, and Barbara Castle, Secretary of State for Social Services.

Shirley Williams, her hands clasped together, beamed a smile at a photographer who called her name. She wore a dark long sleeved blouse and fashionable long line diamond-patterned waistcoat suit. A full yard away from her, Labour stalwart Barbara Castle stood in a check classic shirtdress, which made her look trendy and younger than her 64 years.

Harold stood uncomfortably behind the pair, bending slightly forward at the insistence of the photographers to get him in the shot. These were women from the vanguard of modern feminism, determined to shake the comfortable male-dominated world of British politics. The bright hopes of their respective generations, both, at one time or another, shared the ambition, or perhaps the dream, that one day they would be the first woman Prime Minister of the United Kingdom of Great Britain and Northern Ireland.

The photograph caption? "A Yorkshire Rose between two thorns." Perhaps not.

Nevertheless, he looked so uncomfortable that it would perhaps be true to say that Harold would rather be at his desk.

A pile of official papers awaited him to read ahead of tomorrow morning's meeting with Taoiseach Liam Cosgrave. The Irish Premier had asked for the meeting through the British Ambassador to Dublin as soon as news of the change of Government emerged.

Cosgrave was anxious to make sure that the two countries signed the Sunningdale Agreement as soon as possible as Wilson grappled with a worsening economic situation and a difficult time ahead in the House of Commons.

The power sharing agreement was Cosgrave's top priority. To Wilson Sunningdale, it was just the tip of an information iceberg demanding his attention.

The Northern Ireland situation was as complex and

intricate as three-dimensional chess. In Opposition, in autumn 1971, Wilson had used his time and intellect to try to assist the Heath Government by presenting a 16-point plan to resolve the "troubles".

The Tory Prime Minster welcomed, in principle, Wilson's 15-year program to pave the way for the unification of Ireland, and then Heath wisely let it be lost in the mists of time and politics.

Wilson's earlier Government in the late sixties had witnessed the outbreak of sectarian violence in Northern Ireland and muddled through from year to year. How Heath, through his administration's reckless overreaction and clumsiness, had inflamed the situation to such an impasse Wilson would never understand.

Harold shook his head. He and his ministers would do better this time, much better.

Jack soon tired of watching the scrum of photographers caper around the Premier and his Cabinet and headed for his meeting nearby in the Ministry of Defence.

Wilson shut the door behind him and sat at his desk. Finally, it was time for him to open the box of papers for the meeting with the Taoiseach. The Prime Minister had already agreed the agenda for the meeting and quickly skimmed through the papers until he reached some newly arrived material attached to a short note marked "SECRET COVERING TOP SECRET".

It was from an assistant private secretary at the Foreign and Commonwealth Office, Michael O'Donel Bjarne Alexander, to the Prime Minister's Private Secretary (Overseas Affairs), Thomas Edward Bridges, The Lord Bridges, or Tom, as Wilson knew him.

"I enclose four copies of a brief prepared for the use of the

Prime Minister at his meeting with the Taoiseach, Mr. Cosgrave, tomorrow morning. It has been agreed with the Northern Ireland Office.

A Top Secret brief on Army Plain Clothes Operations (Defensive Brief D) is included but, because of its classification, has been kept separate from the main brief.

I am sending copies of this letter and enclosures to Reid (Northern Ireland Office), Mumford (Ministry of Defence), Sir John Hunt (Cabinet Office) and Hetherington (Law Officers' Department).

Yours ever, Michael Alexander."

Civil Servants provide Defensive Briefs for politicians to give them a convincing "line", but not a wholly revealing answer, to tricky off-agenda questions sometimes thrown in maliciously during important talks. Background briefs covered the items on the agenda.

Labeled "SECRET" the briefing line up for tomorrow's meeting was:

Background briefs:

1. Ireland: The Coalition Government and the North
2. The Security Situation
3. Border Security
4. Commission on Law Enforcement
5. The Council of Ireland
6. Irish State Case at Strasbourg
7. EEC: Cross-Border Projects
8. EEC Questions

Defensive Briefs:

A. Detention
B. Littlejohns

C. The Price Sisters
D. Army Plain Clothes Patrols in Northern Ireland
E. Policing
F. Human Rights
G. Sterling Balances
H. Oil Supplies and Export Licencing
I. Rockall/Anglo-Irish Continental Shelf

Wilson scanned down the list and retrieved Defensive Brief D from the papers. He saw it had an "Annex A" attached to it from Army HQ Northern Ireland entitled "Draft Statement By HQNI" with the word "Draft" clumsily scrubbed out in HB pencil. The document looked a last minute addition.

Wilson started to read the document.

TOP SECRET

MEETING BETWEEN THE PRIME MINISTER AND THE TAIOSEACH
FRIDAY 5 APRIL 1974
ARMY PLAIN CLOTHES PATROLS IN NORTHERN IRELAND

Plain clothes teams, initially joint RUC/Army patrols, have operated in Northern Ireland since the IRA bombing campaign in Easter 1971. Later in 1971, the teams were reformed and expanded as Military Reaction Forces (MRFs) without RUC participation. In 1972 the operations of the MRF were brought under more centralised control and a higher standard of training was achieved by establishing a Special Reconnaissance Unit (SRU) of 130 all ranks under direct command of HQNI.

2. The term "Special Reconnaissance Unit" and the details of its organisation and mode of operations have been kept secret. The SRU operates in Northern Ireland at present under the covername "Northern Ireland Training and Advisory Teams (Northern Ireland)" – NITAT(NI) – ostensibly the equivalent of genuine NITAT teams in UKLF and BAOR.

3. The prime task of the SRU is to conduct covert surveillance of terrorists as a preliminary to an arrest carried out by security forces in uniform. The SRU may also be used to contact and handle agents or informers and for the surveillance and protection of persons or property under terrorist threat. The SRU works to a great extent on Special Branch information and the Special Branch have a high regard for it.

4. Men who have served with the SAS are serving in the SRU but no SAS units are operating in Northern Ireland. One officer and 30 soldiers serving with the SRU since early January are to resume service with 22 SAS by 7 April. Their presence with the SRU went undetected until the Robert Fisk article in *The Times* on 19 March.

5. *What do the Irish Government know about plain-clothes patrols and SAS involvement?*
The statement at Annex A, which was prepared by the Ministry of Defence in consultation with

the Northern Ireland Office and the Foreign and Commonwealth Office, was handed to the Department of Foreign Affairs in Dublin. In answering a question in the Dail on whether he would protest to the British Government against the use of the SAS in Northern Ireland, Dr Fitzgerald said that he had no suggestion that SAS troops were operating in Northern Ireland.

6. *Line to take*
Plain-clothes patrols are a perfectly legitimate activity for the Army in Northern Ireland and their existence has been public knowledge for a long-time. Nobody who wishes to see an end to the violence could wish to deny the Army the use of any effective means of defeating terrorism by the imposition of unreasonable constraints on a legitimate mode of operation.

Northern Ireland Office
Great George Street
London SW1
2 April 1974 **TOP SECRET**

Wilson was puzzled. This was the first time he had seen such a briefing and his predecessor Ted Heath's ministers had been vehement in their denials of SAS involvement in Northern Ireland. From those honourable members' assurances, Wilson was certain that was the case. Yet here it said an officer and 30 men who had been operating in the province "are to resume service with the SAS…". An exercise in semantics or was that sentence structured to mislead?

He pondered.

He turned to Annex A, which was attached to defensive Brief D. In comparison to the other briefing material, it was a scruffy document and bore evidence of a single, now obsolete, perforation – perhaps it had been part of another file at one time.

It bore no secrecy marking not even the customary "Restricted".

The Prime Minister read on.

Draft Statement by HQNI
ANNEX A

It has been alleged from time to time that murders and other major crimes committed in Northern Ireland have been the work of the SAS.
Clearly the terrorist organisations have found it convenient to encourage this belief as a means of evading the responsibility, which is properly theirs.

The facts are as follows.
No SAS unit has been or is stationed in Northern Ireland.

It has been readily acknowledged in Parliament and to the press that the Army in Northern Ireland undertakes plain clothes patrols.
The reason for this is quite simply that soldiers operating in uniform and with service vehicles are easily recognisable at a distance and plain clothes are therefore adopted on certain occasions where effective surveillance is essential. As far as practicable, the Army works in conjunction with the police on these occasions, as at all other times. The value

of these patrols has been amply borne out.

The training which soldiers who volunteer for service with the SAS receive would be particularly valuable in any plain-clothes operations; but in order the more readily to refute hostile propaganda about SAS involvement in Northern Ireland, the policy has been to avoid employing such soldiers on these duties in Northern Ireland until some two or three years after their SAS Service has ended. However, the overriding consideration must always be the operational needs of the situation and we must be free to use whatever measures are most appropriate to counter the current terrorist threat. On this account, the normal embargo may be waived when necessary. The first occasion on which this has in fact been done has been during the past three months when, in order to maintain the level of plain-clothes patrols, use has been made of a number of volunteers whose experience with the SAS had been acquired only just beforehand.

These and all other soldiers employed in plain clothes duties are required to conduct their activities within the law and remain subject to the civil law and to military discipline at all times. Any suggestion that they are employed to carry out assassinations or to create inter-sectarian suspicion is nonsense. The fact that such claims are made is in itself an indication of the degree to which the plain clothes surveillance patrols hurt the terrorists.

Wilson pushed his hair back over his forehead. It may have been unwise to give this briefing to the Irish. It was unclear, but was perhaps an admission that SAS men of one kind or another had been operating in Northern Ireland for years – just not in SAS badged units.

This was not a good time to learn about this bag of tricks. Cosgrave was certain to raise the question and Wilson was going to have to deal with it as best he could.

There was a quiet tap on the door made by a woman's polished fingernails and Wilson looked as he put the document to one side. It was Marcia Faulkender, his political secretary. She wanted to discuss the meeting with the Taoiseach in some depth and a new radical project aimed at a Northern Ireland settlement should Sunningdale fail.

Wilson settled down for a long night.

Light flooded through the window as Jack Gillespie headed for Seat E4 and D4 in the Reading Room of the National Archives in Kew, West London.

He carried the two inch-thick bundle of documents he had taken from the Perspex collection locker to the modern circular workstation and sat down.

He was still puzzling over the mix up at the Reader Registration Desk where, after struggling with the on-line computer self-registration software, he was told by the human interface, Rhiannon, that the reason he found it impossible to register was simple. His details were already registered.

"It happens from time to time," she said sweetly as he had his digital photograph taken for his Reader's Ticket.

"Have you been here before?"

"No this is my first time."

"Expires 23/9/2012," Jack read some 30 seconds later on

the red credit card style ID. "Hope not."

He smiled.

Rhiannon handed Jack his electricity bill and his driving licence.

"Siegriste – such an unusual name," she said, "You don't meet many of them."

"One's enough," he replied.

A student using one of the Reading Room camera stands swore under her breath as her prized 10.1 Megapixel Sony Cyber-shot DSC-H20/B Digital – compact with its impressive Carl Zeiss Vario-Tessar wide-angle lens – fell from its mounting.

Jack looked at his Nokia N73 mobile phone, which he would use to capture any images he would take home with him from the Archive. He felt like Mr. Bean – an inadequate, amateur. He quickly stuffed the mobile back into his jacket pocket on the back of his seat.

Jack returned to the documents piled in front of him. He flipped over the buff cover. Photocopied press cutting, press cutting, more press cuttings.

"This is going to take all day."

Then there was a random loose page about arms sales to South Africa. Jack clumsily flipped forward in the file, straining the string fastening that was keeping the documents together. The scholarly looking man at the next workstation gave Jack a hard look. The researcher was wearing white cotton gloves. Jack's chubby fingers were bare, as were his forearms except for the fading-to-black "Celtic AFC" and fading-to-pink "MRF" tattoos.

Jack had forgotten to get a pair of gloves, but he did have an HB pencil without a rubber on the end. He unconsciously displayed it to his "neighbour". Mr. Bean was *present and correct* Sergeant Major.

He looked down at the documents again. He had flipped it open to a page where a yellow label with his name and seat number on it had separated the pages.

A red stamp cried out from the top of the page.

> "**TOP SECRET**
> MEETING BETWEEN THE PRIME MINIS-TER AND THE TAIOSEACH
> FRIDAY 5 APRIL 1974
> ARMY PLAIN CLOTHES PATROLS IN NORTHERN IRELAND"

This was the very document he had been told about and travelled from Spain especially to see. He had tried to view it online but was told that was not possible for these papers. Purchasing a facsimile was also ruled out.

EasyJet was the answer.

Now as he started to read, the torture of cramped economy seating was ameliorated. This was First Class.

It was the only occasion he had seen official confirmation that the MRF – his Military Reaction Force – actually existed.

But wait...

"Later in 1971, the teams were reformed and expanded as Military Reaction Forces (MRFs) without RUC participation."

Forces? That's plural. There was only one – us. One officer and 30 men. Three call-signs Nine-Zero, Eight Zero and Seven Zero.

Jack didn't like this at all. Then...

"In 1972, the operations of the MRF were brought under more centralised control and a higher standard of training achieved by establishing a Special Reconnaissance Unit (SRU) of 130 all ranks under direct command of HQNI."

Bollocks! That didn't happen until late 1973 at the earliest.

Jack looked round just to be sure he didn't say any of that out loud.

No, Mr White Gloves was still engrossed in the Jewish branch of the Cunningham family tree.

Jack read on. He noted the existence of Annex A; he would look for that in a minute. Then he retraced his steps back a bit…

"4. Men who have served with the SAS are serving in the SRU but no SAS units are operating in Northern Ireland. One officer and 30 soldiers serving with the SRU since early January are to resume service with 22 SAS by 7 April."

"Hang on. That's the MRF, but the timing is all to cock!" exclaimed Jack. This time it was aloud.

"Sorry… sorry… sorry," Mr. Bean bobbed up and down to everyone present.

Jack took out his Nokia and photographed page after page.

He read Annex A. It seemed accurate but not written by a military hand, Jack surmised. The document seemed to confirm the operating environment of the MRF and at the same time, confirm by denial the unit's true purpose:

"…in order to maintain the level of plain clothes patrols, use has been made of a number of volunteers whose experience with the SAS had been acquired only just beforehand.

These and all other soldiers employed in plain clothes duties are required to conduct their activities within the law and remain subject to the civil law and to military discipline at all times. Any suggestion that they are employed to carry out assassinations or to create inter-sectarian suspicion is nonsense. The fact that such claims are made is in itself an indication of the degree to which the plain clothes surveillance patrols hurt the terrorists."

A denial that said too much and perhaps said it all. Anyway, it was more than enough to send Jack back to the Costas floating on air – who needs an aeroplane?

Whoever drafted these two documents knew about the MRF and its purpose, denied it beautifully, and then shifted the tectonic plates of time so that 1974 slid nicely over 1973 and 1972. Moreover, they "forgot" all about the SBS involvement.

Just like Tony Blair, Wilson had a dodgy dossier. However, for Jack their erasure was his closure.

As his orange liveried plane's undercarriage left the Luton tarmac, Jack finished reading the documents from Wilson's meeting. Cosgrave had never raised the issue of the SAS in Northern Ireland.

"It was the elephant in the kitchen," clichéd Jack.

The rest, as they say, is history.

• • •

Jack was as pleased as punch. He dived into the pool. It had been a hot and sticky journey back to the Finca but worth it. He had not imagined he belonged to a unit that did not exist. It is now official – it did. It was just that it needed Doctor Who and the Tardis to write the regimental history.

He broke the surface halfway down the azure oval-shaped pool and pushed his hands forward, ready for the first of many lengths of breaststroke.

"Not bad for a septuagenarian," he beamed.

Jack swam strongly for the far wall of the pool and stretched out to touch it to turn for a second length. Suddenly he was sinking to the bottom of the 1.4-metres of water. He was still conscious.

Jack tried to stand up, he was well within his depth, but his legs would not move. They would not work at all – nothing was getting through from his brain.

He knew he had to get his head above water soon as the seconds were ticking away.

His arms flapped like a large sea bird trying to leave the water after voracious feeding. His fingernails ripped out as one hand went over top edge, hit the rough joint of the non-slip tiles and was then dragged back into the deep by Jack's dead weight.

His arms flapped one last time and he was gone.

Glossary

9MM	9 Millimetre round
AFC	Association Football Club
ASAP	As Soon As Possible
AVRE	Armoured Vehicle Royal Engineers (AVRE) is the title given to a series of armoured vehicles operated by the Royal Engineers (RE) for the purpose of battlefield engineering support
Absinthe	A distilled, highly alcoholic (45%–74% ABV) beverage
Admin	Administration
Ammo	Ammunition
Angle Irons	Member of the Royal Anglian Regiment
Armalite	American .223 Rifles
BBC	British Broadcasting Corporation
BEA	British European Airways
BMC	British Motor Corporation
Berserker	A rash Chess playing style characterized by frenzied attacking with one or two pieces, perhaps with little regard for strategy or danger

Blighty	Armed Services name for the United Kingdom
Bovka	Bovril and Vodka – Hangover Cure
C	The head of MI6
CO	Commanding Officer
C4	Plastic Explosive
Carpe Diem	A phrase from a Latin poem by Horace popularly translated as "seize the day". The phrase is part of the longer Carpe diem quam minimum credula postero – "Seize the day, trusting as little as possible in the future.", and the ode says that the future is unknowable, and that instead one should scale back one's hopes to a brief future, and drink one's wine.
Chubb	Padlock manufacturers
Cpl	Corporal
DJ	Disc Jockey
FLOSY	Federation for the Liberation of South Yemen
FN	Fabrique Nationale de Herstal – a Belgian arms manufacturer
Freds	IRA informers
GT	Grand Tourer – a car trim and/or engine designation
Go doolally	UK Military slang Originally 'doolally tap', meaning unbalanced state of mind
Goon	A thug
Greens	British Soldiers in Northern Ireland
HMG	Her Majesties Government
HQ	Headquarters
IRA	Irish Republican Army

ID	Identify, Identification
Jock	Slang for a person from Scotland
LP	Long Player – a 12-inch vinyl record album
Luppers	Fingers – Polari British gay slang
MOD	Ministry of Defence
MP	Member of Parliament
MRF	Military Reaction Force
Mae dy fam yn llyfu cociau mul	"Your mother licks donkey dicks"
Mags	Weapon magazine, magazines
MC	Military Cross, a top British gallantry medal
Micks	Derogatory name for Irish people
Moggie	Derogatory word for cats
Mufti	Civilian dress worn by someone normally in Military uniform
Murut	Tribe in Borneo
NAAFI	The Navy, Army and Air Force Institutes
NUJ	National Union of Journalists
Nitty Gritty	The heart of the matter
Nom de guerre	A name assumed by individuals engaged in a military enterprise or espionage, usually in order to conceal their true identity. Literally, 'war name'
OC	Officer Commanding
OP	Observation point
One over the Eight	UK military slang for one drink too many
Op's Officer	Operation's Officer
Op's Room	Operations Room
Paddy	Slang for Irish person – sometimes derogatory

Papist	Derogatory slang for a Catholic
Parnellite	A supporter of Charles Parnell in his advocacy for Irish Home Rule
Popish	Catholic person
Prod	A disparaging term for a Protestant
RAF	Royal Air Force
REME	Royal Electrical and Mechanical Engineers
RMP	Royal Military Police
RPM	Revolutions per minute
RSM	Regimental Sergeant Major
RTB	Return to base
RUC	Royal Ulster Constabulary
Radu Ulan	Head of Murut Tribe Borneo
RSPCA	Royal Society for the Prevention of Cruelty To Animals
Rupert	Slang for British Officer
SAS	Special Air Service
SBS	Special Boat Squadron
SLR	Self Loading Rifle
Sapper	Lowest rank in The Royal Engineers
Scouser	Native of Liverpool
Sgt	Sergeant – army rank
Sitreps	Situation Reports
Sixes and Sevens	A state of total confusion and disorder
Skedaddle	Quickly disappear
Slainte	Irish for Good Health/Cheers – an Irish toast
Slime	Members of the Intelligence Corp
SLR	Single Lens Reflex – a 35mm camera
SMG	Sub Machine Gun
Spook	Spy – MI6 or MI5 Intelligence Officer
Squad	A three- or four-man team

Taff	Slang for a man from Wales – sometimes derogatory
Taig	Derogatory term for Catholics
Tourette's	a rare and bizarre syndrome, most often associated with the exclamation of obscene words or socially inappropriate and derogatory remarks
US	United States
UVF	Ulster Volunteer Force
Ulu	"Jungle" in Malay
VCP	Vehicle Check Point
WIA	*World in Action* – a TV documentary programme